Europe-Asia-Pacific Studies in Economy and Technology

Manfred Kulessa (Ed.)

The Newly Industrializing Economies of Asia

Prospects of Co-operation

With 17 Figures

Springer-Verlag Berlin Heidelberg New York
London Paris Tokyo Hong Kong

Dr. jur. Manfred Kulessa
Development Policy Forum
German Foundation for International Development
Villa Borsig, D-1000 Berlin 27, FRG

ISBN-13: 978-3-642-75707-5 e-ISBN-13: 978-3-642-75705-1
DOI: 10.1007/978-3-642-75705-1

Bookbinding: J. Schäffer GmbH u. Co. KG, Grünstadt
2142/7130-543210

It is of vital importance that frontiers are open and that there are no impediments to trade between our countries. The EC must also stand by this basic principle with regard to the Single European Market. Partnerships can only work under these circumstances. I am aware that the conditions for forming partnerships still vary considerably. Some countries are in a far better position to do so than others. Nonetheless, particularly this trade fair here in Berlin demonstrates a great deal of hard work and precision, innovation and boldness which enable you to take the risk of forming partnerships.

The progress we need is the kind of progress that allows such partnerships to work. This trade fair contributes to this in the same way as trade fairs have done since mediaeval times, when Europe was not yet economically developed: people meet and get to know what the others are able to accomplish, and the information thus acquired leads to an interest in trading with each other. Trade is the soundest form of mutual aid: both sides give and take at the same time. Both partners remain aware of the value of their own achievements. This can develop into partnerships from which all parties reap material benefit and which strengthen their confidence in themselves.

RICHARD VON WEIZSÄCKER
President of the Federal Republic of Germany

Preface

Where development is concerned, our language and perhaps our way of thinking often appear somewhat distorted. If anything, the Asian economies with their most impressive and dynamic growth should logically be called developing countries. Instead, we call them threshold countries, newly industrializing countries (NICs) or newly industrializing economies (NIEs), the latter term taking into account the Chinese argument that Hong Kong and Taiwan should not be considered countries.

During the eighties, when Latin American NICs became the main victims of the debt crisis, the NIEs of East Asia (EANIEs), the little tigers or dragons, presented most impressive examples of growth through orientation to world trade, fitting well into the Japanese 'flying-geese' concept.

Naturally, questions were raised as to the reasons for this success, the lessons other countries could draw from it, and the outlook for the future. At the same time, the established industrial countries wanted to know what NIE competition might mean for them. In 1988, the OECD published a study entitled "The NIEs - Challenge and Opportunity for OECD Industries". The NIEs had become a fashionable object of research and debate.

In Western Europe, where countries are preparing for a period of further integration and East-West cooperation, it seems worth-while to also consider the role of the EANIEs and the options for cooperation they represent. Moreover, the NIEs themselves are following development in Europe with some concern and are trying to adjust to the new situation as it emerges.

Against this background, an international round table was convened by the Development Policy Forum of the German Foundation for International Development in cooperation with the Asia Pacific Society, Cologne. The meeting took place at Villa Borsig, Berlin (West), from 25 to 29 September 1989. More than 60 scholars, politicians, government officials and representatives of the business community took part. Most of the contributions to this volume are papers submitted to the round table. A summary of its deliberations, its programme and a list of participants have also been included.

Thus, we are not offering a comprehensive reference book on the NIE phenomenon, but a record of authentic presentations reflecting the views of involved observers at the end of the decade. The main purpose of our meeting was just that: to provide a forum for presenting the NIEs, their situation, future plans, hopes and concerns, and for a discussion of ways to enhance cooperation between them and Germany and Europe. Participants were invited from the four classic EANIEs, namely Hong Kong, Korea, Singapore and Taiwan, and from Thailand and Malaysia, two countries rapidly approaching NIE status, though they still prefer not to be so identified while they certainly belong to the group of Dynamic Asian Economies (DAE). In Berlin, they met their counterparts from Germany and other European countries.

Our meeting coincided with the international import fair "Partners for Progress". On this occasion, the Federal President, Dr. Richard von Weizsäcker, extended invitations to a reception. With his kind permission, we have included his word of greeting to the guests from abroad.

We believe that the expert documents produced for and at the round table are relevant to the present international debate on the status and potential role of the NIEs on the options for strengthening their cooperation with Europe. Therefore, we would like to submit them to a wider audience.

At the same time, I am glad of another opportunity to thank all the authors for their contributions, Theodor Leuenberger and the Asia Pacific Society for their cooperation, and Wolfgang Hillebrand and Philippe Régnier for their competent and conscientious support in preparing the report of the meeting.

January 1990 MANFRED KULESSA

The German Foundation for International Development (Deutsche Stiftung für internationale Entwicklung - DSE) is a government-supported public institution with a mandate of dialogue and training in the field of international development cooperation. Its Development Policy Forum convenes meetings in support of North-South and South-South dialogues.

Europe - NIE Partnership in Development Policy

Address given at the International Round Table by
Hans-Peter Repnik
Parliamentary State Secretary
to the Federal Minister for Economic Cooperation
Bonn

It is a pleasure for me to welcome you all, and especially our guests from Asia, and to convey to you the best wishes of the Federal Government and the Federal Minister for Economic Cooperation.

The North-South dialogue plays an essential role in our efforts to assume a joint responsibility for the one world which is our common home. For this reason, the Federal Government supports the work of the Development Policy Forum of the German Foundation for International Development (DSE), and is pleased that this conference is being devoted specially to the dialogue with the emerging industrial nations of Asia. I think that an open exchange of this kind outside the framework of official contacts can benefit all concerned, and also that we may expect it to generate ideas for strengthening international cooperation.

Based on the detailed introductory paper prepared by Mr. Schomerus, the main areas of global trade in goods and services were highlighted where we in Europe, and you in Asia too, see our main opportunities and challenges and where our political principles must prove themselves in practice. I believe that, if we view things from a higher vantage point, we will see that, essentially, we share common interests.

This certainly goes for development cooperation. The Federal Government cannot but welcome the fact that, in the shape of the NIEs, the traditional industrial countries now have partners willing to play their part in fighting poverty and creating the basis for a life in human dignity throughout the world. It is the express wish of the Federal Government that your nations should join us in assuming a common responsibility for global development. We are pleased to see that the NIEs are establishing international development funds and intensifying their efforts in the field of bilateral and multilateral development cooperation - an area where your countries, as was the case with Germany after World War II, are becoming recipients rather than donors.

In recent years, the Federal Government and the governments of Korea and Singapore have gradually reduced the level of their development cooperation thanks to the economic progress these two countries have achieved.

In comparison with these countries' own efforts, the contribution of German development assistance has been modest but of lasting significance in certain sectors such as vocational training.

This conference will examine the question whether the NIEs can be models for other developing countries. An exemplary feature of our development cooperation, and without doubt one of the factors responsible for the economic success of Korea and Singapore, has been the determination, skill and flexibility with which our two partners have pursued their long-term development strategies whilst ensuring a stable and predictable economic environment.

Development cooperation's South-South dimension can assume a new qualitiy if the NIEs are willing to contribute their special experience, technical skills and economic strength to the cause of international cooperation. Here I would refer in particular to the need for support for the world's poorest countries, some of which are to be found in Asia and indeed in your neighbourhood.

In the coming days, you will discuss the relations between Europe and the NIEs of Asia. Wherever such discussions take place they do so against the backdrop of the historic events and developments of our times which we all are following with a mixture of anxiety and hope: the Uruguay round of multilateral negotiations on GATT; the reform movement in the socialist countries which may lead to a restructuring of international relations; recent developments in China; the completion of the European Single Market; the emergence of a multipolar world – to name but the most obvious.

However, as somebody concerned with the formulation of development policy, I would like also to draw this conference's attention to other global problems confronting us: the international debt crisis, population growth and the continuing devastation of our natural environment.

If you will allow, I would like to say a few words on this last issue. Like Europe, the NIEs have chosen the path of industrial modernization. Today we know that this path has placed an enormous burden on the environment and now poses an acute threat to the bases of humanity's existence. Whether old or young, all the industrial nations are in the same boat. We must assume a common responsibility for ensuring that our way of life and modes of production are oriented more to the needs of the environment and for preserving our most important natural assets worldwide. We offer our cooperation in this field, and hope that you too will make a contribution to developing and to applying environment-friendly technologies and to repairing environmental damage in industrial and developing countries and avoiding it in future.

I hope that despite the intensity of the Forum's programme you will take this opportunity to get to know the Federal Republic and Berlin as well as the people who live here and their hopes and concerns.

Contents

THE NIEs OF ASIA - CHANCES FOR INCREASING COOPERATION

Summary Report

by

Wolfgang Hillebrand **Manfred Kulessa** **Philippe Régnier**

The meeting was organized by the Development Policy Forum of the German Foundation for International Development (DSE, Berlin West) in cooperation with the Asia Pacific Society (Cologne) with the purpose of intensifying the dialogue between the Asian NIEs and their German and European partners on economic and development policies, thus serving mutual interest and understanding. The case of the NIEs and Western Europe and the various perceptions on both sides were to be presented, including the further integration of the Asian NIEs into structures of international coordination and multilateral cooperation.

A group of about sixty experts from governments, international organizations, and the scientific and business communities from the NIEs (Korea, Taiwan, Singapore, Hong Kong), Thailand and Malaysia, the Federal Republic of Germany and other European countries participated in the meeting. This International Round Table also coincided with the official opening of the 27th Overseas Import Fair "Partners for Progress" in Berlin.

The meeting was convened at a time of historic evolutions and major new trends both in Asia and Europe, and world-wide, such as the multilateral trade negotiations of the Uruguay Round in GATT, the reform movements in the majority of socialist countries and the possible emergence of new East-West relations, the recent events in China, the completion of the EEC internal market by 1992, the economic cooperation efforts in the Pacific region, the emergence of regional blocs and greater international coordination.

Europe-Asia-Pacific Studies in Economy and Technology
Kulessa (Ed.)
The Newly Industrializing Economies of Asia

About 30 working papers were submitted by scholars and officials as background documents which outlined the main areas of interest and concerns from both Asian and European viewpoints, as well as from wider international perspectives. A lively discussion raised a multitude of key issues throughout the three days of the meeting. There are certainly various loose-ends remaining from our deliberations, but we do identify some major trends in the arguments and views brought forward. The magnitude of the materials presented and the very numerous contributions during the discussions make it impossible to cover the event fully in a short report. Let us nevertheless try to highlight some of their salient features which can be divided into three sections:

I. Asian Views on Relations between Europe and Asian NIEs

II. German and European Views on Relations between Europe and Asian NIEs

III. Areas of Consensus or Controversy

Of course, the division between sections I and II is not intended to separate our Asian friends from Europe or vice versa, but to clarify the positions expressed during the meeting. Beyond obvious geographic and cultural distances between the two regions, many differences and similarities were observed on both sides and also within each group or sub-group of national economies analysed.

Any report has to deal with the problem of imperfect generalisation and synthesis and it is impossible to do full justice to all the opinions and views expressed. But all of us left this International Round Table with the feeling of better communication among Asian and European friends; we hope this short report will further contribute to this major goal.

I. Asian Views on Relations between Europe and Asian NIEs

Most presentations were characterized by a relative self-confidence, underlining the economic importance of NIEs in the Asia/Pacific region. The NIEs should remain, together with Japan, the major centres for future growth on the eve of the next Pacific century, even if their rapid development has still been too short to be able to assess their global strength and weakness in the long run.

They should not be considered in Europe as an economic shock or threat but as valuable partners for bilateral, inter-regional and international cooperation in many fields (trade, industry and technology, finance and other services).

Several key elements will contribute to the future scenario:

- Global trade patterns are likely to change fundamentally because of the emergence of three major regional blocs (North America - Europe - Northeast Asia) and world globalization of business flows, mainly among multinational firms.

- Japan and NIEs will increasingly invest overseas, first in Asia but also in North and Central America and Europe.

- Europe may even become a subcontractor to Japan and NIEs in some sectors or sub-sectors; subcontracting will be much more of a two-way business relationship.

- NIEs will remain engines of growth in Asia and beyond, with new types of possible East/West (Asia/Europe) economic partnerships in the two regions and elsewhere.

- Compared with the USA and Japan, Europe was thought to be on the decline until quite recently. The European Single Market in 1992 and a relative decline of the USA are new factors of change, whereas Japanese growth will continue. The world is becoming multi-polar, including the NIEs and new potential NIEs in Asia and America.

- If Europe misses the train for more liberal policies and cooperation (not confrontation) with the NIEs, it could contribute to more economic coordination among Asian nations, especially Japan/NIEs/ASEAN.

- The concept of gradual intraregional industrialization or flying geese is just a concise way to describe a global process of division of labour in the Pacific region. It can only be further implemented if a free regional and international business environment is guaranteed, for the benefit of all nations.

Regional and international issues are perceived as follows:

1. Role of ASEAN:

- This organization has achieved increasing political cohesion, internally (peaceful coexistence of the 6 member states) and above all externally (Indochina), but economic cooperation is still very loose and difficult. The final aim is more economic coordination but not integration.

- Following Japan, the Asian NIEs are investing more and more in the ASEAN countries, but Malaysia and Thailand do not consider themselves emerging NIEs.

- In the case of greater protectionist pressures from Europe and USA, ASEAN would seek more intense intra-regional economic relations and coordination in the Pacific region.

2. Role of EEC:

- The NIEs have major worries about the rising protectionism in both the EEC and USA.

- There is some major concern about a potential "Fortress Europe" in 1992. Concerns about investment concentration within the EEC, preferential agreements with the ACP countries, new priorities for more cooperation with Eastern Europe.

- The FRG and perhaps a few smaller EEC countries like the Netherlands are seen as the best guarantors of a liberal and open EEC market.

3. NIEs' anxieties and fears in interregional and international economic relations.

- The NIEs face a series of selective protectionist or safeguard actions in trade, especially from USA and Western Europe, the EEC anti-dumping policy being an example. The same goes with restrictive measures in the field of direct investment versus trade (local production content) and increasing resistance from the industrialized countries to transfer high technology to the NIEs, which heavily rely on capital- and technology-intensive industries.

- The NIEs are ready to do their share in achieving free trade. In fact they have already embarked on major liberalization and deregulation of their domestic markets, but they should not be expected to make unilateral sacrifices. This is why they are in favour of their gradual integration into international economic multilateralism (rights and obligations for all member nations).

- The NIEs will increasingly participate in international governmental and non-governmental organizations and they would agree to some kind of coordination mechanism. They have welcomed informal dialogue with the OECD and will or could join OECD committees. Korea will not formally join in the very near future. The economic success stories of the NIEs are felt to have been too short to assume further rapid growth in the long run. Some of them experienced trade deficits and huge foreign debt until recently (like Korea), or sudden economic recession because of world market fluctuations (like Singapore in 1984-85).

TAIWAN is a very special case as cooperation had to be conducted without normal diplomatic relations in the absence of formal relations, even at the consular level, for many years. The Republic of China faces severe difficulties in joining interregional or international negotiations (like OECD or GATT). Most European countries have considerably neglected the rapid economic boom in Taiwan, probably because of excessive fear (especially among European businessmen) of possible reactions in the People's Republic of China. Europe has begun to realize the economic strength of Taiwan, and bilateral economic relations have been registering a sharp increase since 1985-86. But many Europeans, particularly those who dream of the Chinese market, are not yet sufficiently aware of the economic crossroad location of Taiwan, reinforced further by China's instability since 1989 which will probably continue for a few years to come. In the interest of all (including China), Europe should support the participation of Taiwan in economic multilateralism in order to ease Taiwan's trade and financial surpluses and to curb exclusive bilateral relations and the frequent confrontations between the USA and the Republic of China.

HONG KONG: Since June 1989, Hong Kong has been facing the very sensitive issue of 1997. However, there is long-term confidence because Hong Kong will remain a key door between China and the world economy, especially its booming neighbours. Positive change in China may be expected. As for Singapore, international business freedom in Hong Kong and on world markets is a precondition for the future health of the local economy.

KOREA: Korea is facing a major period of political and socioeconomic transition, with several uncertainties yet to be overcome: sharp social inequalities, difficult conditions of labour, overconcentration and overregulation of the economy are major issues.

Beyond current adjustments, Korea's economic future looks promising even if the targets for the year 2000 might be too ambitious. Various policies will be accelerated such as industrial diversification, R & D, trade and gradual financial liberalization, income redistribution, development of small and medium-sized firms.

Together with Singapore, the NIEs are requesting the EEC to:

1. Stick to a liberal trade policy.
2. Reactivate investment in the NIEs and the Pacific region.

3. Consider relocation of industries in both regions, with all kinds of possible subcontracting and business complementarity or matching.
4. Allow access to technology and know-how not only from/for big firms but also from/for small and medium-sized firms which are quite a force in many European countries.

II. German and European Views on Relations between Europe and Asian NIEs

A. Role of FRG/EEC and Asian NIEs in the world economy; the present state of EEC/NIE interdependence and future trends

1. Europe (EEC countries and EFTA) is still a dynamic economic power and the major trading bloc in the world. Western Europe is not on the decline but has been going through vast industrial restructuring and 1992 is a challenge for strong revival and development. European business is concentrating on the relevant markets which are viewed in the following order of priorities:

- Western Europe (EEC/EFTA) and new potential opportunities in Eastern Europe because of current changes and reforms there.

- Northern America with the new perspective of the Free Trade Zone between USA and Canada, and the close association of Central American economies.

- Japan and Northeast Asia.

Although growth rates are impressive, the domestic markets of Asian NIEs are still considered to be relatively small, even somewhat marginal. <The 4 markets combined in terms of GNP

are slightly larger than the economic potential of Spain (some US $ 350 million)>.

2. Two-way trade between EEC countries and Asian NIEs has developed quite considerably in recent years. As a trader, the EEC is not a marginal player in Asia, nor is the EEC market a marginal one for Asian NIEs, but remains number 3 after USA and Japan in the Asia Pacific region. In terms of foreign direct investment and technology exports, EEC countries are clearly underrepresented in Asian NIEs. Even so, European business is increasingly aware of business opportunities in Asia. (For example, a "product show" to be organized by the EEC Commission in Korea has drawn considerable interest among European companies (400) only 40 of them were interested in the Korean market three years ago).

3. The possible impact of one single integrated market after 1992 will benefit new linkages between EEC and Asian NIEs:

- The creation of the European Single Market will introduce new types of business dynamism, both inward and outward. Concentration and competition on a bigger scale should contribute to all kinds of national deregulations and to easier access to European markets for outsiders.

- European companies are already preparing for the challenges ahead, and their restructuring in both labour and financial terms is concentrated in Europe for a few transitory years before further or stronger expansion overseas.

- There will be winners and losers in Europe after 1992. Losers will call for protectionist measures, and some sub-sectoral protectionism cannot be ruled out. But the overall effect of "1992" will be a move towards a more liberal environment for entrepreneurship both internally and externally. Some speakers were, however, not so sure whether it would really induce a move towards a more liberal and competitive environment with negotiations in the industrial sector among member states being very difficult and time-consuming.

- Among the so-called "Third World countries" it is the weaker ones such as the ACP countries which will face increasing difficulties in maintaining their existing preferential and economic relations with the EEC. For strong competitors such as the Asian NIEs, the Single Market will be more of an opportunity to increase business than a threat.

- Europe will not become a fortress or a closed trading bloc in 1992. But serving the Single Market will only be possible for countries offering products which are highly competitive in terms of price and quality.

4. Whether or not the Asian NIEs will be able to compete in the world market in the 1990s will depend on their access to high technology and their capacity for fostering domestic technological capabilities with know-how imported from abroad. There are two scenarios:

- The pessimistic scenario, namely a tendency towards technological protectionism in OECD countries and increasing barriers to international technology diffusion.

- A more optimistic scenario, provided that the key players (namely the multinationals) realize that a zero sum game will have detrimental effects for all concerned.

  Even so, moving ahead in the global technological race will become increasingly difficult in the 1990s. This is a real challenge for Asian NIEs, probably a much more serious one than trade protectionism.

B. The management of EEC-Asian NIE interdependence: policy issues

1. There was full agreement that the present institutional framework for managing the interdependence between the EEC and Asian NIEs is inadequate. More informal contacts are needed as well as new approaches for improving the formal institutional framework. But skeptical views regarding the possibilities of EEC/NIEs policy coordination were also expressed: policy coordination is already an enormous task among EEC countries. But there is larger scope for more frequent consultations between the EEC and Asian NIEs and for fairer competition between their economies.

2. Policymakers from the German side stressed that the strengthening of ties between Asian NIEs and EEC countries is a big chance for Europe and a real challenge for entrepreneurs and for themselves. EEC countries and Asian NIEs should, however, not only concentrate on bilateral issues but should also address issues of global significance such as structural poverty, debt protectionism, population growth, environmental protection.

3. Key decision-makers both in Europe and Asian NIEs should be aware of the ongoing changes affecting the network of global economic and political structures. Both sides will have to cope with fairly new phenomena such as increased global interdependence, and the resulting decreasing significance of national boundaries, and the evolution of a multipolar power system implying the eclipse of the "Pax Americana" as well as the "Pax Japonica".

4. Future relations between the EEC and Asian NIEs should be based on the principle of "multilateralism". The European integration process emphasizing both economic and political

goals is not tantamount to the emergence of a trading bloc more or less closed to the outside world. The European approach is much in accordance with the concept of "open regionalism" and with GATT rules.

5. Asian NIEs were recommended to adopt a liberal approach as regards domestic policies and external economic relations. They should in particular accept the established international rules of the game in such fields as intellectual property rights protection, GATT principles, and various codes of conduct.

6. The informal and formal institutional framework should develop step-by-step. In the short term, emphasis should be placed on "policy discussion", but not on "policy coordination". This could be done at several levels:

- between EEC countries and individual NIEs;

- on a bilateral basis between the EEC-Commission and individual NIEs;

- between EEC and formal Asian organizations such as ASEAN, ADB, or more informal regional fora in the Pacific basin;

- through informal consultations between OECD and Asian NIEs, either individually or as a group (like the first meeting in Paris this year). As an excellent example, the EEC/ASEAN dialogue has proved to be extremely open and helpful and it has gradually developed institutional links. In general, German and EEC policymakers felt that Asian NIEs should also strengthen regional cooperation, including the formulation of a more ambitious concept for the long-term future.

7. As regards the special case of Taiwan, the following approach

adopted by the EEC and OECD was explained. OECD and EEC recognize the political weight of the People's Republic of China (member of the UN, member of the Security Council) and its future role as a key economic power in the long run. Although there is no way in the foreseeable future to establish formal political relations with Taiwan, EEC and OECD have made it clear to the People's Republic of China that Taiwan will be considered a full partner in the fields of trade, investment, technology transfer, cultural relations etc. As in the past, Taiwan will also be asked to participate fully in informal consultations within NGOs and some GOs. This should provide sufficient bases for long-term intensified cooperation, at least in concrete and practical terms.

8. For the shaping of future improved relations, the NIEs should develop more lobbying in Brussels; the various EEC institutions are certainly very accessible to all governmental and non-governmental representatives.

9. Beyond the principles of "multilateralism" (a free market approach internally and externally), some clarifications were also put forward concerning OECD countries' active industrial and technology policies, including OECD governments themselves spending enormous amounts of money (some US $ 100 billion a year) on strengthening their tech- nological base. The same observation is also valid for the Asian NIEs, namely Korea, Taiwan and Singapore. Hong Kong, which has so far adopted a non-interventionist approach, is obviously losing the technological race compared with its neighbours. On both sides then, real policies versus declared policies should be reassessed for more direct and practical talks, beyond pure rhetoric.

III. Areas of Consensus or Controversy

1. All participants agreed on the following:

- They recognise obvious trends toward globalisation of the world economy.

- They believe in a multilateral system of free trade as a common goal.

- They are against unilateralism, exclusive bilateralism, or closed regionalism.

- They would like to see gradual liberalisation in new areas of international business flows like services, government procurement, food supply, technology and know-how.

- They are in favour of increasing all kinds of links between Europe and the NIEs to overcome various misunderstandings and suspicions, and to build relations of confidence between the two groups of countries.

- They would support all kinds of instruments for promoting more cooperation between Europe and the NIEs, and in particular the integration of NIEs into international coordination structures. Consensus appeared to emerge even on the mechanisms of such coordination through informal or more formal dialogue frameworks.

2. Lessons to be learned from the economic success of the Asian NIEs:

Most observations tend to agree on the specificity of the Asian NIEs' experiences and on their limited relevance as models for less developed countries. However, there is much to be learned for both LDCs and rich nations, although there is much debate and controversy about the nature of the lessons to be drawn. This situation is directly related to the diversified perceptions of the Asian NIEs' success and of clear-cut differences among the NIEs.

- The take-off of the NIEs occurred under very specific historical circumstances and after massive US support (in the case of Korea and Taiwan), factors which are too often underestimated.

- Macroeconomic analysis has favoured either the free market approach or more seldom the role of public intervention (Korea, Singapore, Taiwan), but most observers have neglected an attempt to combine the two for a better explanation of the NIEs' success.

- Microeconomic analysis to detail the sharp differences among the 4 NIEs is still lacking in many fields (potentials of local private entrepreneurship, large-scale industrial policy, role of small and medium-sized firms, investment and saving correlations).

- The patterns of local politics, culture and social values have also played a very important role.

- The 4 Asian NIEs neither propose a single model of development nor should they be put into one too simplistic a basket by most of their competitors - USA and EEC in particular.

- Some of the NIEs' experiences should inspire other nations, for instance the key role of highly skilled human resources or the high rates of savings to feed domestic investment.

- The NIEs could offer more financial and technological assistance to LDCs, something they have already started doing by increasing investment to Southeast Asia and elsewhere.

- But the economic success of the NIEs is still too short a story (compared with the OECD nations) to allow an assessment of whether the NIEs will remain strong economies in the long run and whether they will be able to manage their close dependencies on world markets, particularly in a few industrial sectors.

- Asian NIEs are still small economies and not yet major engines of growth by world standards.

3. Some thoughts on the rapid industrialization process on a world scale.

After Europe, the USA and Japan, the Asian NIEs have embarked on rapid industrialization which (if the concept of flying geese is partly accepted at least) is also taking place in some regions of highly populated Asia (China, India, ASEAN).

- This type of rapid industrial development pattern has reached significant portions of the populations concerned but leaves the majority of the Asians largely out of the game. The minority beneficiaries should now consider how to involve the masses at the grass roots. This might mean the addition of other types of instruments to promote true development for "all".

- Rapid industrialization and authoritarian rule bring some key questions for the near future: social and political change or transition is then needed in all 4 NIEs (which is a well-known process in Europe).

- Too rapid industrialization and urbanization are now creating some major environment protection problems, at least as bad and sometimes much worse than in OECD countries (bearing in mind the small size of the NIEs). Protection of the environment and the quality of human life are becoming major concerns in both industrialized and newly industrialized countries. This is sufficient proof that new roads for more balanced economic and social development have to be explored for the sake of both rich, developing and poor nations.

In many ways, the experiences of the Asian NIEs are new contributions to the globalisation of the world economy and world affairs in general. They are the most recent illustration of transnational economic flows, multipolarism and the relative decline of national and regional frontiers. The emergence of the NIEs and the various challenges their integration into international cooperation poses clearly show that no nation or region will be able to play world leader any more. World affairs are becoming more competitive but also more unstable.

This International Round Table had the merit of presenting basic facts, avoiding formal rhetoric, and above all overcoming misconceptions and suspicions through frank dialogue and friendship. This was certainly a contribution to greater international cooperation and understanding on the long road to world globalisation.

Part One

The Asian NIEs and the Asia-Pacific Region

KOREA: A NEWLY INDUSTRIALIZING ECONOMY MARKET OPENING, INTERNATIONALIZATION AND INTERNATIONAL COOPERATION

Han Young-Soo
Director
Import Division Bureau of International Trade
Ministry of Trade and Industry
Government Building Complex II
Kwacheon

1. Market Opening and Internationalization on a Continuing Course

From 1980 to 1987, the share of the Asian NIEs (4 countries) increased from 1.1 % to 1.8 %, and the trade volume from 4.1 % to 6.7 %. The group's trade balance was transformed from a deficit of 11.6 billion dollars to a surplus of 22.9 billion dollars.

In the same period, Korea's share of world trade volume increased from 1 % to 1.8 % and what had been a chronic trade deficit finally moved into surplus in 1986. Today Korean industries in various sectors are leaders in worldwide production, including shipbuilding, televisions, VTRs, iron and steel, semiconductors, textiles, automobiles and cement.

The world economy may now be characterized by several phenomena. First, multi-polarization, the decline of the American economy and the growth in economic strength of Japan and the NIEs. Second, broadened globalization in that multinationals account for a third of world production. Third, the rise of trading blocs and protectionistic practices exemplified by the Single European Act and unilateralism in American trade policy. Neo-protectionism is based on "selectivism" and "unilateralism", and is seen in the increased demands of the NIEs to open markets and to implement policies of macro-economic adjustment, such as currency realignment.

Europe-Asia-Pacific Studies in Economy and Technology
Kulessa (Ed.)
The Newly Industrializing Economies of Asia

Trends in the world economy spur Korea to open its market in the name of reciprocity. But more than this, it must be recognized that market opening and internationalization is a responsibility Korea must bear as increasingly strong participant in the international economy, considering its recent rapid economic growth. Also, in order for Korea to join the ranks of advanced countries, last year the Korean government abolished the regulation for currency transactions (IMF article 8) and Korea is now preparing to adhere to GATT article 11, regarding the import liberalization of agricultural products and is planning to seek membership in the OECD.

2. Status of Market Opening and Internationalization of the Korean Economy

Market opening and internationalization are somewhat difficult to define; however, they might be distinguished in relative terms. "Market opening" may be regarded as a relatively passive concept, while "internationalization" is a more active concept. Market opening from the simplest conception refers to the liberalized goods and in the broadest conception means free access to goods, capital and services. Internationalization in broad terms includes domestic market opening with emphasis, however, on outward-oriented activities including overseas investment. I would like to proceed with an explanation of two areas; import liberalization and capital flows.

2.1 Import liberalization and the widening of market access

Import liberalization in Korea commenced in the late 1970s and has been accelerated since 1984. This is evidenced by the jump in the import liberalization ratio, from 53 % in 1977, to 69 % in 1980, 85 % in 1984, to 92 % in 1986 and 95.5 % as of September

1989 (99.5 % for manufactured products and 76.1 % for agricultural products). According to the latest import liberalization schedule (1989-1991), the overall liberalization ratio will reach 97.3 % by 1991 (99.9 % for manufactured products and 84.1 % for agricultural products).

Import liberalization has had a favourable effect on the economy; consumers have benefited, resources are allocated more efficiently and fair competition has been encouraged. It has, however, also ushered in an adverse set of circumstances in the farming community as well as for small and medium-sized industries. Apart from import liberalization, since 1987 the Korean government has continued to streamline individual laws so as to adapt Korea's trading system, specially import procedures to the GATT Code.

With the removal of non-tariff barriers, a reduction in tariffs has been accelerated. According to the tariff reduction schedule for 1981-1993, the average tariff will be lowered from 18.1 % in 1988 (16.9 % for manufactured items) to 7.9 % in 1993 (6.2 % for manufactured products), a level comparable to that in OECD countries!

The Surveillance System, which protected industries from liberalization, was abolished at the end of 1988 and, in its place, a Safeguard System and Anti-dumping Code was developed.

2.2 Capital flow liberalization and corporate internationalization

The liberalization of capital flows has occurred in various sectors (including currency transactions), however, this paper will address only the liberalization of investment and capital markets, and then, the internationalization of corporations.

Liberalization of investment

- Foreign investment in Korea has been rapidly liberalized since 1984. The liberalized ratio currently stands at 97.5 % in the manufactured sector and 60.8 % in the services sector. Advertising, wholesaling of pharmaceuticals and foreign trade agencies are scheduled for opening in a few years.

- Overseas investment has also increased rapidly since the nation began to record a trade surplus in 1986. The Korean government plans to liberalize foreign direct investment in real estate and financial assets as well, and incentives to promote investment will also be offered.

Internationalization of capital markets

Capital market internationalization has followed from the Korea Fund and the Korea Europe Fund, since 1981. The government also recently formulated a plan for the opening of the Bond Market (1989-1992) which will allow foreign direct investment in that market in 1992.

Internationalization of corporations

Internationalization of corporations means usually a complex system of export-import operations, international marketing and capital investment, with a worldwide information system. Today, the Korean company is still far from this advanced stage so that an investment abroad is more aptly termed an overseas operation rather than a multinational one.

To date the object of foreign direct investment has primarily been to secure natural resources, advanced technology and to deflect protectionism. Scale of investment is small (80 % of investment is below million dollars) and the investment region generally tends to be in the Asian countries and North America. Thus, internationalization of the Korean company is in an early phase and not yet a leading force in the global market in spite of the recent rapid growth in overseas investment.

3. Challenges to the Korean Economy and Directions for International Cooperation

Recently, the Korean economy has faced problems never before experienced. Market opening has forced firms to face great competition in the domestic market. Also as a result of the democratization process in the labour market wages have increased by more than 20 % annually, while productivity has increased by only about 14 %. Difficulties have been encountered in terms of unstable production.

The Korean won has appreciated by 32 % since the G-5 meeting of September 1985. In 1988, the won appreciated 15.8 % against the dollar while the Japanese yen and the Taiwan NT $ were stable or depreciated slightly against the dollar.

Wage rises and appreciation of the won against the dollar have slowed Korean exports, while changes in consumer patterns and expansion of the domestic market have effected a rise in imports. As a result the trade surplus has dropped. Furthermore, appreciation of the won and labour disputes have discouraged investments by firms. The economy has been led by consumption rather than exports or investment.

Such problems require both structural adjustment and external cooperation. The direction of internal structural adjustment may be summarized as follows:

- Industrial structure policy; development of high-tech industry (micro-electronics, mechatronics, aerospace, new materials, fine chemistry etc.), structural adjustment for declining industries (enhancement of competitiveness, production of high-value-added products).

- Industrial organization policy; keep markets competitive, promote medium-sized firms.

- Technology policy; increase in R&D (2 % of GNP in 1989 up to 3 % in 1991), introduction of advanced technology, strengthen external cooperation.

Structural adjustment is also a problem for Korea which is caused by a change in the international division of labour. It may be solved by international cooperation. Structural problems of advanced countries, regardless of their problems endogenous in the development of the economy of market, are caused by the rise of Japan and the NIEs. The structural problems of Korea and other NIEs, apart from problems caused by limited technology development, are caused by the rise of other developing countries and neo-protectionism in advanced countries.

The industries of comparative advantage of NIEs will shift from textiles, shipbuilding, iron and steel, to capital and technology-intensive industries such as automobiles, machinery and electronics in the 1990s. Advanced countries will maintain comparative advantages in such areas as biotechnology, aerospace, new materials etc. Considering changes in the international division of labour, NIEs and advanced countries should find the proper domestic structural adjustment to their internal and external economic situation. Intra-industry cooperation between NIEs and advanced countries may be pursued in the following manner:

- technical and capital cooperation with advanced countries in the area of high-tech industry such as electronics and new materials,

- intra-industry cooperation in the process in the area of mechanics and non-ferrous metals,

- product differentiation in the area of textiles and chemistry.

4. The Directions for Cooperation with the EC

The trade pattern of Asian NIEs is characterized by two imbalances; overdependence on the United States and Japan and regionally imbalanced trade. The trade dependence of NIEs on the United States and Japan is high; exports depend heavily on America, imports on Japan. The trade share of the EC, though, is only about 10 %.

35.3 % of Korea's exports are to the United States and 30.7 % of imports are from Japan. The EC accounts for 13.4 % of exports and 11.7 % of imports. This is also the case of capital flows and technology transfer (see table).

The relatively low dependence on the EC is due to various factors; the numerous languages, customs, industrial standards etc., lack of competitiveness in industrial technology compared to the United States and Japan, the passive marketing by EC firms in Asian countries. The effect of the Single European Act on NIEs is not yet clear but the cooperation between the NIEs and the EC seems very probable. Superficial trade relations between the NIEs and the EC would show great room for expansion of mutual economic cooperation.

In terms of the ratio of the current bilateral trade volume with regard to their potential import-export market, "Exploitation Degree (E)" can be defined as follows (here, in light of the ANIES-EC trade relations):

$$E^{x}_{an \rightarrow ec} = \frac{X_{an \rightarrow ec}}{X_{an}} \Big/ \frac{M_{ec}}{M_{w}}, \qquad E^{x}_{ec \rightarrow an} = \frac{X_{ec \rightarrow an}}{X_{ec}} \Big/ \frac{M_{an}}{M_{w}}$$

$$E^{m}_{an \leftarrow ec} = \frac{M_{an \leftarrow ec}}{M_{an}} \Big/ \frac{X_{ec}}{X_{w}}, \qquad E^{m}_{ec \leftarrow an} = \frac{M_{ec \leftarrow an}}{M_{ec}} \Big/ \frac{X_{an}}{X_{w}}$$

X = export, M = import, an: ANIES, w: world
$X_{an \rightarrow ec}$ = ANIEs' export to EC, $M_{an \leftarrow ec}$ = ANIEs' import from EC
E^{x} means E for export market (E^{m} for import market)

(If E = 1.0, then it indicates equilibrium; E > 1.0, over-exploitation; E < 1.0, under-exploitation)

The E between EC and NIEs stands far below 1.0 (approximately 0.2 - 0.4 respectively).

Considering E, the possible sectors for cooperation are chemical products (SITC 51, 55 - 58), non-ferrous metals (66), iron and steel (67), special machines (72), other machinery (74), electrical machinery (77), transport equipment (79), scientific instruments (87), and optical instruments (88).

Fields and modalities for the expansion of intra-industrial cooperation between NIEs and EC should be chosen on the basis of mutual benefit taking into consideration overall factors such as problems related to the respective industrial readjustments and other non-economic factors. In this regard, both sides would further their mutual cooperation in such fields as iron and steel, shipbuilding and automobiles in which the EC countries are actually suffering structural difficulties.

Let me introduce some directions for economic cooperation, especially between the EC and Korea, in two areas; trade cooperation and industrial cooperation.

First, for trade cooperation, it is necessary to relax trade frictions to induce a favourable trading environment through efforts such as continuous import liberalization and tariff reduction, streamlining of import procedures and strengthening the government's support of private efforts for market diversification.

Second, for industrial cooperation, the following directions merit pursuit:

- improve the laws and regulations related to foreign investment such as license procedures, tax and finance system to make a favourable environment for mutual investment activities including those in fields of manufacturing, banking, insurance and maritime industry;

- deepen mutual cooperation between sectoral private associations in the area of textiles, footwear, electronics and iron and steel;

- technology transfer to Korea by the EC in the field of high-tech industries and promotion of joint-venture projects on a small and medium scale;

- for cooperation in telecommunications and scientific technology, exchange of information, joint feasibility studies, joint conferences and exchange of some scientists and experts.

5. Concluding Remarks

So far I reviewed market opening, the problems of Korean economy as one of the NIEs, and direction for economic cooperation. I suggested cooperation between the EC and the NIEs to reduce the heavy dependence on the United States and Japan.

Korea had an annual growth rate of more than 12 % from 1986, but now faces problems due to such rapid economic development, an economy which might be considered "overheated" with regard to the "potential GNP growth", as well as the democratization process. Korea will overcome current difficulties considering its economic performance in the past and the experience of two oil shocks in the 1970s as well as the politico-economic crisis in 1980.

Now, the Korean government is making a long-term economic plan for the year 2000 which predicts that Korea will become an advanced nation by that time and stresses international economic cooperation over the long term.

Cooperation between the EC and the NIEs should be developed in the intra-industrial or "horizontal" level, so that it will benefit both sides and should be followed by the positive adjustment of advanced countries and a healthier industrial structure of the NIEs.

The relationship between Korea (as well as other NIEs) and the EC will be pursued to expand mutual cooperation. In this respect, the Single European Act and its effect on the Korean economy and taking advantage of opening the Korean market and internationalization for the part of the EC countries should continue to be examined.

External Economic Relations of Korea (by Region)

(Unit: $ US Mil., %)

		Period	World	USA	Japan	EC
Trade	Export (A)	1988	60,696	21,404 (35.3)	12,004 (19.8)	8,132 (13.4)
	Import (B)	1988	51,811	12,757 (24.6)	15,929 (30.7)	6,042 (11.7)
	(A) + (B)	1988	112,507	34,161 (30.4)	27,933 (24.8)	14,174 (12.6)
	(A) - (B)	1988	8,886	8,647	-3,925	2,090
Capital Flow	Foreign Investment in Korea	'62-7.'89	4,626	1,326 (28.7)	2,332 (50.4)	417 (9.0)
	Korean Investment abroad	'68-7.'89	1,173	382 (32.6)	34 (2.9)	47 (4.0)
	Foreign Loans	'59-7.'89	38,366	8,298 (21.6)	7,928 (20.7)	8,598 (22.4)
Introduction of Technology (number)		'62-7.'89	5,516	1,400	2,873	719

Notes: ( ) means importance in percentage
Sources: Ministry of Trade and Industry, Ministry of Finance

KOREA 2000: ECONOMIC AND SOCIAL TARGETS AND DEVELOPMENT STRATEGIES

Hak-Yong Rhee
Professor, Director
Institute of Economic Research
Korea University
5-1, Anamdong, Sungbuk-ku
Seoul 136-701

1. Economic Success and New Challenges

It is widely recognized that the Korean government's policy shift from an "inward-looking" strategy to an "outward-looking" one in the early 1960s was a tremendous success. In fact, it was so successful that the annual average growth rate of real GNP increased from 4.1 percent before the policy shift to 9.6 percent for the entire period of 1962-1979. This period of rapid growth may be regarded as a critical experiment not only for the development strategy in a resource-poor and poverty-stricken country but also for the necessity of economic planning in a basically market economy (see Edward E. Mason et al., 1980). It is indeed remarkable to recall that the development strategy overcame the hardships of the first oil shock in the later part of 1973.

In addition to the policy shift from import substitution to export promotion in the early 60s, there was an important policy shift in the early 70s, namely the shift of the government's emphasis from labor-intensive light industries to heavy and chemical industries. It is rather difficult to evaluate the validity of the latter policy shift, but in view of the Korean economic performance in the 80s, it does seem to be working. The second policy shift steered economic and social development of Korea toward quite a different path from those of the other Asian NIEs such as Taiwan (for different industrial structures and economic performances in Korea and Taiwan, see Hak-Yong Rhee, 1987).

Europe-Asia-Pacific Studies in Economy and Technology
Kulessa (Ed.)
The Newly Industrializing Economies of Asia

The shift of development path in the early 70s changed the industrial structure such that the share of heavy and chemical industries in GDP, as well as in exports, rose much faster than in Taiwan, and such industrial restructuring imposed numerous costs in terms of higher inflation, severe fiscal deficits, rapidly rising foreign debt, and finally greater economic concentration and widening income inequality. In my opinion, these economic costs of rapid growth caused the social unrest in the late 70s which culminated in the assassination of the late President Park on October 26, 1979.

Due to the political upheaval following the president's assassination, together with the second oil shock, the Korean economy in 1980 experienced the first negative growth since the Korean War. When the new government came into power the following year, the policymakers were determined to remedy the economic ills of the 70s. The first policy priority was to stabilize prices through sound fiscal policy and tight control of the money supply. The stated policy objective was "equity as well as growth" which was another big shift from the popular catchphrase "growth first and distribution later" of the 70s.

Beyond all expectations, the stabilization measures of limiting the growth of money supply to 10 percent and balancing the budget, together with authoritarian rule, brought inflation under control, that is, below 5 percent from 1982. This first success of price stability gave tremendous confidence to the government, the business community, and the people as a whole. Gradually, the price stability encouraged savings and reduced speculative activity, which was known to be the chief villain for worsening income inequality.

At the same time, the world economic environment was favorable to the Korean economy in the middle of the 1980s. The favorable exogenous conditions were described by what was called the "three lows", namely the falling oil price, lower interest rates in international capital markets, and the falling value of the US dollar in Japan and Europe. All this boosted the Korean economy from about 1984, and the economic boom continued until 1988. Of course, the 1988 Summer Olympics in Seoul was another favorable factor. The remarkable economic success in terms of growth is shown in Table 1.

One can observe a couple of dramatic changes by looking at economic performance. The first is the trade surplus, which Korea experienced for the first time in 1986, that reached about three billion US dollars. This is also reflected in the excess of the savings rate over the investment rate. This reduced our foreign debt from approximately 45 billion US dollars to less than 30 billion in 1988. It is expected that sometime this year the country will become a net creditor country. The second interesting change is the fall of the exchange rate, which also started from 1986.

The remarkable economic success has brought many new challenges. The first challenge is the stronger pressure from our major trading partners such as the USA, Japan, and EC countries to further open our domestic markets. The most controversial and painful area is the agricultural sector, where import liberalization has brought some violent resistance, despite the government's promise to provide bailout programs. It appears that our government will have to struggle with endless demands for improving economic conditions in the rural sector. Another challenge, perhaps more important and more difficult, is the stronger demands from labor not only for higher wages but for better working conditions and shorter working hours. These labor demands have turned into violent strikes and confrontations with police in many cases. Not only blue-collar workers but also some white-collar professionals such as teachers and bank employees are trying to form trade unions. The political democratization since 1987 has influenced these stronger labor movements.

At the same time, there is a growing feeling among intellectuals as well as policymakers that the government has to play a stronger role in relieving the worsening inequalities in income distribution. The increasing economic concentration due to the growing economic power of the dominant business conglomerates is blamed for the distributional inequality. This implies that in the future some economic efficiency may have to be sacrificed to improve equity.

2. Economic and Social Objectives

2.1 Economic objectives

Projections for major economic indicators in Korea up to the year 2000 were made by the Korea Development Institute (KDI) in 1985. Those projections, together with the actual figures for 1988, are shown in Table 2.

There is no problem with population projection; the population will be around fifty million by 2000, with the growth rate reaching around 1.2 percent.

According to KDI projections, the annual average growth rate of GNP for 1985-90 will be 5.6 percent and 8.2 percent for 1990-2000. Considering the fact that the annual average growth rate for 1981-88 was 9.9 percent, the KDI's projection for 1985-90 seems to be too conservative. If the growth rate for 1989-90 is 5 percent (the actual growth rate for the first quarter of 1989 was 5.7 percent despite some violent labor strikes), the GNP in 1990 will be over 120 billion dollars in terms of 1984 constant prices. Thus the GNP projection for 2000 should be adjusted accordingly.

The per capita GNP projection should be adjusted by the difference between actual and estimated growth. The actual per capita income in 1988 has already surpassed the projection for 1990. It is expected that per capita GNP in 1990 will be over 3,000 dollars in terms of 1984 prices.

Considering the actual figures for 1988 and assuming the projected growth rates for the 1990s, one can say that the level of per capita GNP in Korea by the year 2000 will reach that of countries whose per capita incomes were around ten to twelve thousand dollars in 1988. This means that our per capita GNP will roughly double in the next ten years.

The KDI projections show that the trade volume will be about 350 billion dollars in current prices by the year 2000, the trade being roughly balanced and both exports and imports growing by 12.5 percent per annum. Although the trade volume roughly doubled during the period of 1984-88, with exports growing by more than 17 percent per annum for the period, one should remember that any projection of trade volume incorporates numerous exogenous variables over which a small country like Korea has no control. Based on the performance of the past couple of decades, the KDI projections seem to be neither too conservative nor too optimistic.

2.2 Social objectives

The first social objective is to maintain a "free and stable" society. This may imply that Korea wants to develop and maintain a western style democracy.

The second social objective is to have a "prosperous, dynamic, and efficient society" so that the levels of income and consumption will reach those of the advanced countries. This target seems to imply that market mechanisms will be enhanced and thus fewer controls will be imposed. Indeed, the Korean government has tried to lift controls in such areas as credit allocation and the use of foreign exchange, to name just two.

The last, and perhaps the most difficult, objective is to have an "equitable and just" society by providing equal opportunity for education, employment, fair competition, and an "equitable standard of living". To achieve this objective, the government is expected to take a stronger role in redistribution.

The most pervasive social problem in Korea today seems to be the public antagonism toward the "haves" whether it involves wealth or political power. At the same time, income inequality is getting worse, simply because of insufficient policy measures for redistribution. One example is a rather higher tax on wage income than on capital income, which had been necessary for encouraging capital accumulation during the 60s and 70s. It is essential that stronger redistributive policies be instituted in the near future, implying that income distribution may improve in the future at the expense of higher growth.

3. Development Strategies

3.1 Expansion of economic base

Korea is basically a trade-oriented country, the total trade volume being more than eighty percent of GNP. Trade has been and will be the engine of economic growth in Korea. This implies that the economic expansion should be made in such a way as to improve our international competitiveness.

Rising wages and increasing social burdens require industrial restructuring in such a way that new investments are directed into capital and technology-intensive areas rather than those of the past. This does not mean that our investments should all go to heavy industries; even in the light industries such as textiles, new investments should be guided into those products which yield higher value added and higher labor productivity. Of course, businesses will seek those areas, and government policies should be adjusted to act as stimulators, rather than barriers.

Industrial restructuring requires continuous technological improvement. Since it is becoming extremely difficult to get technology transfers from advanced countries, particularly in the area of high-tech industries, Korea intends to invest much more in technological development, including investments in basic science education and research.

The stated strategy for expanding the economic base is to maintain the current domestic savings rate. This is necessary for maintaining high levels of investments both at home and abroad not only for expanding physical capital but also for improving human capital.

3.2 Promotion of national welfare and regional development

Economic expansion alone is not sufficient to satisfy the social goal of becoming an "equitable and just" society no matter how vague and subjective the goal may be. For this purpose, the Korean government intends to strengthen regional economic bases by dispersing industrial locations into rural areas so as to increase non-farm incomes of farm households.

At the same time, the government is planning to impose stiff capital gains taxes. In particular, it is expected to expand wider application of the concept of "public property" for land in order to stop speculation on land and capital gains from such activity. I also expect higher property taxes in general, including higher taxes on capital income, than in the past. In other words, there will be stronger tax policies and transfer payment programs directed at income redistribution in general.

According to the government's strategy, stronger environmental protection is an essential policy for promoting national welfare. Thus, we expect to see stronger government regulation and increasing expenditures for environmental restoration and protection.

3.3 Active participation in international cooperation

As mentioned above, Korea's basic economic growth strategy is trade promotion, due to such obvious reasons as poor natural resource endowments, a smaller domestic market, increasingly built-in economic interdependence with other countries, and so on. The trade volume in Korea is already within the top ten in the near future. Thus, it is widely recognized, at least among policymakers, that Korea should bear wider responsibilities for maintaining the world trade regime through vigorous pursuit of import liberalization in domestic markets and active participation in trade liberalization movements in the international community. It is felt in Korea today that "rapid economic growth could be sustained only in parallel with its degree of market opening and internationalization" (Ministry of Trade and Industry, p.15).

Korea's active commitment to opening up domestic markets is reflected in both tariff reductions and dramatic reductions in the number of restricted items for imports. Average tariff rates were cut almost in half between 1983 and 1989, from 23.7 percent to 12.7 percent. This will be further reduced to 7.9 percent by 1993. The average tariff rate for manufactured goods is even lower; it was reduced to 11.2 percent from 22.6 percent in 1983, and it will be lowered to 6.2 percent by 1993. The restricted items for manufactured goods are only 41 out of a total of 8,278, showing an import liberalization rate of 99.5 percent. The import liberalization rate for agricultural and fishery goods are 74.7 and 34.2 percents respectively (ibid., pp. 18-19).

Korea is actively seeking so-called "South-South cooperation", that is, closer economic relations with other developing countries. The government has already set up the "External Aid Fund", currently about 50 million dollars but expected to be increased to 500 million dollars per year in the next couple of years. Numerous restrictions on foreign direct investments have been lifted to encourage our business community to invest abroad, particularly in developing countries. It is reported, in fact, that our direct investments in ASEAN countries have been increasing rapidly during the last year or so. Most of this direct investment is made in light manufacturing, such as footwear, textiles and clothing, and electronics, where labor costs play a relatively important role.

Both the business community and the government are actively trying to improve our economic relations with communist countries such as China, Russia, Eastern European countries, and North Korea. The recent events in Beijing cooled down the fever a bit, but it appears that our business community treats the socialist bloc as a new frontier for its business expansion.

4. Concluding Remarks

Economic expansion and development in Korea for the last three decades in terms of per capita GNP, trade volume, structural transitions, technological adoptions, viability of sustained growth, and above all the recognition as one of the NIEs in the international community has been beyond most economists' expectations. It is not difficult to recognize, however, that such phenomenal economic growth and structural changes were possible due to international political stability, together with coerced austerity on the part of the majority of the population, and conducive international trade environments.

Perhaps as inevitable result of the rapid economic growth, the country is going through some serious internal social challenges as well as external adjustment problems. The internal turmoil is associated with the political democratization that started in 1987 after more than twenty-five years of authoritarian rule, and can be classified as severe labor disputes, acute conflicts between the wealthy and the non-wealthy, disparity between rural and urban economic conditions, and increasing economic concentration. The external problems are associated with increasing responsibilities and commitments to becoming a fair and responsible trade partner in the international arena.

The economic picture described by the KDI projections is based on the assumption that Korea will somehow overcome most of the internal, as well as external, challenges that the country is faced with. According to local reports, the single labor dispute at Daewoo shipyard during June, 1989, brought about a loss of more than one hundred million dollars without counting indirect effects. For most of the social conflicts, there is no instant cure; people have to learn through a painful learning-by-doing process. This implies that the economic growth rate in the 90s will have to be slowed down, first because it is most unlikely to allow another authoritarian system, and secondly because democratization in political decision-making as well as economic policy formulation is considerably costly in terms of economic efficiency. With all this in mind, the picture of Korean economy by the year 2000 given in Table 2 may in fact be too rosy.

Table 1 Recent Performances of the Korean Economy [1)]

	1980	1983	1985	1987	1988	Annual average 1981-88
Real GNP Growth Rate (%)	-4.8	11.9	5.4	12.7	12.2	9.9
Per Capita GNP (US $)[2)]	1,592	2,002	2,194	3,098	4,040	
Consumer Price Index (%)	28.7	3.4	2.5	3.0	7.1	6.2
Saving Rate (%)[3)]	23.7	28.1	29.5	36.9	38.1	31.3
Investment Rate[3)]	32.8	29.7	30.0	29.9	30.2	30.6
Current Balance (100 mil. US $)	-53.2	-16.1	-8.8	98.5	141.6	
Exports (100 mil. US $)	175.1	244.5	302.8	472.8	607.0	
(Growth Rate, %)[4)]	(16.3)	(11.9)	(3.5)	(36.2)	(28.4)	(17.3)
Imports (100 mil. US $)	222.9	261.9	311.4	410.2	518.1	
(Growth Rate, %)[4)]	(9.6)	(8.0)	(1.6)	(29.9)	(26.3)	(11.8)
Exchange Rate (W/$)[5)]	659.9	795.5	890.2	792.3	684.1	

1) Bank of Korea, Principal Economic Indicators (1989) 6; Revised National Account (1989) 3.
2) In terms of current prices.
3) Percentage of GNP.
4) Over the previous year.
5) Rate at the end of the year.

Table 2 Major Economic Indicators[1)]

	Unit	1984	1988	1990	2000	Average growth 1985-90	Annual rate (%) 1991-2000
Population	Million	40.6	41.8	44.1	49.4	1.38	1.14
GNP	Billion US $ in 1984 price	81.1	110.4	112.2	247.5	5.6	8.2
Per capita GNP	US $ in 1984 price	1,999	2,641	2,542	5,016	4.1	7.0
GNP deflator	1980 = 100	133.0	153.1	163.5	240.8	3.5	3.9
Comm. exports	Billion US $ in current price	26.3 (29.2)[2)]	(60.7)[2)]	53.4	173.2	12.5	12.5
Comm. imports	Billion US $ in current price	27.4 (30.6)[2)]	(51.8)[2)]	51.8	168.2	11.2	12.5

1) KDI, National Long-Term Development Perspective (in Korean), (September 1985) p.228.
Economic Planning Board, Korean Economic Indicators, various issues.
2) Total exports and imports.

References

1. Bank of Korea (June 1989) Principal Economic Indicators.
2. Bank of Korea (March 1989) Revised National Account.
3. EPB (1988) Social Indicators in Korea.
4. KDI (1985) National Long-Term Development Perspective (in Korean).
5. Mason E. S. et al. (1980) The Economic and Social Modernization of the Republic of Korea. Council on East Asian Studies, Harvard University.
6. Ministry of Trade and Industry (Republic of Korea) (1989) Free and Fair Trade.
7. Rhee H.-Y. (January 1988) Industrial Structure and Economic Performances: Korea and Taiwan. The Journal of Asiatic Studies 79:171-190.

KOREA'S LONG-TERM TRADE PROSPECTS AND POLICIES TO THE YEAR 2000

Lee Young Sae
Director
Import Division
Bureau of International Trade
Ministry of Trade and Industry
Government Building Complex II
Kwacheon

I. Introduction

Since 1986, the benchmark year in which Korea made the first trade surplus in its history of economic development, Korea has turned into a surplus economy. Not only has it entered an era of surplus but it has also surfaced as an eye-catching country in the world economy, emerging as the 12th biggest trading country of the world by recording a hundred billion dollars of combined import and export trade in 1988. Owing to the cumulative surplus in trade since 1986, Korea is also expected to become a net creditor country from 1990. Underlying this surprising performance in trade are many factors, both internal and external. The relatively favorable world trade environment during the last quarter of a century, except for recent protectionist tendencies among industrialized countries, has contributed to the success of the Korean economy. World import volume increased on average by 5.1 % a year from 1970 to 1987. The GATT system worked fairly well with only occasional minor modifications up to the 1980s, although the world economy was suffering from stagflation sparked off by two consecutive oil shocks in the 1970s. This rather favorable world environment was well matched internally by government support for an outward-looking policy. Various incentives were given to promote exports, for instance: export financing loans, tariff exemption on imports of intermediate goods and capital equipment to be used for promotion of exports and maintaining relatively low exchange rates, etc. It goes without saying that trade was the

Europe-Asia-Pacific Studies in Economy and Technology
Kulessa (Ed.)
The Newly Industrializing Economies of Asia

driving force behind Korea's economic development. Therefore, it was possible for the Korean economy to grow so fast that one can only compare its performance to the record of Japan, Taiwan and Germany in recent history. However successful the past performance of the Korean economy might have been, it is quite a different matter whether or not the Korean economy will grow as fast in the future. Particularly in the case of trade, there are many aspects to be considered in judging what the future trend will be under the anticipated new conditions of world trade. Now is the time for the existing trade policy strategies to be designed to suit the new environment in the 1990s. This is what this paper intends to do. Following this introduction, a number of expected changes in the world trade environment in the coming decade will be described. Then, Korea's trade will be forecasted until the end of this century, based on assumptions regarding a few exogenous variables such as world import volume and the growth rate of Korea's GDP. Finally, the directions of this new trade policy will be briefly discussed.

II. Changes in the Trade Environment in the 1990s

In the coming decade, some significant changes in the environment of world trade are foreseeable. By 1992, the European Single Market will have been completed if the on-going project keeps to its schedule. Threatened by the unification of the EC bloc, the US and Japan will be motivated to move towards regionalization of the Pan-Pacific basin countries. The GATT system will be strengthened if the Uruguay Round is ratified by member countries in one form or another. Above all, the socialist countries, including the USSR and China, will concentrate on their economic development through open-door policies which will obviously help the world economy to grow smoothly and rapidly. Developing countries, particularly the Southeast Asian countries, have embarked on vigorous industrialization and will emerge as newly agro-industrializing countries in the 1990s. The world economy will be more decentralized and divided into three or four economic regions as a result: Pan-Pacific region, EC Single Market, Asian NICs and/or socialist countries. If trade imbalance is reduced to a still significant but manageable level among industrialized countries, the foreign debt problems of a number of developing countries, which made the protectionist world trade environment even cloudier, will also remain stable. With foreseeable change in the world trade environment, technological innovation will further accelerate and, as a result of technical change, industrial structures will change in favor of the high-tech service and information sectors.

All these changes in the world economy in the 1990s will have mixed effects on Korea's trade performance. The Development of economic blocs will undoubtedly hinder Korea's trade as it pursues globalism. Korea is now exporting to about 125 countries and importing from more than 106 countries. If Fortress Europe, for example, continues to develop after 1992, which many non-European countries are worried about, it will make it difficult for the Korean economy to have mutual beneficial relations with European nations through trade. On account that the US trade deficit does not seem to be decreasing to any significant degree, perhaps to less than 100 billion dollars, bilateral pressure to open Korean domestic market will continue to be heavy in all sectors, ranging from agriculture to services and including intellectual property rights.

Challenges to the Korean economy do not come only from outside; there are serious internal challenges, too. Labor unrest and wage hikes following strikes are one of the important factors which could jeopardize the Korean economy by critically weakening international competitiveness. In 1988 alone, wages in the manufacturing sector rose by as much as 22 %, which far exceeded the 7 % increase in labor productivity. Pressure to raise the Korean won against major currencies including the US dollar are expected to be heavy in the 90s, as long as Korea maintains its trade surplus. Rising wages on the one hand and a higher exchange rate on the other hand force a shift to capital- and technology-intensive import substituting industries from labor-intensive and export-oriented ones. However, barriers to a smooth change in industrial structure lie ahead. Sophisticated manpower urgently needed in high-tech industries is in short supply whilst there continues to be an excessive supply of labor in the conventional low value-added industries. The existence of labor unions makes it difficult for labor to move from sector to sector.

III. Trade Prospects in the 1990s

Before forecasting Korea's trade in the 1990s, a number of assumptions should be made regarding the rate of growth in world imports and Korean gross domestic product, on which Korea's export and import are largely dependent. Taking into consideration the world trade environment outlined in the previous section and the forecasts of world imports published by major international forecasting institutes such as WEFA and DRI, world imports in the coming decade are expected to grow by 4.8 % each year up to the year 2000. However, growth in world trade will not be smooth and steady throughout the period. Dividing the entire period until 2000 into three phases, relatively slow growth in world trade can be expected during the first phase which extends to 1992. This is because the cloudy and protectionist environment of world trade will continue during this phase and the world economy can be expected to slow down conspicuously, no matter how soft or hard the landing is. During the second phase, from 1993 to 1996, world trade will accelerate owing to the favorable trade environment: conclusion of the Uruguay Round, emergence of Asian NICs, recovery of the US economy, and completion of the European Single Market, etc. In the final phase, there is a worry that world inflation will be rekindled and the world economy will again slow down.

Domestically, the Korean economy is expected to grow at 7.3 % a year up to the year 2000, which is much slower than its performance in the past. Particularly, during the first phase, owing to the unfavorable environment of world trade and the rising demand for democratization and equality, the economy will slow down. But during the second phase the economy will speed up again, mainly as a result of a favorable external environment and the establishment of new arrangements based on equity between the "haves" and "have-nots" which will lead to the revitalization of the Korean economy. During the third phase, the economy will reach a new equilibrium which will be slower but steady and balanced. Other important variables in forecasting Korea's trade are price variables such as exchange rate movements, changes in wages and productivity, world import price index, etc. However, the bases on which they are assumed will not be explained here.

Taking into consideration this rather conservative forecast for the Korean economy, it seems that export performance will not be like it was in the past. Based on the regression estimated from 1970 to 1987, the elasticity of exports in real terms with regard to the world import volume is 3.25 while the elasticity with regard to the relative price of Korea's export unit price divided by world import unit price is approximately minus one as eq. 1 below depicts. This means that as world import volume increased by 1 %, Korea's export increased by about 3.25 %. But it is difficult for us to assume that this elasticity will continue in the 90s for reasons which will be explained below. One of the reasons why elasticity will be lower in the 1990s is simply that if the economy grows, the growth rate of exports and of the economy itself cannot be as fast as before. Another reason that is more characteristic of the Korean economy is that, on the one hand, an unfavorable external trade environment would impair steady export growth while, on the other, the competitiveness of Korean products would be weakened by an internal environment unfavorable to the exporting sector, i.e. pressure to raise the exchange rate and wages and to eliminate policy incentives for exports. Therefore, the elasticity of exports with regard to the world import demand will steadily fall to 1.6 by 2000. The export unit price, which reflects the price competitiveness of Korea's export goods, will depend on three variables; real wages adjusted for labor productivity, index for import unit prices and exchange rate. According to the estimates from 1970 to 1987 as reported below in eq. 2, a 1 % increase in real wages adjusted for labor productivity pushed up the export unit price by 0.33 % and a 1 % increase in the import unit price pushed it up by 0.44 % while a 1 % increase in the exchange rate lowered it by 0.3 %. It is assumed that these elasticities will continue in the 1990s with only marginal changes in their magnitude. Based on these two equations, Korea's exports are expected to grow by 13 % in nominal terms and 9 % in real terms each year up to the year 2000.

. Export Equation

$$\ln(EXPKOR/EUVKOR) = \underset{(-12.966)}{-16.9769} + \underset{(19.182)}{3.2585} * \ln(IMPWOR/IUVWOR)$$

$$\underset{(-2.918)}{-1.0150} * \ln(EUVKOR/IUVWOR)$$

R = 0.9853 D.W. = 0.797
EXPKOR: Korea's Exports, million dollars, in custom bases
EUVKOR: Korea's Export Unit Value Index, dollar base 1980 = 100
IMPWOR: World Imports, billion dollars

. Export Unit Value Equation

$$\ln(EUVKOR) = \underset{(5.993)}{2.9158} + \underset{(5.900)}{0.3309} * \ln(WGEIDX/(GDPMAN/EMPMAN))$$

$$+\underset{(7.381)}{0.4423} * \ln(IUVKOR) - \underset{(-3.081)}{0.2918} * \ln(EXCAVR)$$

R = 0.9903 D.W. = 1.568

EUVKOR: Korea's Export Unit Value Index, dollar base 1980 = 100
WGEIDX: Wage Index, 1980 = 100
GDPMAN: GDP of Manufacturing, billion dollars, 1980 constant price
EMPMAN: Manufacturing Employment Index, 1980 = 100
IUVKOR: Korea's Import Unit Value Index, dollar base, 1980 = 100
EXCAVR: Exchange Rate, Period Average, ₩/$

The forecast for imports to the year 2000 is based on the same methods as those used for exports. Demand for imports in real terms increases by 1.4 % as GDP grows by 1 %, whilst decreasing by 0.3 % as the ratio of import unit price adjusted for exchange rate to wholesale prices increases by 1 %. The income elasticity of imports is expected to decline in the 1990s if the economies of scale are taken into consideration. But market-opening and elimination of non-trade barriers will offset the scale effect to some degree. Therefore, import demand in nominal terms is expected to grow by an average 12.1 % per year while in real terms it will grow by 9.0 %. Thus Korea's exports will amount to 208.3 billion dollars in 2000 while imports will be about 204.4 billion dollars, which is slightly less than the volume Germany is exporting and importing now. The combined forecast for exports and imports shows that the trade balance to the year 2000 will remain in surplus. But the surplus relative to total trade volume is expected to narrow from 8 % in 1988 to only 1 or 2 % in 2000. The degree of openness or the ratio of trade reliance, which is defined as the ratio of the value of imports and exports to GDP, is likely to decline slightly from 68 % now to 65 % in 2000.

. Import Demand Equation

$$\ln(IMPKOR/IUVKOR) = \underset{(-2.549)}{-2.7337} + \underset{(38.968)}{1.4008} * \ln(GDPKOR) \underset{(-1.864)}{-0.3285} * \ln((IUVKOR * EXCAVR)/WPIKOR)$$

R = 0.9915 D.W. = 1.528

IMPKOR: Korea's Import, million dollars, in custom bases
GDPKOR: Korea's GDP, billion won, 1980 constant price
IUVKOR: Korea's Import Unit Value Index, dollar base, 1980 = 100
EXCAVR: Exchange Rate, Period Average, W/$
WPIKOR: Korea's Wholesale Price Index, 1980 = 100

Regional trade is expected to approach equilibrium in the long term. Trade with the US will grow at below-average speed so that the share of US trade in Korea's total trade will shrink from 35 % at present to about 27 % in 2000. However, trade imbalances with the US will become negligible because it is expected that imports from the US will grow faster than exports to the US. According to the regional forecast, the growth rate of exports to the US is expected to be 8.5 % while that of imports from the US will be 13.1 %. In contrast, exports to Japan will grow faster than imports because yen appreciation against Korean won is expected to prevail in the long run and import substitution of capital goods in Korea will continue. The share of trade with Japan and the EC is likely to remain at the same level as it is now, and trade balances will be attained with these countries by 2000.

However, trade with developing countries, especially with China, is expected to increase sharply, as anyone can imagine. Bilateral trade with China will amount to more than 20 billion dollars in 2000, growing at 18 % a year average in the 1990s. China's share in Korea's total trade volume will double by 2000 making it Korea's third largest trading partner. Trade with developing countries will also grow rapidly because it is expected that countries such as those of Southeast Asia will maintain complementary relations with Korea in trade as their industrialization accelerates. Korea can provide these newly agro-industrializing countries with the machines and equipment using appropriate technology and at low prices which they badly need. They will also have better market access as Korea's domestic market grows, incomes improve and more market-opening is achieved.

The commodity composition of Korea's trade will also change significantly in the coming decade. Machines, electronics and automobiles will be the leading export industries, their share in total exports will grow from 35 % at present to 50 % in 2000. However, some sectors in the high-tech industry such as microelectronics, robotics, fine ceramics, mechatronics, aerospace and bio-tech will rapidly get a competitive edge in the late 1990s if adequate and opportune investments in these sectors are made with government support. Import composition by use is expected to change in the 1990s, as industry shifts towards resource-saving and technology-intensive sectors. Fewer imports will be required for the production of high-value-added exports, which means the import component ratio of export goods will fall. Development of the capital goods industry will also make the Korean economy less dependent on imports of investment goods, especially from Japan whose share is about 30.7 % of total Korean imports. However, imports of consumer goods will increase as the standard of living goes up and non-trade barriers to foreign goods fall as a result of government measures in the coming surplus era.

IV. Direction of Trade Policy in the 1990s

In spite of the many obstacles and barriers lying ahead internally as well as externally, as explained already in this paper, it seems that Korea will emerge as one of the major trading countries in the coming decade, ranking 10th in the world by trading volume. A moderate but solid trade surplus will be maintained, unless unexpected shocks from abroad or at home deal a critical blow to the Korean economy. Therefore, international pressure on Korea to take a more active role and greater responsibility in shaping world trade will increase, to the degree where it will be almost impossible for Korea to resist. Bilateral pressure on Korea to open its domestic market is expected to be even heavier and is building up faster than the Korean economy's ability to adjust. In the world market, trade conflicts with industrialized countries will be very likely to occur in the field of high-tech which is now in its infant stage in Korea but has a promising future. Korea will also be chased by developing countries in the field of low-value-added products. Therefore, it is very likely that trade conflicts with developing countries will also occur, both in the domestic market and in the world market. Domestically, surplus creates many new problems. Among other things, it tends to unsettle the economic stability which was obtained with great effort during the 1980s. Another problem is that it tends to disturb balanced growth among sectors.

Trade policy in the 1990s should be designed to solve all the above-mentioned problems the Korean economy is expected to confront in the coming decade. Therefore, the new policies are targeted at 1) internationalization of the economy, 2) expansionary but balanced growth of trade, and 3) maintenance of competitiveness of industry in the world market. First, as for the internationalization of the economy, Korean business companies will have to abide by the fair and just multilateral rule in world market, and the government will have to cooperate with major trading partners on policy coordination by participating in international institutions such as the OECD. Internationalization means Korea's assuming a more active role and greater responsibility in maintaining free trade in the world market. Therefore, Korea has to provide developing as well as developed countries with more access to its domestic market by eliminating tariff and non-tariff barriers. Second, in order to ensure growing but balanced trade, it is essential to keep the economy stable. Without price stabilization, it is impossible to envisage steady and balanced growth. By balanced growth, what is meant is a balance between exports and imports, tradable and non-tradable sectors and different regions. Third, to promote trade by enhancing the competitiveness of industrial products, it is necessary to create new leading export industries. In the 1990s, high-tech industries such as mechatronics, robotics, bio-tech, aerospace and microelectronics, and capital goods will have to emerge as leading export sectors. In order to induce investment in these sectors, the government should support the training of high-tech manpower and the smooth transfer of manpower from conventional sectors to high-tech industries. Investment funds for these industries should also be mobilized and financed through the intermediation of the financial sector. Speculative investment in land or real estate, however, prevents funds generated by an economic surplus from flowing into the manufacturing sector and should, therefore, be discouraged. It is very undesirable that in Korea speculative investment should have generated higher wind-fall profits than manufacturing in recent years because this accelerates the hollowing-out of the manufacturing sector. Above all, labor unrest should be calmed whatever the effort or cost, simply because at present it is rapidly eroding the vitality of the Korean economy. However, labor problems should be neither suppressed nor ignored but solved on the grounds that the economic cake has to be distributed rationally among workers and owners.

TAIWAN: CLAIMS AND STRATEGIES TOWARDS EUROPE

Sho-Chieh Tsiang
Professor, President
Chung-Hua Institution for Economic Research
75 Chang-Hsieng Street
Taipei 10671

With a population totalling 320 million and a combined GNP exceeding 4 trillion US dollars, the European Economic Community (hereafter the EEC) is an economic entity comparable in all dimensions to the United States of America and much larger than Japan. Yet Taiwan (the Republic of China), one of the four remarkable NIEs on the Asian Pacific rim, seems to have rather neglected the EEC in its spectacular expansion of trade until very recently (i.e., until after 1985).

For various reasons, both geographical as well as political, Taiwan had concentrated its trade development mainly on the US and Japan. The resulting rather lopsided development of trade can be readily observed from tables 1 and 2.

From these tables, it may be observed that although the EEC is a market comparable in size to the US it managed to occupy only less than one half, sometimes even less than one third, of the share of the US in the total volume of Taiwan's trade. The EEC's share has been even smaller than that of Japan which is much smaller in terms of population and aggregate GNP.

This lopsided development of Taiwan's trade is not the fault of Taiwan alone. The European countries are at least equally responsible for it. The most important reason for the lack of closer trade relations between Taiwan and the EEC is the lack of diplomatic and consular relations between the two entities, which greatly hampers the development of trade. At the moment not a single EEC country maintains diplomatic recognition of the Repub-

Europe-Asia-Pacific Studies in Economy and Technology
Kulessa (Ed.)
The Newly Industrializing Economies of Asia

lic of China in Taiwan. Presumably, they gave us up as a lost cause very early on and flocked to recognize the People's Republic of China, fully expecting us to perish soon in the ruthless contest for survival.

Somewhat to their surprise, however, we managed not only to survive, but also to prosper to become one of the important trading nations in the world. Today, we rank as the 12th largest trading nation in the world, and hold the second largest foreign exchange reserves, next only to Japan. Thus Taiwan should by no means be belittled as a worthy future trade partner of the EEC.

Unfortunately, until very recently great difficulties and inconveniences were imposed upon any Taiwan merchant who wanted, say, to travel to Europe to negotiate business with his European counterparts. He had to go through the EEC countries' representatives in Hong Kong, or to file applications directly with the ministries in these countries to obtain visas to travel to Europe. It was no doubt a very time-consuming and troublesome process.

In contrast with the EEC's attitude of abandonment towards Taiwan, both the US and Japan adopted a shrewder course by maintaining *de facto* official representatives in Taiwan with full authority to perform most of the consular services, even after they severed diplomatic relations with Taiwan. In this way, they successfully prevented the lack of formal diplomatic relations from hampering the development of trade, and, not surprisingly, Taiwan's trade with these two countries continued to grow much faster than its trade with the EEC countries.

Moreover, the lack of political relations has also deprived us of the regular channels for consultation and discussion. This in turn has led to discriminatory and unfair treatment and the inevitable retaliatory action. For instance, the non-recognition of Taiwan as a legitimate political entity led the EEC countries to exclude Taiwan from the "Generalized System of Preferences" (GSP), while according the privilege of tariff preference to most other developing countries with which Taiwan had to compete in the EEC market. Thus Taiwan was put in a very unfavorable competitive position. In contrast, the US continued to recognize us as being legitimately qualified for the GSP treatment together with our chief competitors. It was only recently that the US announced that we, in addition to several of our competitors, were being graduated from GSP. This is therefore no longer an issue for us now, but, until our graduation from GSP, it constituted another reason why our trade with the EEC lagged far behind our trade with the US.

Furthermore, without proper channels for mutual consultation, Taiwan was often subjected to varying forms of unilateral discrimination which dealt great blows to our trade. At present, there are still in effect a number of import quotas on different categories of commodities imposed unilaterally by the EEC countries on Taiwan products; e.g., on textiles by the whole EEC, on footwear by France, Italy and the U.K., color television sets by the U.K., umbrellas by West Germany and Italy, non-metallic zippers by Spain, etc. Since there is no way to negotiate the removal or reduction of these unilateral restrictions on our exports, it is natural that we would retaliate by denying the most favored nations treatment to the EEC countries and, in particular, by not letting them enjoy the special favorable treatment given to some of the US products. By the same token, in terms of government procurement, Taiwan has also discriminated against the EEC in favor of the US.

Nevertheless, despite all these retaliatory measures, Taiwan has been promoting trade liberalization as a self-elected and publicly announced policy course since the beginning of the 1980's. The effective tariff rate of Taiwan, as measured by the ratio of customs revenues to the aggregate value of imports, has been reduced from 11.62 % in 1979 to 5.66 % in 1988, and is scheduled to be further reduced to 3.50 % by 1992. As to non-tariff barriers, notably some cumbersome import licensing procedures and import restrictions that used to be in force, they have been either eliminated already or are in the process of being eliminated. This explains why the EEC's exports to Taiwan (or Taiwan's imports from the EEC) have expanded from $ 1.61 billion in 1980 to $ 6.15 billion in 1988. If the EEC's trade with Taiwan is further normalized to the level of Taiwan's trade with the US or Japan, both exports and imports between the EEC and Taiwan can be doubled again very quickly, as the EEC is still largely an untapped market for the Taiwan traders.

Thus, in order to develop trade relations between Taiwan and the EEC on a normal basis:

1. It is much to be hoped that the EEC countries would at least follow the example of the US and Japan in exchanging trade representatives with Taiwan with *de facto* consular authorities and power to negotiate in matters of trade and tariff.

2. Secondly, the EEC countries should help Taiwan join the Gatt and OECD, and certainly not try to block her admission for fear of offending the PRC. Since Taiwan ranks as the 12th largest trading nation in the world, she should be able to contribute more to the development of free trade in the world as a member country of these organizations than as an excluded outsider.

3. Although we have been repeatedly assured that the GATT specifically rules against the raising of tariffs and protection against outsiders in connection with the formation of regional free trade areas or customs unions, it is well-known, however, that there are always ways to circumvent such GATT regulations. For instance, the newly promulgated

(August 1988) anti-dumping and anti-subsidy measures of the EEC appear to lend themselves readily to such uses. That is to say, whenever a member country of the EEC finds that certain outside products are threatening the sales of its own products, it can always invoke the 1988 anti-dumping or anti-subsidy measures against the competing products on the grounds that these outside products are making too fast an inroad into the EEC market. Even as early as January 1988, the EC Council of Ministers in Brussels passed a resolution put forward by the French that included limiting the imports of umbrellas from Mainland China as well as Taiwan on grounds of dumping practices, because the French umbrella manufacturers had become increasingly concerned with the large quantity of low-priced umbrellas from Asia which has caused the sales of their own more expensive brands to dwindle.

The legal appeal against an accusation of dumping in a foreign court is always very difficult and costly. For a merchant of a non-European country that does not even enjoy the diplomatic recognition of the EEC authorities, such legal appeals are very unlikely to be of any avail. This is what we are most worried about with regard to the impending full integration of the EEC in 1992.

We would very much hope that the members of the EEC would purge themselves of the protectionist idea of turning the integrated European market into a preserve for members alone, from which non-members are excluded, or at least in which they are not welcome. Such a stance would inevitably lead to the formation of countervailing free trade areas or customs unions from which the EEC countries would be excluded. In this way, the world would be partitioned into trading blocs which would maintain fairly free trade between their own respective member countries, but between the blocs, trade would be restrained not only by tariffs but also by the so-called anti-dumping or anti-subsidy measures on account of real or alleged cases of dumping or subsidies.

It is to be earnestly hoped that international organizations such as the GATT will be able to prevent effectively the anti-dumping and anti-subsidy measures from being abused in the direction of trade restrictions.

4. Finally, we hope that the advanced industrialized countries of the EEC will look upon the newly industrialized countries of Asia with sympathy and friendliness; for they have pointed out a way toward solving the so-called North-South problem with which most rich advanced countries have ostensibly expressed their concern. The traditional method of aiding the impoverished developing countries involves the granting of more loans and aid to these countries to help their reconstruction and to raise their standard of living directly. Its results, however, have so far been rather disappointing. Even though many developing countries have accumulated huge debts, there is no sign that they have thereby attained the capacity to maintain a continuous self-sustained growth.

   The Asian NIEs, on the other hand, demonstrated that, by adopting a more sensible and sound growth policy, they were able to wean themselves from foreign aid and loans early on and to achieve continuous self-sustained growth with domestically generated savings. Within a period of a little over a single generation, they have all grown from a very low level of real income per capita to a fairly affluent level comparable to that of the poorer members of the EEC. It seems, therefore, that the experience of the Asian NIEs should provide some useful lessons for the solution to the North-South problem.

In particular, the case of Taiwan should be especially significant, because it provides not only a hope to the impoverished South that persistently failed to take off into self-sustained growth, but also a sharp contrast with Mainland China, whose inhabitants are of the same ethnic stock, and share the same historical and cultural background as the people of Taiwan except that they are now under Communist rule. The far superior economic achievement of Taiwan as compared with that of Mainland China has sufficiently convinced the people of Mainland China that the free market economy adopted by Taiwan is much superior to the Marxist centrally planned economy. They had even gone so far as to openly request economists from Taiwan to help them in reforming their economic system just before the interruption of the tragic Tien-An-Men incident. The abrupt change in the political climate following the incident has temporarily made such cooperation impossible to continue, but nevertheless the example of the economic success of Taiwan remains a strong inducement for Mainland China to reform its economic system in a liberal direction. It is our earnest demand, therefore, that the other countries of the world will respect the right of the people of Taiwan to live independently of the Communist regime of Mainland China and will refrain from stymieing Taiwan's effort to seek her continued prosperity and growth by trading with the free world.

Table 1 Percentage distribution of Taiwan's Trade (Exports and Imports) With Major Market Areas of the World)

(in percentages)

	EEC	US	Japan	Rest of the World	Total
1980	11.4	28.9	19.0	40.7	100.0
1981	9.8	29.5	19.1	41.6	100.0
1982	9.8	30.7	16.5	43.0	100.0
1983	9.8	35.2	17.8	37.2	100.0
1984	9.1	38.0	18.4	34.5	100.0
1985	9.4	38.4	17.7	34.5	100.0
1986	11.0	38.2	20.0	30.8	100.0
1987	12.8	35.5	21.3	30.4	100.0
1988	13.6	33.0	21.4	32.0	100.0

Source: Monthly Statistics of Trade, The Republic of China.

Table 2 (a) Taiwan's Exports to and Imports from Major Market Areas of the World

In Absolute Amounts

(billions of US dollars)

	Exports to				Imports from			
	EEC	US	Japan	Rest of the World	EEC	US	Japan	Rest of the World
1980	2.90	6.76	2.17	7.98	1.61	4.67	5.35	8.10
1981	2.65	8.16	2.45	9.35	1.64	4.77	5.93	8.86
1982	2.38	8.76	2.37	8.69	1.87	4.56	4.78	7.68
1983	2.53	11.33	2.48	8.78	1.94	4.65	5.59	8.11
1984	2.81	14.87	3.19	9.59	1.96	5.04	6.44	8.52
1985	2.73	14.77	3.46	9.76	2.06	4.75	5.55	7.74
1986	4.31	19.00	4.55	11.93	2.74	5.42	8.26	7.75
1987	7.04	23.64	6.96	15.90	4.27	7.63	11.82	10.79
1988	8.84	23.43	8.77	19.55	6.15	13.00	14.82	15.68

Source: Monthly Statistics of Trade, The Republic of China.

Table 2 (b) Taiwan's Exports to and Imports from Major Market Areas of the World

In Percentage Distribution

(in percentages)

	Exports to				Imports from			
	EEC	US	Japan	Rest of the World	EEC	US	Japan	Rest of the World
1980	14.6	34.1	11.0	40.3	8.2	23.7	27.1	41.0
1981	11.7	36.1	10.9	41.3	7.7	22.5	28.0	41.8
1982	10.7	39.4	10.7	39.2	9.9	24.2	25.3	40.6
1983	10.0	45.1	9.9	35.0	9.6	22.9	27.5	40.0
1984	9.2	48.8	10.5	31.5	8.9	23.0	29.3	38.8
1985	8.9	48.1	11.3	31.7	10.2	23.6	27.6	38.6
1986	10.8	47.7	11.4	30.1	11.3	22.4	34.2	32.1
1987	13.1	44.1	13.0	29.8	12.4	22.1	34.3	31.2
1988	14.6	38.7	14.5	32.2	12.4	26.2	29.9	31.5

Source: Monthly Statistics of Trade, The Republic of China.

THE CASE FOR TAIWAN'S ROLE IN THE OECD

Raymond J.M. Chang
President
Institute for National Policy Research
114, Chienkuo N. Road Sec. 2
10433 Taipei

I. Coordination in Trade and Macroeconomic Policies

The two major crises in the international economy in the 1980s that Taiwan should be highly concerned about are:

One, the neo-protectionism led by the US. Protectionism by nature is contagious, destructive, and revengeful, a fact which should not slip from people's memory. There are examples in the not too distant past: in the 1930s, as the major countries around the world competed to raise tariff barriers, protectionism led to a spiral shrinkage and the tragedy of the Great Depression as a result of mutual retributions and impacts (Kindleberger, p. 291). A major task for the international economy now is to persuade countries to follow strictly the GATT's spirit of free trade and principle of joint consultation in order to mitigate the protectionist crisis. Topics that should be discussed include trade, investment, the services industry, agriculture, and intellectual property rights.

Two, the international financial crisis aggravated by the global trade imbalances. International trade, investment, credit and other economic activities depend very much on a stable international financial system. In the 1980s, capital flows among countries increased, becoming more rapid and more frequent as international financial institutions were internationalized. Major countries therefore must consult on foreign exchange rates if they are to solve the trade imbalance issue and maintain international financial stability. In addition, consultations are

Europe-Asia-Pacific Studies in Economy and Technology
Kulessa (Ed.)
The Newly Industrializing Economies of Asia

also needed on the fiscal and monetary policies which will supplement the weaknesses of trade and exchange rate policies.

Since Taiwan has benefited from an open international system, it naturally should contribute what it can to the system's continuity and stability. Calls to this effect have been made in the joint declaration at the OECD's ministerial conference, the joint communique of the G-7 financial ministers' meeting, and by economic and financial leaders of OECD countries. The Institute of International Economics (IIE) in the US has collected the views of 33 economists from 13 countries and made an official statement about Taiwan (IIE, 1987). The following are brief analyses of the root causes of the two crises and of how Taiwan can join the international community in helping to solve them.

1. Coordination of Trade Policies

1.1 The root cause of protectionism is the shift of comparative advantages in international trade.

In the 1960s, the US employed comparative advantages in international trade in almost all industries. But beginning in the 1970s, these advantages gradually shifted to latecomers like Japan and West Germany and even some NICs. In some industries, the US comparative advantages turned into comparative disadvantages. Such industries included textiles, steel, automobiles, electrical and electronic consumer goods.

As comparative advantages shifted, the need arose to adjust industry. This in turn led to uncertainty within the international economic order. Industries losing comparative advantages necessarily led to lower profits for their capital owners, reduced rent for their land owners, and rising unemployment. However, owners of production factors like capitalists, landlords or workers, through various power operations, always brought about rigid prices of production factors, making it hard for international industrial adjustment to succeed and creating social and political unrest. For an individual country, new and old industries will encounter different challenges in the race with foreign competitors; the result of success or failure will cause the problem of profit redistribution among industries. This means serious rifts will occur among different interest groups advocating different external economic policies. For instance, traditional industries are inclined to protectionism, while high-tech industries and services industries are inclined to free trade. This will cause international social, political and economic uncertainty in a world of increasing interdependence.

Industries facing threats from international competition can react by choosing one of the following strategies:

- to develop new technologies to maintain their comparative advantages;
- to move the capital out of the country, to make use of relatively cheap labor in other countries, or bring in low-cost foreign workers;
- to demand the government to protect them.

Theoretically speaking, advanced countries may be in a disadvantageous position as some of their industrial advantages have been nullified by a number of latecomers. But their high-tech R & D, and accumulated capital resources should play an active role in the face of international competition and act on the principle of international division of labor. This is exactly the gist of the spirit of free trade. The long-term solution should be the first two of the above three alternatives. Governments should revise their overall industrial policy in this direction. However, free and democratic countries allow their interest groups to work out solutions by check and balances, which usually does not lead them to the first two alternatives. Industries would demand protection via interest groups, political forces, or unions which influence government decision-making. This is usually case-convenient, expedient, and effective in the short-range.

Interest groups have to consider only the cost-benefit ratio when lobbying; they do not have to consider consumer interests, the overall long-term economic planning for the country, or fair play in international competition. Much less do they have to consider whether short-term protection can reach the goal of their long-term survival. Protectionism has been proved to have six evident shortcomings for the US: a. the trade coverage of special protection is growing; b. special protection is costly to consumers; c. special protection diverts scarce resources to America's least promising industries; d. special protection is associated with huge quota rents, largely accruing to foreign producers; e. special protection has come to impede new initiatives for trade liberalization; and f. special protection is highly inequitable between industries (Hufbauer, pp. 20-22).

In short, the limitations inherent in Western democracies make it difficult to allow technological renovation and flows of production factors (capital moving out or labor moving in) - adjustments which are good for the world. These limitations also make it difficult to stop the surge of protectionism.

1.2 Taiwan should join in the OECD's coordination activities to combat protectionism.

Protectionism is extremely harmful to international trade and global economic prosperity. As Taiwan's trade dependency is near 100 %, it is easy to imagine that the erosion of the free trade principle would have a great impact on Taiwan's economy. Taiwan's GNP ranked 11th against the 24 members of OECD; its manufactured exports ranked 11th in the world, accounting for 2.5 per cent of the world total. Therefore, Taiwan is obliged to join efforts to maintain and strengthen the GATT spirit. Taiwan should do the following:

a. In respect of trade policy, Taiwan can join OECD countries in coordinating tariff and non-tariff barriers.

Taiwan's tariff rate is higher than that of OECD members; but its non-tariff barriers are lower than those of the US and Japan (Chang, pp. 1-6). The main cause of Taiwan's high tariff rate in the past was that it was not a GATT member, and thus was excluded from GATT's multilateral negotiations. In recent years, Taiwan has once again lowered its tariff and non-tariff barriers. Taking 1984 - 88 as an example, Taiwan reduced tariffs five times, resulting in 234 items being placed on the duty-free list and duties on another 7,128 items being reduced. The real effective tariff rate fell from 7.7 % in 1984 to 6.1 % in 1988. Currently, the nominal tariff rate on raw materials is 0 - 2.5 %, that on semi-finished products 0 - 10 %, and that on finished goods 5 - 15 %. The real effective tariff on finished goods in 1988 was only 4.9 %. During the same period, the real effective tariff on agricultural products was 10.6 %. This was because Taiwan's farmers are characterized by advanced age and low technical level; it would be difficult for them to switch to other non-farming jobs. Therefore, tariff protection for farm products is higher than for industrial products. Similar cases are seen in other advanced countries.

Import control measures are the best example of non-tariff barriers. In January 1989, Taiwan adopted the Harmonized

System (HS) for categorizing commodities in line with the prevailing international practices. Under this system, 8,798 items are listed as Taiwan's import commodities, of which 8,532 items or 97 % may be imported. Among them, 5,860 items or 67 % can be imported without import licenses. Only 2,672 items require import licenses to be imported, of which 953 items require import permits from the Board of Foreign Trade. Another 1,719 items require permits from designated government units (such as banks). As many government units are authorized to issue import licenses and the procedures for applying for them are very simple, importers can get permission very easily. Applications usually are accepted immediately without any conditions on import quantities and so on. Except for items whose import is controlled for reasons of national security, social order, education, culture, public health etc., others are controlled to protect Taiwan's farmers who have difficulty switching to other jobs. In brief, no products are prevented from being imported in order to protect domestic products. Because of this, the total value of imports accounts for 40 % of Taiwan's GNP, a high ratio that is second to very few in the world (Chang, p. 15).

In summary, there has been a great improvement in recent years in Taiwan's tariff and non-tariff barriers, making Taiwan's trade barriers similar to those of advanced countries.

As Taiwan was not a contracting party to GATT, it did not participate in GATT's seven rounds of multilateral trade negotiations. We believe, however, that if Taiwan is permitted to join international organizations, it could testify to its own successful experience in developing its economy by advocating free trade, thus convincing other developing countries not to doubt the GATT spirit. When coordinating policy with the OECD countries, Taiwan will adhere to such a conviction. Taiwan should also make it known that it is willing to adjust its tariff and non-tariff barriers to the same level as advanced countries. The OECD would be happy to see an NIC providing its members with an open market; it would also be delighted that one more force has joined in protecting the free trade system. From Taiwan's standpoint, it indeed has to pay a price for joining OECD coordination on lowering trade barriers. But the price, compared with the price it paid while its currency fluctuated drastically against foreign currencies, is not too high. Moreover, multilateral coordination exerts a multilateral binding force, and is sometimes more favorable than bilateral coordination.

b. Taiwan can coordinate agricultural policy with OECD countries.

Both Taiwan and OECD countries face the difficulty of adjusting their agricultural structures. Compared with industrial products, Taiwan imposes higher tariff and non-tariff barriers on agricultural products. But compared with OECD countries, Taiwan's agricultural protection is not high. About 25 % of Taiwan's agricultural population is aged 55 or above, and 90 % of farmers are poorly educated and not skilled. It is not easy to teach them new methods or train them for new jobs. This problem should be jointly solved with OECD members, so that favorable conditions can be created for the production, consumption and trading of farm products.

c. With regard to trade in services, Taiwan can also coordinate its policy with OECD countries.

International trade in services is booming as a result of technological development and convenient communications. But GATT did not incorporate trade in services into the system of international norms in time (Hufbauer, 1985, pp. 66-70). Taiwan's services industry is still in the initial stage of development. Taiwan should dedicate its efforts to developing this industry on a long-term basis into the 21st century. If Taiwan opens trade in services, and introduces well-established service industries from abroad, whose quality and technology will help evaluate local industry, then Taiwan's services sector may grow, like its manufacturing industries in the past, and win a niche in the international market. Taiwan should support the proposal to extend the GATT spirit to the services sector.

In conclusion, the trade policy which GATT has propagated over the years is no longer the only source of leverage in today's international economy because in the 1980s the sphere of international activities and exchanges expanded rapidly. It would be necessary to incorporate investment, services, and agriculture into international economic policy, which in turn must be mapped out jointly by various countries. This means that the GATT spirit must be extended to cover the above-mentioned areas. If Taiwan can join in OECD coordination of the international economic policy in its capacity as a NIC, it will certainly increase the efficiency of OECD coordination.

2. Coordination of Exchange Rate Policies and Macroeconomic Policies

2.1 The swift international flows of capital have endangered international financial stability.

It has been emphasized that if international economic policy coordination can be performed in the framework of GATT, the international economic crisis can be alleviated to a certain extent, and the determination to counter protectionism in numerous countries can be strengthened. But the internationalization of financial institutions in the 1980s led to rapid flows of capital among countries. The swift movements of huge volumes of capital among countries resulted in exchange rates that cannot ensure international trade equilibrium. Trade imbalance, plus expectation, aggravates the uncertainty in international finance, which in turn influences the stability of international trade.

The US was plagued by severe trade imbalances in the 1980s. As the US dollar is a key currency in the world, and the US a major promoter of GATT and supporter of military security of all free countries, its trade imbalance could lead to an escalation of world protectionism, and an unstable US dollar and a chaotic financial order could endanger world peace and security. Taiwan, as the country with the third largest trade surplus both with the world and with the US, has a role to play which should not be ignored. Taiwan's trade barriers are merely a secondary reason for its trade gap with the US; the major reason lies in the structural imbalance. In spite of this, Taiwan should still consult the OECD on exchange rate and macroeconomic policies so as to effectively improve the structural imbalance with the US.

2.2 Taiwan should participate in OECD coordination of exchange rates and macroeconomic policies.

a. Participate in international coordination of exchange rates.

The drastic appreciation of the New Taiwan Dollar has inflicted damage on all Taiwan's export and import industries. The influence is far greater than the lifting of tariff and non-tariff barriers for individual industries. Furthermore, coordination of exchange rates requires neither lengthy negotiations by the executive nor approval by the congress. A major effect can be had through government intervention and even expectation. Therefore, the main purpose of coordinating exchange rate policy is to make it reflect a country's real international trade competitiveness.

Taiwan's foreign exchange holdings are the second largest in the world (though part of them originate from the flow of short-term international hot money). If Taiwan's government sector tries to change their manner as deposit on the international market (i.e. by redistributing the proportions of various currencies), this certainly will have some impact on the international financial market. Therefore, Taiwan's role cannot be ignored if international coordination of exchange rates is to be really effective. And Taiwan should also fully demonstrate its willingness to participate in exchange rate coordination to help stabilize the international financial market.

From Taiwan's standpoint, it would not make much difference whether exchange rate talks were held multilaterally or bilaterally with the US. However, multilateral talks within the OECD would be much more significant than bilateral talks with the US alone.

b. Participate in coordination of monetary and financial policies.

Taiwan should change its demand structure so that its domestic demand can be speedily expanded to avoid overdependence on foreign demand. Through public investment, domestic demand can be expanded towards more public goods, of which there is a severe shortage now. This means that in order to cope with the current international and domestic economic situation, and in order to alleviate the cost for economic development, increasing domestic demand by way of public investment will be a key method of sustaining the country's economic development. Priority in such efforts should be placed on improving the quality of life. In order not to cause inflation in goods of the non-trading sectors (such as land and labor), huge amounts of foreign goods should be used in construction projects. The following three areas should be the main content of Taiwan's public investments:

- The quality of housing and the environment: more housing units, efficient prevention and disposal of air, water and solid wastes;
- Recreation facilities: national parks, community parks, stadiums, and museums of history, traditional objects, science, oceanology and electronics;
- Transportation and telecommunications: these are the best ways to promote efficient utilization of the nation's land resources. If a high-speed railway can be built which shortens south-north transportation to two hours only, many urbanization problems, such as population concentration, sky-high housing prices, traffic congestion, and rising crime, can also be alleviated.

II. Taiwan's Participation in OECD Development Assistance Programs

The US's ability to share the burden has declined because of its twin deficit. In the meantime, other advanced countries must take a greater share of the responsibility. They must cooperate closely with one another in order to push ahead effectively with international assistance programs. Against such a backdrop, Taiwan should make the following efforts:

(1) Taiwan should make a contribution commensurate with its economic strength, to international assistance programs, a move which would make up for the shortage in international assistance and cooperation. Though Taiwan is burdened with extremely high military spending in order to ensure its own security, it should still set aside 0.2 - 0.3 % of GNP for participating in international assistance programs.

(2) Taiwan is obliged to help maintain peace and stability in Asia. Though it cannot achieve this purpose militarily, it should help Southeast Asian countries attain continued economic growth by strengthening trade and economic exchanges with them. This could help the Southeast Asian countries to avoid political and social instability which might be caused by economic problems. What these countries most need now is the Mini-Marshall Plan proposed by the US Secretary of State James Baker and calling for joint efforts to help the Philippine economic recovery.

(3) As Taiwan's economy is not large, the economic assistance it can afford to give other countries is limited. Therefore, Taiwan should dedicate itself to promoting its development experience to help developing countries enhance their own capabilities. This means that Taiwan should make good use of its resources, and introduce systematically to developing countries its experiences in land reform, foreign trade development, and industrial development. Taiwan can exchange views with political leaders, decision-makers and academics of the developing countries.

(4) Research institutes and schools in Taiwan should invite technical and academic personnel from developing countries to study for a period of time, so that they can gain a good understanding of the decision-making and social situations in Taiwan. After returning to their countries, the technicians and academics can serve their countries. Also, they can improve their countries' trade, economic, investment and cooperative ties with Taiwan with their knowledge of Taiwan. This would also alleviate Taiwan's overdependence on the US market.

(5) The government of Taiwan should design tax incentive measures, establish insurance programs for overseas investment, and even offer low-interest loans to encourage its people to invest in Southeast Asian countries. This would help solve the problems of employment, capital accumulation, foreign-exchange shortage and technical backwardness in these countries.

(6) Taiwan should break out of its political impasse and set up Taiwan Special Funds as soon as possible in international economic organizations of which Taiwan is not a member, such as the World Bank, and the Inter-American Development Bank (IDB). As for the Asian Development Bank (ADB), in which Taiwan is already a member, it should actively take part in its Asian Development Fund activities.

(7) Taiwan's official foreign exchange reserves are mostly deposited in the US. However, developing countries need them more than the US. Besides, excessive funds in the civilian sector in Taiwan tend to cause inflation in non-trade sectors such as land (real estate) and the stock market. Therefore, Taiwan's government should figure out ways to encourage international financial groups such as the World Bank, the International Monetary Fund, and regional economic bod-

ies like IDB and ADB and the African Development Bank to issue bonds for assisting developing countries. Such bonds bear low interest but are high-risk. The government can use its Overseas Economic Development Cooperation Fund (OEDCF) to make up for the differences, so that idle funds in Taiwan can be well used internationally.

(8) Taiwan should learn from the way the US and Japan operate ex-im banks, in order to give more concrete assistance to developing countries in their foreign trade. This could help solve their foreign debt and foreign exchange problems.

III. The Problems Involved in Taiwan's Joining OECD

1. Eligibility

1.1 The OECD convention does not clearly define the conditions government must meet to become a member. It just says that "any Government prepared to assume the obligations of membership" "may" be invited to join the organization. Broadly speaking, "prepared to assume the obligations of membership" means willing to make joint efforts to achieve the aims of the organization and fulfill the obligations it defines for members. This is largely contained in Articles 1-3.

1.2 From the analysis of Chapter I, it can be seen from the economic indicators that Taiwan's economic power has surpassed some OECD member countries. So Taiwan should be eligible to join OECD. The Trilateral Commission suggested that the following four requirements should be met if a government wishes to join OECD: First, per capita income should exceed SDR 2000; secondly, it should be among the first twenty largest exporters of manufactures; thirdly, it should have a reasonably liberal external economic policy and domestic political system; and fourthly, it should be willing to assist backward countries. Taiwan naturally meets all those requirements. From the perspective of the international economy, both Taiwan's economic capability and its current emphasis on "internationalizing and liberalizing" its economy show that Taiwan is qualified to apply for membership of OECD. It is in the political arena that Taiwan might meet with some difficulties owing to Communist China's blocking tactics and the nomenclature issue.

2. Difficulties:

2.1 Article 16 of the OECD Convention states that an applicant must deposit an instrument of accession "with the depository Government", and Item 2 of Article 14 says "the Government of the French Republic" is "hereby designated as depository Government". Article 21 stipulates that "Upon receipt of any instrument of ratification, acceptance or accession ... the depository Government shall give notice thereof to all the Contracting Parties".

2.2 Article 16 says "The Council may decide to invite any Government prepared to assume the obligations of membership to accede to this Convention. Such decisions shall be unanimous, provided that for any particular case the Council may unanimously decide to permit abstention, in which case, notwithstanding the provisions of Article 6, the decision shall be applicable to all the members." The Article 6 ruling is that "decisions shall be taken and recommendations shall be made by mutual agreement of all members".

Therefore, if Taiwan files an application, it must first of all fill in an application form stating its willingness to assume the obligations of membership, and then deposit it with the depository Government, i.e. the French Government.

Upon receipt of it, the French Government will notify all members and the secretary general, who will call a "council" to decide on the case.

2.3 Judging from OECD entry rules, Taiwan may encounter the following two difficulties politically:

First, the nomenclature issue. As the applicant must be a "Government", Taiwan cannot but be flexible in this regard.

Secondly, the "unanimous" issue. Taiwan must call for OECD countries' attention to its membership, so that those which might find it difficult to cast a "yes" vote for Taiwan can at least be persuaded to abstain from voting.

3. Actions

3.1 Taiwan should form a task force, say, an OECD Action Group, to deal exclusively with Taiwan's entry into the OECD. Its jobs would include liaising with the OECD as soon as possible and studying ways to encourage other Asian NICs to join the OECD. Among the four Asian tigers, Hong Kong and Taiwan face political difficulties. Singapore and South Korea are not enthusiastic about joining the OECD at the moment. Still, Taiwan should make it known that it is willing to join the OECD. The economies of Hong Kong and Singapore are too small; their focus is the financial sector, and they have no solid industrial base. As for South Korea, its liberalization programs obviously lag behind those of Taiwan. Therefore, Taiwan should serve as a good example for Asian tigers in joining the OECD.

3.2 Taiwan should notify the OECD in the most unequivocal terms that it is willing to join the organization, and at the same time try to reach a certain extent of understanding with

through exchanges of students and technical personnel and academics. Taiwan therefore should participate in DAC's coordination activities. Even though Taiwan must carry a heavy defence burden, it should allocate 0.2-0.3 % of its GNP to international assistance activities annually.

- Besides heightening its awareness of its international obligations, Taiwan should also keep a flexible political position toward Mainland China. With the maintenance of the international economic order as a target, Taiwan should not allow political ideology or the name issue to influence its international role.

- The OECD countries should be aware of Taiwan's importance in participating in international economic activities, and boldly remove political hindrances to Taiwan's joining international activities in order to achieve the primary aim of maintaining the international trading and financial order and international cooperation. Before difficulties involving Taiwan's joining the OECD can be solved, the OECD should take the initiative and invite Taiwan to participate in economic policy coordination and DAC activities, two important activities which are helpful to achieve a breakthrough in the current international economic impasse.

- Mainland China should also realize that an orderly international economic environment is a necessary prerequisite for opening up towards the rest of the world. Taiwan's participation in international coordination activities would contribute to such an orderly international economic system, which should also be in the interest of Mainland China. Therefore, Mainland China should take a more flexible attitude toward Taiwan's joining OECD activities. Further isolation of Taiwan would inevitably create more hatred and distrust between Taiwan and Mainland China and foster sentiments for Taiwan's independence. Taiwan would then be forced to rely even more on its military defense. Mainland China's flexibility in this matter would, however, create an atmosphere conducive to trade, investment and technological exchange between the two sides of the Taiwan Straits, thus paving a way for peaceful and healthy relations across the straits.

- Last but not least, the US should recognize that Taiwan's joining the OECD can help the US in several aspects. First, anti-American sentiments, which might be harbored as a result of US pressures in the several rounds of bilateral trade talks with Taiwan, can be reduced. Indeed, it is extremely unwise for the US to bear the whole burden of the bilateral trade talks alone but share the benefits from the talks with others. We believe multilateral trade negotiations can appease bilateral hostilities. Secondly, as the US struggles to reduce its budget deficit, she is unable to commit more foreign assistance to some strategic allies, such as the Philippines. It is time to encourage Taiwan to assume international responsibilities through international economic organizations such as DAC in the OECD.

Therefore, it would be advisable that the US administration do its utmost to overcome the difficulties. It is also recommended that the US Congress pass a resolution in support, as it did in the case of the Asian Development Bank in 1983.

References

1. Baldwin R. E. and Krueger A. O., eds. (1984) The Structure and Evolution of Recent US Trade Policy. Chicago and London, The University of Chicago Press.

2. Balassa B. and Noland M. (1988) Japan in the World Economy. Washington DC., Institute for International Economics.

3. Bergsten C. F. (1987) The New Era in Economic Relations Between the United States and the Republic of China. Remarks before the Eleventh Joint US-ROC Business Conference. New Orleans.

4. Bergsten C. F. (1988) America in the World Economy: A Strategy for the 1990s. Washington DC., Institute for International Economics.

5. Bergsten C. F. and Cline W. R. (1985) The United States - Japan Economic Problem. Washington DC., Institute for International Economics.

6. Brick A. B. (1988) The Case for Taipei's Membership in International Economic Organizations. Washington DC., Backgrounder of Asian Studies Center, Heritage Foundation.

7. Chang R. J. (1988) Taiwan's International Economic Relationship with the US: Challenges and Future Prospects. Unpublished manuscript.

8. Destler I. M. and Odell J. S. (1987) Anti-Protection: Changing Forces in United States Trade Politics. Washington DC., Institute for International Economics.

9. Hufbauer G. C., Berliner D. T. and Elliott K. A. (1986) Trade Promotion in the United States: 31 Case Studies. Washington DC., Institute for International Economics.

10. Hufbauer G. C. and Schott J. J. (1985) Trading for Growth: The Next Round of Trade Negotiations. Washington DC., Institute for International Economics.

11. Huntington S. P. (Winter 1988/1989) The US - Decline or Renewal? Foreign Affairs, pp. 76-96.

12. IIE (1987) Resolving the Global Economic Crisis: After Wall Street. A Statement by Thirty-Three Economists from Thirteen Countries. Washington DC., Institute for International Economics.

13. Kindleberger C. P. (1973) The World Depression. 1929-1939. Berkeley, University of California Press.

14. Murakami V. and Kosai Y., eds. (1986) Japan in the Global Community. Japan, University of Tokyo Press.

15. OECD (1985) Twenty-Five Years of Development Co-operation: A Review. Reported by R. M. Poats. Paris, OECD.

16. OECD (1987) Interdependence and Co-operation in Tomorrow's World. Paris, OECD.

17. OECD (1988a) The Newly Industrialising Countries: Challenge and Opportunity for OECD Countries. Paris, OECD.

18. OECD (1988b) Voluntary Aid for Development: The Role of Non-Governmental Organisations. Paris, OECD.

19. OECD. Activities of OECD in Various Issues. Paris, OECD.

20. OECD. Development Co-operation in Various Reports.

21. Paliagne G. J. and Shuey R. D. (1986) Foreign Aid - A Policy Overview. Issue Brief, Congressional Research Service, Washington D.C.

THE SIGNIFICANCE OF TAIWAN'S REJOINING GATT

Arthur K. Yeh
Vice President
Administration Division
Institute for National Policy Research
114, Chienkuo N. Road Sec. 2
10433 Taipei

1. The Significance to Taiwan

Once Taiwan enters GATT, Taiwan will benefit from tariff and non-tariff concessions from other contracting parties to GATT. As Taiwan is an export-oriented economy whose trade dependence, according to 1988 statistics, is as high as 105 %[1], it must win reciprocally favorable treatment from its trading partners either in export or import. But as Taiwan does not have diplomatic ties with its major trading partners except the United States, bilateral negotiations with them have to be conducted surreptitiously, not to say signing bilateral agreements. Currently the US, Japan, the EC and Australia accord to Taiwan most-favored-nation treatment, which, however, is a unilateral commitment, without any binding force. If Taiwan joins GATT according to the principle of the most-favored-nation treatment, it will receive the same treatment concessions as other contracting parties do. It will not need to protect its trade interests only by resorting to bilateral negotiations with other countries. Moreover, it will have access to trade and economic information through GATT and to participate in multilateral trade negotiations which will prevent other countries from making unilateral unfair demands on it. And even if trade disputes erupt, it can refer to GATT for recommendations or rulings. This means trade relations between Taiwan and other countries can be ensured and stabilized, which will cer-

---

[1] Directorate General of Budget, Accounting and Statistics (DGBAS) (June 1989) Monthly Statistics of the ROC. Measured by EXP - IMP/GDP, figures in current values.

Europe-Asia-Pacific Studies in Economy and Technology
Kulessa (Ed.)
The Newly Industrializing Economies of Asia

tainly contribute to the development of Taiwan's external trade.

On the other hand, Taiwan, after its joining GATT, will not be allowed to take discriminatory measures to other contracting parties. Nor can Taiwan take protectionist measures at will to protect domestic industries. During the last four decades, Taiwan, as a developing country, has taken such measures as foreign exchange control, high tariffs, export subsidies and restrictions on imports and exports. These measures, true, have laid a good foundation for Taiwan's industry and helped score a good economic performance. In recent years, controls on foreign exchange have been lifted and export subsidies gradually eliminated. Import duties have also been lowered by a substantial margin, though controls of several import items are still there.

Quite a few import controls currently in force in Taiwan, such as the quota on Korean passenger cars and the restraints on the imports of tyres, automobiles and motorcycles from all countries other than Europe and the US, are obviously violating GATT's principle of the most-favored-nation treatment. Moreover, there are still controls on or conditions for the imports of several hundred industrial and agricultural items. Requests for the opening of the market for these items will certainly be made during negotiations over Taiwan's entry into GATT.

Taiwan's domestic industry, faced with the above-mentioned threats for market opening, will certainly have difficulties in adjusting itself to the new situation in the short term. But from a long-range point of view, except some special cases involving agricultural products, protracted or excessive protection will prevent the domestic industry from normal development and lower its competitiveness on the international market. On the contrary, opening the market to foreign products will force the domestic industry to sharpen its competitive edge. Therefore, the pressure of tariff reduction and market opening, which will come following

Taiwan's entry into GATT, will give Taiwan a good chance to review its industrial policy and set up new development guidelines. The industrial level of Taiwan can thus be elevated through international competition.

In the 1980s, Taiwan has experienced the first decade since its withdrawal from the United Nations. During the decade, Taiwan has shown its economic vitality by successfully developing its foreign trade through the so-called "substantive diplomacy". But on the other hand, it has tasted the bitterness of being ousted from the international community and begun to reexamine its foreign policy. In recent years the People's Republic of China, which has become more and more active on the international stage, has also tried persistently to isolate Taiwan. The PRC has tried to create the impression in the international community that Taiwan was a "local" administrative unit of Peking. Taiwan itself, on the other hand, has had to face an increasingly complicated situation in its economic relations with foreign countries, with whom trade talks were getting more and more frequent. These developments together with a rising democratic awareness at home, have aroused people's concern over Taiwan's international status.

For Taiwan, international trade is the most significant one among various international activities or organizations. Trade is a major medium for Taiwan to communicate with the international community. It is also the major international activity which can best inspire the self-assurance of the entire Taiwanese people. Therefore, the success in Taiwan's bid to rejoin GATT is a key to the problem of rebuilding Taiwan's self-confidence in reentering the international community.

On the other hand, Taiwan will have to negotiate with over two thirds of contracting parties to GATT in the process of its accession to the Agreement in accordance with Article 33 of GATT. This would enable Taiwan to have official dealings with between

60 and 90 countries with which it has not had diplomatic ties since 1971. For both Taiwan and these countries, negotiations and the conclusion of bilateral agreements in accordance with GATT practice would be tantamount to recognizing each other's sovereignty. The GATT membership also provides a legal basis for Taiwan and other contracting parties to have official relations with each other and therefore helps enhance their diplomatic ties.

As the PRC has applied for joining GATT, it is expected that the two governments across the Taiwan Straits will both become contracting parties to GATT. This will set another precedent following the Asian Development Bank, in which both sides tacitly agreed that the other side had sovereignty over the territory under its control, at least over external trade or other matters governed by GATT. Furthermore, if both governments across the Taiwan Straits do not invoke Article 35 of GATT to prevent them from applying GATT to each other, the two governments have to negotiate with each other and conclude a bilateral agreement on trade concessions as mentioned above. This would lead to the first ever official contacts between both sides of the Taiwan Straits, and have both sides recognize each other's sovereign power.

Besides, if Taiwan becomes a contracting party to GATT, it can participate in ministerial meetings of GATT and GATT-sponsored multilateral trade negotiations wherein to coordinate international trade policy in a more responsible and significant way. In addition, Taiwan will be able to set up formal diplomatic channels for a possible establishment of full diplomatic ties with other countries through its official representative in Geneva. Through GATT Taiwan could also develop its liaisons with IMF and the United Nations which have close ties with GATT. In short, GATT membership would provide sound channels for Taiwan to return to the international community.

2. The International Significance

Taiwan's joining GATT would have a great significance not only to itself, but also to the international political economy. Taiwan's commodity trade ranks 13th in the world, next only to the Group of Seven (the US, West Germany, Japan, France, Great Britain, Italy and Canada), the Soviet Union, the Netherlands, Belgium, Hong Kong, and Switzerland[2]. Compared with the latter four countries, Taiwan, however, has a population of over 20 million, and its foreign reserves, amounting to US $ 74 billion, are second to Japan alone. Judging from either its current economic strength or its potential of development, Taiwan should be a major trade nation.

But on the other hand, because Taiwan is not a contracting party to GATT, Taiwan can only abide by GATT rules indirectly - mainly through the US-ROC bilateral agreement, which, however, cannot be generally applied to other contracting parties to GATT. But the main purpose of the Uruguay Round is to develop a more open, viable and durable multilateral trading system and to promote multilateral instead of bilateral negotiations. If Taiwan, as a major trade nation should be forced to continue its trade dealings through bilateral negotiations, this would be a great irony of the Uruguay Round. Moreover, the major subjects for negotiations in the Uruguay Round, such as the trade in services, investment measures and intellectual property rights, are all of considerable concern to Taiwan. If Taiwan cannot coordinate with GATT efforts in this regard, the Uruguay Round will certainly achieve much less than it expected.

Therefore, as Taiwan remains an outsider to GATT, the more its trading status is enhanced, the more the defects in the world trading system are revealed. If such an important trade nation

----

[2] GATT (1988) International Trade 87-88. Volume II, p. 7

should be under no GATT governance, it would not only be a challenge to the credibility and performance of GATT, but also have an unfavorable "demonstrating effect" for the majority of contracting parties to GATT. On the contrary, if Taiwan joins GATT, GATT's representation will be even more comprehensive and the world trading system more healthy. Moreover, since Taiwan's efforts on liberalization and internationalization are at a critical juncture, GATT membership will assure Taiwan of an equal footing in international trade and relieve Taiwan's business community of apprehension over unfair competition in the international market. This will then accelerate Taiwan's efforts in opening its market to foreign competition and promote its import trade which will consequently bring substantive benefits to all countries.

In fact, Taiwan's entry into GATT is also beneficial to each contracting party individually. This is particularly true for the US. In all previous trade negotiations with Taiwan, the US alone paid the price. But what the US gained from the negotiations has eventually been shared by other countries. Once Taiwan becomes a contracting party to GATT, while its trade policies and practices will be monitored internationally under GATT surveillance, all its preferential treatments granted to other countries will be accorded to the US. This is certainly to the benefit of the US. Still more, it will have strategical significance for the US in the Asia-Pacific area, if the entry into GATT by both Taiwan and the PRC should bring about improvement in their relations. Japan and the European Community would also be glad to see Taiwan's entry into GATT, for Taiwan, once being a contracting party, can no longer impose discriminatory import quota or restrictions on their products. This will no doubt help to promote their export trade with Taiwan. As for the developing contracting parties, given Taiwan's ample foreign reserves and strong buying power, most of them would welcome Taiwan's joining GATT, even more so if Taiwan does not apply for GATT membership as a developing country.

From the standpoint of international politics, whether or not Taiwan successfully joins GATT will have a great bearing on stability in the Asia-Pacific area, which has had the fastest economic growth in the world since World War II. This area has also been tapped as a main driving force for the world's economic growth in the 21st century[3]. The stability of the Asia-Pacific area is thus closely linked to the well-being of the whole world.

The antagonism between Taiwan and the PRC has, however, been an unpredictable variable to the stability and prosperity of Asia-Pacific. The growing trade and economic exchanges across the Taiwan Straits[4] do not mean their animosity has lessened. The PRC government has permitted imports of Taiwan products, encouraged Taiwanese to invest on the mainland, and repeatedly asked Taiwan to open direct trade with the mainland to pave the way for a peaceful unification. But on the other hand, all signs tell that the mainland's trade policy towards Taiwan indeed is but part of its united front tactics. Facing with a centrally planned economy, which is controlled by hostile Chinese communists who can turn the economic exchanges into deathly economic sanctions any time, Taiwan of course can by no means open direct trade with the mainland.

2. Preliminary Conclusion

Between 1950, when Taiwan withdrew from GATT, and 1979, when the Tokyo Round was held, Taiwan's foreign trade was small in size,

----

[3] Asian Development Bank, Asian Development Outlook 1989, p. 1

[4] Yu-jun Lin, Liangan Maoyi Yinian Huigu (Annual Review of Taiwan-Mainland Trade), Economic Outlook, April 10, 1989, pp. 9-11

its export and import markets concentrating in the US and Japan. To cope with the difficult situation it faced after withdrawal from GATT, Taiwan has to win support from the two countries, which did grant GATT concessions as well as GSP to Taiwan. As a result, before the Tokyo Round, Taiwan's withdrawal from GATT did not have much impact on Taiwan's foreign trade.

In the 1980s, however, trade frictions among all countries increased with the global economic recession. After many rounds of bilateral negotiations with the US and European countries, Taiwan gradually realized the disadvantages of holding bilateral trade negotiations. The Uruguay Round of multilateral trade negotiations and the PRC's formal application to join GATT, together with the liberalization of Taiwan's domestic politics, eventually converged into a strong national consensus for seeking GATT membership.

The new situation in the 1980s, in fact, is a brand new and acid test for Taiwan. The favorable environment it had enjoyed in the old international trade system was disappearing. The international community has demanded Taiwan take a greater share of responsibility and obligation. In order to maintain its economic achievement, Taiwan must have a sound world view on international trade and speed up self-adjustment so that it can adapt itself to the new international trade order. The analysis in this paper shows that Taiwan's joining GATT would not only bring substantive benefits to itself, but also have a positive influence on Mainland China as well as the international politics and economy.

As to the technical problems involving Taiwan's joining GATT, Taiwan can file an application in accordance with Article 33 of GATT. But US assistance will be pivotal. If Taiwan sticks to its "pragmatic diplomacy" policy, aiming at the right of equal participation and stepping out of the psychological complex over the nomenclature issue, then, given the US backing, there is ample room for reaching a compromise with the PRC. Judging from Taiwan's current economic structure, it would not be too difficult for Taiwan to adjust itself if it becomes a contracting party to GATT as a NIC. And if Taiwan speeds up its application to GATT, it can be expected that Taiwan and the PRC will become contracting parties of GATT simultaneously.

THE HONG KONG ECONOMY IN A CHANGING INTERNATIONAL ECONOMIC ENVIRONMENT

Edward K.Y. Chen
Director
Centre of Asian Studies
University of Hong Kong
Pokfulam Road
Hong Kong

The Hong Kong Economy has been growing at a very rapid rate in the past few years after some setbacks in 1983-1984. In both 1986-1987, the growth rate was over 10 per cent. At the same time, the rate of inflation was relatively low in the range of only 3-5 per cent, despite the fact that the Hong Kong dollar devalued quite significantly relative to Japanese and European currencies because of Hong Kong's linked exchange rate system with the US dollar. Economic growth in Hong Kong remained fast even after the October 1987 stock market crash, achieving a 7.5 per cent growth in 1988. But the inflation rate has been increasing quite rapidly since early 1988. The domestic economy has become very overheated and a severe shortage of labour has been developed. It is expected that in 1989 the Hong Kong economy will still be able to grow at 5 to 6 per cent, but inflation rate will certainly become a two-digit figure.

In the past few years, the Hong Kong economy has been undergoing a very rapid economic restructuring, changing from the stage of export-oriented industrialization based on the export of traditional light, labour-intensive manufactured products to a more complex and sophisticated stage of export-oriented industrialization based on the export of more capital- and technology-intensive manufactured products and at the same time, the further development of Hong Kong into an international services centre. In

Europe-Asia-Pacific Studies in Economy and Technology
Kulessa (Ed.)
The Newly Industrializing Economies of Asia

this connection, there are a number of problems facing Hong Kong:

(1) The 1997 issue. Despite the Sino-British joint declaration, there are still a lot of uncertainties about the future of Hong Kong with regard to the change of sovereignty in 1997. Such uncertainties have prevented a lot of long-term investments from happening. At the same time, the problem of brain drain has become increasingly serious. It was estimated that about 100,000 professional and skilled workers left Hong Kong in the past few years. The Tian-an-men Square incident has of course further damaged very significantly the confidence of the Hong Kong people.

(2) Government's non-intervention policy on industrial development. As a result of Hong Kong government's lack of positive support to industry in terms of manpower development and promotion of basic and applied research, the industrial technological foundation of Hong Kong is now well below that of Taiwan, South Korea and even Singapore. Nevertheless, a more positive attitude towards industrial transformation has recently been undertaken by the Hong Kong government.

(3) Lack of physical infrastructure. The Hong Kong government has not been taking a long-term and comprehensive view on the development of physical infrastructure in Hong Kong to cope with Hong Kong's recent development. For example, the government has been very hesitant in taking decisions on building a replacement airport, and the transportation system has fallen short of the requirements arising from Hong Kong's rapid domestic growth and increasing economic ties with China.

(4) The China factor. China has become Hong Kong's number one trading partner and Hong Kong's investment in China accounts for about two-thirds of the total foreign direct investment in China. Moreover, Hong Kong has relocated very signifi-

cantly its labour-intensive production to South China. Hong Kong has also become China's intermediary in the indirect trade between China and South Korea, and between China and Taiwan. However, recent economic and political turmoils in China will certainly lead to a concentration in China's economic activities with the outside world. In consequence, the China factor will become a less favourable factor in the future than in the past few years.

(5) Increased protectionism. In the past few years, western developed countries have become more protectionist in terms of both tariff and non-tariff barriers to international trade. In addition to the quota system, the anti-dumping accusation imposed on Hong Kong's exports to the EEC has become an important concern for Hong Kong manufacturers. At the same time, the formation of a trading bloc, especially the EEC in 1992, will also threaten the multilateral system established under GATT.

Despite these problems, in the context of the changing environment in the global economy and in the Asian Pacific region, we can still be optimistic about the economic outlook for Hong Kong in the intermediate and long term.

For example, the gap in long-term investment has to some extent been filled by investment from outside. In particular, the increase in Japanese investment in Hong Kong has been very rapid. In 1987, Japan became the number one investor in Hong Kong's manufacturing in that year. Traditionally, Japan emphasized much more the investment in the service sector in Hong Kong. The increasing cost of production in Hong Kong's tradition industries has to some extent been overcome by Hong Kong's relocation of industries to lower wage countries such as China, Thailand, and Indonesia. Hong Kong has also been able to penetrate the Japanese market in the past one to two years with considerable success.

Hong Kong has managed to increase its sales in the China market in not only consumer products but also in capital goods and technology. In terms of assistance to industrial development and the building up of infrastructure, the Hong Kong government has to some extent realized these problems and more positive steps will be taken. With regard to increased protectionism adopted by western developed countries, Hong Kong is in a better position to fight back because of Hong Kong's resilience and Hong Kong 's traditional free trade policy.

An optimistic outlook for the Asian Pacific region as a whole can be based on four major developments emerging in the past few years in this region: (1) an increasing degree of complementarity among countries in this region in their industrial production and economic diversification, (2) increased intraregional trade, (3) increased intraregional investment, (4) increased opportunity for greater regional economic cooperation. Hong Kong will have a new role in all these new developments.

Subregional Division of Labour

Hong Kong has been and will be playing a very important role in the increasing degree of complementarity in industrial production in this region. This development can best be described by the flying geese pattern of economic development. We can envisage a group of countries in this region flying together in layers, signifying the different stages of economic development achieved in different countries. The idea is that countries in the higher layer will pass on their outdated industries to the next layer of countries because of changing comparative advantages. Today, this division of labour is not only horizontal in the sense that the entire industrial product is passed on, but also vertical in the sense that the sub-processes may be passed on to other countries in the production of a particular product.

The leader of the flying geese is Japan which is followed by the Asian NIEs. Of the ASEAN countries, Malaysia and Thailand fly closer to the NIEs than the Philippines and Malaysia. South Asia as a group falls far behind the others. China is not just a goose but a huge bird flying side by side with the geese. China has the potential of complementing and competing with various layers of the flying geese at different levels of industrial production. What is emerging from this pattern of development is that countries in this region will engage in different stages of industrial development. Even for countries in the same stage of development, specialization is normally possible for the achievement of complementarity. In the past few years, a very sophisticated pattern of specialization has occurred for example in the manufacture of semi-conductors. Taiwan and South Korea have specialized in wafer fabrication, a highly capital- and technology-intensive production process. Hong Kong and Singapore have become specialized in the design and testing stage which is highly skill and equipment intensive; on the other hand, the Philippines, Thailand and Malaysia concentrate on the highly labour-intensive assembling stage. In terms of technological capability, Hong Kong has generally been lagging behind economies such as South Korea, Taiwan and even Singapore. Nevertheless, this does not imply that Hong Kong will not be able to survive. In the flying geese pattern of development, Hong Kong can still find niches in which it enjoys some unique advantages over the other economies. For example, while in terms of technological level Hong Kong is behind the other ANIEs in the electronic industry, Hong Kong is gaining a competitive edge in some specialized market and consumer-oriented products such as the application-specific integrated circuits.

In the broader spectrum of economic diversification, some kind of specialization within the region has also developed. While South Korea and Taiwan have largely become sophisticated manufacturing bases, Hong Kong and Singapore have diversified significantly into the service sector. This does not mean that Hong Kong will give up manufacturing, but it is inevitable that the relative importance of services will increase. It is anticipated that Hong Kong towards the year 2000 will increasingly become a regional centre in the provision of trade, financial, telecommunication and technological services. As a result, Hong Kong will have a more balanced economy, making better use of its most precious resources - human resources.

Intraregional Trade

Another source of optimism for export-oriented industrialization in the region is the increased importance of intraregional trade. This is most important in view of the slowing down of world trade and the increased extent of protectionism in most developed countries. For a number of reasons, intraregional trade will be of increasing importance. First, the intraregional market has become larger as a result of the rapid increase in income level in the Asian NIEs, the opening up of China, and the restructuring of the Japanese economy. The aggregate GNP of the Asian NIEs, China and ASEAN will soon come to about one-half of Japan's; their markets should not be underestimated. While the per capita income level of China is very low at only about US $ 300, the purchasing power of China's one billion people should not be neglected because the nation-wide average per capita income is misleading. Along the coast and in the economically more developed areas, per capita income is in fact very much within the range of the middle income countries. Although China's economy is going to experience a period of consolidation and slowing down, there is no question that the modernization programmes and open door policy will still to some extent be maintained.

The Japanese market is of course huge in terms of purchasing power. Japan is now the second largest economic power whose GNP is half that of the United States. The problems of the Japanese market in the past were related to the inward-looking attitude of their consumers and the non-tariff barriers imposed on imports. After the drastic appreciation of the yen, Japan has switched from its conventional export-led economic growth to a domestic demand-oriented type. Hong Kong's ability to penetrate the Japanese market is also impressive. In 1987, Hong Kong's export to Japan increased in real terms by 42 %, while the increase in exports to all markets was only 23 %. In the first half of 1988, Hong Kong's export to Japan compared with the same period in 1987 increased in real terms by 13 %, while only an 8 % increase was recorded for all markets. In the China market, Hong Kong of course enjoys advantages over other countries. It is not inappropriate to label China as Hong Kong's semi-domestic market. The China market is burgeoning, and Hong Kong will get the greatest benefit out of China.

Another reason explaining the increased intraregional trade in this region is a convergence towards free trade policy. While Japan has been making very serious attempts to lift its non-tariff trade barriers, other developing countries in this region such as South Korea, Taiwan, Thailand, Indonesia, and the Philippines are gradually reducing their level of tariffs.

Intraregional Investment

Traditionally, foreign direct investment in this region comes mainly from the developed countries in the west. Later on, Japanese investment became important. Most recently, the Asian NIEs have increasingly become important foreign investors in this region. In fact, Hong Kong is one of the largest foreign investors among developing countries. In 1987, Hong Kong was the number one investor in China, the second largest foreign investor in Indonesia, the third largest foreign investor in the Philippines, Thailand, Singapore and Taiwan, and the fifth largest investor in Malaysia. In making investment abroad Hong Kong firms have been acting as agents of technology transfer. Moreover, making foreign direct investment abroad is a means to relocate industries to the next layer of countries in the flying geese pattern of industrial production. In recent years, Hong Kong has relocated a large part of its footwear and toy industries to Thailand and the Pearl River Delta in China. Of course, making foreign investment is not only of benefit to the host country. Hong Kong, for example, in investing abroad is actually relocating its outdated industries so that the phasing out process can be less painful and more gradual. This outward investment should not be regarded as a sign of lacking confidence in the future of Hong Kong, but should be taken as a positive measure undertaken by the dynamic firms to explore their ownership-specified advantages for greater profitability.

Regional Economic Cooperation

The lack of economic cooperation in this region in the past is not a surprise in view of the fact that there are significant differences among countries in this region in history, culture, economic development strategies, economic system, level of income, and stage of economic development. Significant changes have however occurred in the past few years. Notably, there is a tendency for different economic systems and development strategies to converge. Specifically, we observe a trend of liberalization, deregulation, and privatization in most countries of this region. At the same time, an increasing number of countries has switched to outward-looking policies of industrialization. As a result, the difference in the type and level of economic development has become smaller. But the most important force which will pull Asian Pacific developing countries together is the recent emergence of regionalism or trading blocs in the developed world, leading to a much greater degree of protectionism. Today, we notice the trading bloc of United States and Canada, the trading bloc of Australia and New Zealand, and above all a fortress Europe in 1992. Inevitably, some kind of formal organization consisting of most of the Asian Pacific countries and focusing on trade and development issues will emerge. The formation of a powerful economic bloc consisting of Taiwan, Mainland China and Hong Kong which can be labelled "The Greater China" is already underway. The Greater China has become a de facto economic bloc because of the rapidly increasing interactions in trade and investment among themselves, and their high degree of complementarity in economic resources. Mainland China has very rich natural resources, a plentiful supply of trainable and cheap labour, and a huge potential in conducting basic research. Hong Kong has an ample supply of capital and professionals, the ability to commercialize invention, and all the infrastructures for being a service centre in finance, trade, telecommunication and technology. Taiwan has built up a high level of technological capability to specialize in relatively sophisticated industrial manufacturing. On the demand side, the combined market of Hong Kong, Taiwan and Mainland China is huge. We have yet to see how this Greater China economic concept will be affected by the recent events in China.

In the movement towards greater economic cooperation in this region, Hong Kong can certainly have an important role. No Greater China is possible without Hong Kong acting as a conduit. Hong Kong could also be instrumental in the formation of Asian Pacific economic cooperative organizations and can logically become the headquarters of such economic cooperative organizations. China, Taiwan and Hong Kong have, however, not been invited by Australia to participate in discussions about Asian Pacific economic cooperation to take place later this year. Hong Kong has now to convince the Asian Pacific economies that Hong Kong's role is important and Hong Kong will be an autonomous economic entity after 1997.

Implications for Europe

(1) There is little question that for survival, Hong Kong has to transform its manufacturing industries from high labour intensity to high technology, capital, and skill intensity. Hong Kong has to participate in the subregional division of labour among the Asian Pacific countries which has already emerged in the past few years. Hong Kong has to phase out some of its outdated industries to China and Southeast Asian countries. Conventionally, Hong Kong depends heavily on Japan for technology, machinery and equipment, and semi-manufactures for its manufacturing industries. It is anticipated that in the near future China will depend more on Europe for technology and equipment in its industry transformation and the building up of higher technology industries. There is in fact evidence to show that despite the appreciation of European currencies against the Hong Kong dollar in the past few years, Hong Kong's imports from West Europe has in fact increased not only in absolute term but even in relative terms. Specifically, the import from West Germany has increased; Hong Kong's import from West Germany has increased from 17 per cent of its total in 1981 to 20 per cent in 1988. In the case of Switzerland Hong Kong's import has increased from 11 per cent of Hong Kong's total import in 1984 to 14 per cent in 1988. In the case of Italy, the increase has been from 9.3 per cent in 1981 to 12.4 per cent in 1988. It is in the case of the United Kingdom that Hong Kong's import has decreased significantly in terms of percentage shares. The major imports of Hong Kong from West Germany are chemicals and related products, machinery and equipment for particular industries, electronic semi-manufactures and components, and motor vehicles. From Italy, Hong Kong imports quite significant quantities of manufactured goods classified by materials such as textiles, construction materials, and clothing. In terms of Hong Kong's future direction of industrial development,

the European supplies of technology and equipment seem to be very much in line with the nature and types of industries to be established and further developed in Hong Kong.

(2) As an increasingly mature economy Hong Kong will develop its service sector hand-in-hand with its manufacturing industries. While Hong Kong is already an important international and regional financial centre, there is little question that Hong Kong will further develop in the area of services such as telecommunications, commerce, technology and trade. Owing to the uncertainties related to the 1997 issue, local investment will be much more hesitant than before and local investors will seek to find overseas partners to engage in many of their activities. Multinational corporations undertaking global business activities are of course in a better position to manage the risks that Hong Kong is facing and will face. There are therefore vast opportunities for European investors to invest in the non-manufacturing sectors of Hong Kong. The attached tables show the importance of European investments in such sectors in the past few years. At present, the most important European investors in Hong Kong's manufacturing are the United Kingdom, West Germany, Switzerland, the Netherlands, and France.

(3) Despite the June events in China it is expected that China will continue to maintain an open door policy to trade with western nations and to attract their investment, though the degree of openness has necessarily to be smaller because of the expected changes in China's policies towards more centralization and a smaller private economic sector. To a large extent, Hong Kong's economic relations with China will still be very close and Hong Kong will continue to serve as China's window on the world. In this connection, European countries and other western nations will still find Hong Kong an important base for information gathering and for establishing an

operating base for trading with and investing in China. A less open Chinese economy than before will make Hong Kong even more important as a bridgehead for doing business in China. Moreover, in response to the recent events in China, Hong Kong firms have inevitably to look for opportunities outside China. Hong Kong's firms will become more internationalized and more integrated with the rest of the Asian Pacific towards the 1997. There are therefore plenty of opportunities for European firms to cooperate with Hong Kong firms to do business in the Asian Pacific region at large.

Table 1

European Investment in the Non-Manufacturing Sectors of Hong Kong by Industry, 1987

	European Investment	
Industry	Number of Establishments	Percentage
Banking	28	5.7
Deposit taking company	34	6.9
Business services	14	2.8
- computer programming	5	1.0
- rental	3	0.6
- others	6	1.2
Construction	31	6.3
Communications	2	0.4
Insurance	16	3.2
Publishing	7	1.4
Real estate	1	0.2
Record production	2	0.4
Securities and financial services	19	3.8
Transportation	53	10.7
- airline and air cargo	10	2.0
- freight forwarding	24	4.8
- ship management	17	3.4
- others	2	0.4
Trading		
- chemical products	26	5.3
- electrical and electronic products	31	6.3
- garment and accessories	36	7.3
- industrial machinery	34	6.9
- pharmaceuticals	22	4.4
- others	139	28.1
Total	495	100.0

Source: Ma, A. Y. M. (ed.) (1986) Key European Business in Hong Kong. Dun and Bradstreet (H. K.) Ltd.

Table 2

European Investment in the Non-Manufacturing Sectors of Hong Kong by Country, 1987

	European Investment	
Country	Number of Establishments	Percentage
U.K.	198	40.0
West Germany	77	15.6
Switzerland	49	9.9
The Netherlands	45	9.1
Sweden	21	4.2
France	43	8.7
Italy	13	2.6
Luxembourg	11	2.2
Norway	11	2.2
Belgium	10	2.0
Denmark	10	2.0
Others	7	1.4
Total	495	100.0

Source: Same as Table 1

SOME REFLECTIONS ON PROSPECTS FOR REGIONAL CO-OPERATION IN THE ASIAN-PACIFIC REGION

Syed M. Naseem
Chief
Development Planning Division
United Nations Economic and Social Commission for Asia and the Pacific (UN-ESCAP)
The United Nations Building
Rajdamnern Avenue
Bangkok 10200

The designations employed and the presentation of the material do not imply the expression of any opinion whatsoever on the part of the secretariat of the United Nations concerning the legal status of any country, territory, city or area, or of its authorities, or concerning delimitation of its frontiers or boundaries.

1. Introduction

Regional co-operation efforts in the Asian and Pacific region gained momentum in the post-war period in the wake of decolonization by Western countries. However, the effects of the cold war were so divisive that the movement for regional co-operation did not progress much beyond rhetorical pronouncements and expressions of political solidarity. In the economic fields, the countries of the region were drawn into the North-South stancing through the Non-Aligned Movement and the formation of the Group of 77 in the United Nations. There were few efforts of significance during the 1950s or the 1960s to foster economic co-operation among the region's developing countries. International efforts, both bilateral and multilateral, were focused more on fostering technical co-operation activities and exchange of experience than on linking or integrating these economies to reap the benefits of economies of scale or differences in comparative advantage.

Europe-Asia-Pacific Studies in Economy and Technology
Kulessa (Ed.)
The Newly Industrializing Economies of Asia

The slow movement of regional co-operation efforts in the early post-war decades was also explained by the need for consolidation, integration and development of the national economy, which is an essential prerequisite for effective regional co-operation. By the middle of the 1960s and the early 1970s, however, many developing countries of the region had begun to realize the need for greater economic interaction with their neighbours as their production base broadened and became more diversified. Import substitution, though easy in its initial phases, became more difficult and inefficient as it progressed further and it became imperative that market expansion be sought, whether within or outside the region.

The main economic motivation for regional co-operation among developing countries was to get over the limitations generated by import substitution. It had the advantage of subjecting themselves to some degree of openness without risking severe balance-of-payment problems. Regional co-operation was thus viewed as a middle path between complete self-reliance at one end of the spectrum and total openness of the economy, at the other. Its main rationale consisted in the possibility of increasing the degree of flexibility and the room for manoeuvre in pursuing national development strategies. This increased flexibility was seen to arise from two principal sources: (a) an increase in the economies of scale provided by pooling their resources and exploring the complementarities in their production base, (b) increasing the size of their market mostly through trade diversion but also through trade creation.

In the event, however, the countries of the developing Asian and Pacific region pursued widely divergent strategies of development. While most adopted import substitution as the main vehicle for their initial industrial transformation, others found export promotion - mainly directed towards and assisted by developed countries - to be a more profitable avenue of growth. The establishment of highly protected import substituting industries in most developing countries of the region reduced the possibilities of intraregional trade and specialization in production activities.

2. Past Experiences in Regional Co-operation in Asia and the Pacific

Despite the theoretical attractiveness of regional co-operation, its actual progress in the Asian and Pacific region has been painfully slow. There have been only a few successful attempts to launch effective region-wide schemes of economic co-operation among developing countries of the region. Among the successful ventures, e.g. Asian Highway, Asia Pacific Telecommunity and the establishment of a number of commodity trade agreements, including those relating to pepper, rubber, tin and coconut have been established under the auspices of ESCAP (or ECAFE in earlier years). The Asian Development Bank, which was also established at the initiative of ESCAP and in the face of considerable resistance from a number of countries, has concentrated mainly on the supply of finance and technical assistance to individual countries, rather than on fostering regional economic co-operation and financing of regional projects as its major concern. There have also been less successful attempts to forge a regional payments union of tariff preferences among selected groups of countries in the form of Bangkok Agreement. Both have lacked universality and their impact has been rather modest, despite several efforts to make them more effective and broad-based.

Much more seems to have been achieved in the realm of subregional co-operation. Of these, ASEAN has been the most effective, but SPC and SPEC in the Pacific and SAARC in South Asia have emerged as established forums of subregional co-operation. However, in terms of economic integration and policy co-ordination their achievements are as yet modest, at best.

The road to regional and subregional co-ordination in Asia and Pacific is paved with good intentions. Unfortunately it has led to few tangible results. To analyze the reasons for this, it would be necessary to examine in detail the above institutional arrangements. Although such an exercise would be rewarding and will have considerable lessons for evaluating future options, it cannot be attempted in this brief paper.

3. Future Prospects of Regional Co-operation and its Likely Role in Stimulating Growth

The recent resurgence of interest in regional co-operation in the Asian and Pacific region stems mainly from the phenomenal growth of some of the leading economies of the region. Led by Japan's post-war economic performance which made double-digit annual growth rates a norm rather than a freak occurrence, the NIEs in the 1960s and 1970s (as well as in the late 1980s), China and some of the ASEAN economies have repeated the performance in the 1980s, while the rest of the world has remained largely sluggish during the last decade. Other major economies in the region, especially India have also shown remarkably resilient if less sustained growth during the 1980s. These economies constitute a highly significant proportion of the world's population, GDP and, most importantly, foreign trade.

Much of the world's attention has understandably centred on Japan, the NIEs and the ASEAN countries, which have shared certain common characteristics during the process of their development. Among these, the following seem to have been most significant: a high and rising ratio of exports to GDP, continuing increases in ratio of manufactures to total exports, a highly dynamic private entrepreneurs class, a dedicated and generally well trained labour force, as well as governments willing and able to intervene to ensure continuing high rates of growth and competitiveness of their exports.[1] These three groups of economies have also represented three waves of industrialization in Asia, beginning from the 1950s to the present decade.

These three waves of industrialization and the concomitant dynamism brought to the Asian and Pacific region have occurred without any formal arrangements for regional or subregional co-operation among the three groups of countries. Yet there has been a growing perception of interdependence among them and of their impact on the world economy. It is the nature of this complex interdependence and the need for avoiding the strains not only among them but also on the world trading system as a whole that have generated the pressures for seeking some formal arrangements for regional co-operation. These dynamic economies of Asia and the Pacific depend for their survival on an open world trading system and access to the markets of developed economies to which a predominantly high proportion of their exports are destined. With the increase in protectionist pressures in developed countries, and the emergence of trading blocs among them, the future of Uruguay rounds negotiations has become increasingly uncertain. As a result, these countries are faced with the problem of articulating an appropriate response in a co-ordinated manner to the challenges confronting them. A number of options seem to present themselves.

The first and the most commonly discussed option is to form a trading bloc under the leadership of Japan. This conforms to the perception that the world would eventually divide itself into three or four major economic blocs: the North American bloc, the

---

1 Some authors have also considered common cultural characteristics, represented by a shared use of chopsticks and practice of Confucian values as a highly important factor in explaining their success.

European bloc, the socialist bloc and a Japanese bloc. Sometimes the proposition is made in terms of leading currencies: US dollar, ECU, rouble and the yen. This rather extreme scenario is unlikely to find much favour in the Asian and Pacific region which has a commitment to an open trading system and which has strong traditional links with both the American and European markets.

A second option is often presented as a loose union of Pacific rim countries consisting of the NIEs, ASEAN, Australia, New Zealand, Japan and USA. Both the membership and the nature of economic ties within such a grouping are not clearly spelled out. In some instances China, Pacific island countries and even Canada, Chile and Argentina are mentioned, while in others, Hong Kong, Taiwan Province of China, among the NIEs, and Brunei Darussalam, among ASEAN are excluded.

Both the composition of the countries and the likely agenda of the proposed meeting arouses concern on analytical, as well as political grounds. Analytically, the concept of Pacific rim countries as a source of dynamism in the world economy is of questionable validity. For the recent dynamism of the region is largely an Asian rather than a Pacific phenomenon. The countries of the Pacific region, which are outside the Asian continent, especially Australia, New Zealand, the Pacific island and the Latin American developing economies have in fact shown marked sluggish growth during the 1980s as a result of their dependence on primary commodities and commercial borrowings. The Asian countries, led by the NIEs and China and to a lesser extent by ASEAN and the larger South Asian economies, India and Pakistan have recorded high growth rates during most of the 1980s.

Although trade has been the engine of growth in the economies of many countries in the Asian and Pacific region, the role of domestic demand expansion in many of the large and rapidly growing economies has not been insignificant. It has often served to provide a cushion to the vagaries of the external environment. While trade is an important ingredient of the success story of many Asian and Pacific economies, high levels of investment, often with a high component of foreign direct investment, have also played a significant role. Thus not only trade, but also investment and other resource flows are a matter of equal relevance for the Asian and Pacific region.

There is yet no clear indication about the nature and objectives of such grouping. In its most recent incarnation given to it by the Australian Prime Minister, Mr. Bob Hawke, the new grouping is viewed as a forum for Asian and Pacific governments to promote economic co-operation. The main vehicle for such a consultative forum is envisaged as an OECD-type institution aimed mainly to deal more effectively with emerging international trade issues.

The hesitancy and equivocation with which the proposal has been received in most ASEAN capitals underlines its political weakness. Apprehensions in countries which are presently excluded from the envisaged grouping are likely to be stronger. They arise from a number of considerations. Firstly, the presence and strong initiatives of extraregional and developed countries in the grouping is likely to be viewed with considerable equanimity, if not outright suspicion. Secondly, it could prove divisive and drive a wedge between poor and rich developing countries. Thirdly, it could lead to the weakening of existing arrangements of regional and subregional co-operation, such as ASEAN, SAARC and SPEC, which have yet to see their full flowering as instruments of regional economic co-operation. Fourthly, any grouping which comprises Japan, the NIEs, ASEAN-4 and Australia, at its core, is likely to be susceptible to retaliation by other trading blocs or nations and thus lead to further deterioration in the world trading environment.

The third alternative for regional co-operation in Asia and the

Pacific region has unfortunately not received the attention and articulation it deserves. It arises in the context of the restructuring efforts of developing countries of the region which are trying to find a niche for themselves in the ever changing pattern of international division of labour in the world economy. The opportunity that this provides for market expansion and intraregional trade is insufficiently realized at present. However, it could serve as the basis for a mutually reinforcing development impulse for sustained growth momentum which the more dynamic economies of the region have so far found elusive.

Effective regional co-operation in economic restructuring would be based on broadening the narrow space for development presently available to the developing countries. The rapid growth of the region's developing economies during the last few decades has created considerable room for mutually supportive and complementary restructuring within the developing Asian and Pacific region. The process of differentiation in the region has now increased quite considerably to allow for greater complementarity that makes room for greater interdependence among them. This process is likely to intensify in the coming decade. Japan's need to utilize its surplus, to restructure its domestic economy, to relocate some of its industries and to diversify its export markets will continue to provide the developing Asian and Pacific economies not only a growing market for the latter's exports but also a reservoir for finance and technology transfer. The NIEs can serve the role of a second locomotive in energizing the developing economies of the region, while the ASEAN-4 will be direct beneficiaries of the restructuring efforts in Japan and the NIEs. The crucial question for the 1990s is whether the process of the "flying geese" formation, which helped the East Asian and to a more limited extent the Southeast Asian developing nations to achieve a degree of restructuring, will continue and involve the less dynamic countries of the region. It would seem that this mechanism would not be as effective in the case of countries with a large population, low agricultural productivity and other institutional handicaps. In other words, the third or fourth wave of industrialization in the Asian and Pacific economies have been responsible for the success of Japan and the NIEs.

None the less, the model of transformation through the changing division of labour among Asian and Pacific developing economies will continue to have some degree of appeal and relevance in at least three crucial ways. The growing interdependence among the region's economies in the 1990s is likely to necessitate some degree of policy co-ordination in the developing ESCAP region. If the current trends of closer regional, subregional and bilateral trading relationships continue, the developing economies of the region will also have to consider some mechanism for closer co-operation among themselves. This third alternative of a larger regional framework for Asian and Pacific co-operation through widening complementarity in their economic structure would, therefore, provide greater opportunities for restructuring the economies of the region.

4. The Possibilities for and Constraints on Wider Regional Economic Co-operation in Asia and the Pacific

A wider basis of regional co-operation in Asia and Pacific co-operation can be established through systematic efforts to enhance intraregional trade and investment flows beyond their present levels and scope. The emerging differentiation in the levels of development among the developing countries of the region - represented by per capita incomes ranging from $ 150 to $ 8,000 - are giving rise to complementarities both on the supply side in terms of costs differences and on the demand side in terms of different income elasticities. The complementarities are likely to give rise to inter-sectoral trade among the countries of the region.

Besides inter-sectoral trade, there are considerable possibilities of intra-sectoral and intra-industrial trade which the developing countries of the region have begun to exploit in recent years. These arise, on the supply side, due to complementarity in resources/skills through regional or subregional specialization in production and, on the demand side, as a result of limitation of domestic market size. The potential for such trade is especially evident if the industrialization pattern takes place in the "flying geese" formation, e.g. between Japan and the NIEs, between the NIEs and ASEAN and so on.

The realization of the potential for intraregional trade and investment is beset with many difficulties. First, it has to be realized that intraregional trade, in order to have beneficial effects, should add to and not substitute for interregional trade, especially that with industrialized countries. Secondly, the composition of trade would need to be restructured for it to provide the necessary impetus to trade and development in the region. Thirdly, it is not possible for countries of the region to perceive fully the benefits of wider regional co-operation in an environment of uncertainty when short-term market strategies are more important than longer-term goals. The benefits of wider regional co-operation have often to be balanced against the need for preserving their existing market shares in trade with developed countries. However, the need for a proper assessment of trade opportunities within and outside the region, especially in view of emerging protectionist trends and creation of trading blocs becomes imperative.

5. The Role of Japan and the NIEs in Asian and Pacific Regional Co-operation

In any credible scheme for wider regional economic co-operation in the Asian and Pacific region, Japan and the NIEs will have to play a critically important role. The significance of their role lies in their ability to enhance intraregional flows of trade, investment and technology transfer. Given their success in pursuing an export-oriented strategy and their ability to generate large and continuing balance-of-payments surpluses and their capacity for technology innovation, these countries can contribute greatly to the development of the low-income countries of the region and, in the process, create expanding markets for their industrial products which are beginning to face the effects of protectionism in developed market economies of Europe and North America.

The possibilities of such a role being played by Japan and the NIEs would depend on the following considerations.

(a) The *readiness* or *reluctance* of these economies to vacant their space in the matrix of international trade flows for those countries which follow in their footsteps as late industrializers and to relocate production in ESCAP developing countries more widely than at present;

(b) Their *ability* to sustain their current account surplus over the next decade, in the face of increasing protectionism and mounting international pressure to adjust their external balance;

(c) Their *willingness* to recycle their current account surpluses through an appropriate mix of direct foreign investment, commercial bank lending and concessional aid flows to other ESCAP developing countries;

(d) The *decision* of Japanese firms to invest and to relocate the production in ESCAP developing countries other than the NIEs, or some of the favoured ASEAN-4;

(e) The *absorptive capacity* of ESCAP developing countries in terms of (i) physical infrastructure, (ii) human resources and skill formation, (iii) profitability of private investment, and (iv) nature or degree of state intervention.

It is evident that the success of a wider basis of regional co-operation in the Asian and Pacific region, will depend on the relative perception of Japan and the NIEs regarding two possibilities: (a) their ability to penetrate the protective barriers in Europe and North America, (b) the possibility of low-income Asian and Pacific economies being transformed into attractive future markets for industrial products through the infusion of capital and technology transfers. Some degree of policy co-ordination among developing countries of Asia and Pacific and Japan and the NIEs will inevitably be necessary if regional economic co-operation efforts are to yield beneficial results for all concerned.

Whether new regional or subregional institutions would be necessary or old ones would need to be strengthened and interlinked in order to reflect the emerging realities and aspiration is an issue which requires careful, though urgent consideration. Evidently, there is a need for new or invigorated institutions relating to the promotion of joint investment ventures, intraregional trade and development research, as well as in the important and emerging concerns relating to the protection of environment. There would also seem to be a need for greater interaction or dialogue between subregional groups, such as the ASEAN, SAARC and SPEC. Clearly the time is ripe for putting regional co-operation on the agenda of the region's developing countries in a broader framework with the active participation of Japan, the NIEs and other leading economies of the region.

ASEAN REALITY AND PERSPECTIVE

Sharon Siddique
Senior Fellow
Institute of Southeast Asian Studies (ISEAS)
Heng Mui Keng Terrace
Pasir Panjang
Singapore 0511

1. Overview

ASEAN was formed in 1967 as a regional political organization whose main task was to provide a loosely-structured regional forum where differences amongst member states could be discussed and resolved without resort to confrontation. For twenty-two years there has been peace among ASEAN members, and a united stand on political events within the larger Southeast Asian region (primarily regarding a position on unfolding events in Cambodia). Providing this essential collective climate of regional political stability has been ASEAN's major contribution to the economic and social development of each of the member states.

Given this reality, it will be political developments within the region which will determine ASEAN's future viability. As long as it is considered essential for regional political stability, ASEAN will continue to promote a climate for regional economic and social development in the year 2000 and beyond. This regional social and economic role, however, will evolve slowly, and the pace of this development will bo carefully set by consensus.

2. Social Targets

The ASEAN Secretariat in Jakarta, which was only formed in 1976, has very limited authority and functions. Even these are flexible and subject to periodic reviews. Therefore, an "ASEAN bureau-

Europe-Asia-Pacific Studies in Economy and Technology
Kulessa (Ed.)
The Newly Industrializing Economies of Asia

cracy" in the sense of an "EC bureaucracy" does not exist. Instead, the most important administrative bodies are the ASEAN National Secretariats located in each of the six member states.

How does ASEAN perform as an effective decision-making body given this loosely-structured bureaucratic character? ASEAN's unique management style has become popularly known as "the ASEAN way". This "ASEAN way", which has been developing over the past decades, is considered successful, and it is unlikely that this form of administration and decision-making will change in the next decades.

The ASEAN way is based on three important concepts: *mesyuarat* (discussion); *muafakat* (consensus); and *gotong-royong* (cooperation). Participants in a *mesyuarat* (discussion) only formally raise topics on which agreement is possible. Points of basic disagreement are postponed, and inflexible positions are avoided. Decisions taken are always reached on the basis of *muafakat*, or consensus. Thus there is no casting of votes, no vetoes, and no open expression of conflicts. Even after consensus has been reached on a certain issue, each participant still has the option of whether or not to actively participate in its implementation, and the sensitivities of each participant are taken into account in the spirit of *gotong-royong* (cooperation).

Initially, ASEAN meetings were scheduled amongst senior politicians and civil servants. Over the decades, these ASEAN meetings have generated an increasingly dense network of ASEAN public servants, youth and women's groups, journalists, artists, chambers of commerce and industry, bankers and other professionals, who meet together on a regular basis. As these ties continue over the years, these personal contacts will ensure that the ASEAN way becomes an increasingly important factor in the decision-making process in all levels of society in the member states.

3. Economic Targets

ASEAN has never aspired to be a common market, nor has it ever had as its goal a unified regional economy. Broadly speaking, there are two types of economic development which have been of concern to ASEAN: intra-ASEAN trade, and ASEAN trade and investment with its dialogue partners.

Attempts to initiate governmental economic development cooperation (for example, the AIP - ASEAN Industrial Projects - scheme initiated in 1976) have not met with much success. Present efforts at intra-ASEAN cooperation have therefore shifted to the private sector. Private sector initiatives are channelled through the ASEAN-CCI (ASEAN Chambers of Commerce and Industry), which, in 1986, founded the Group of 14 - composed of two prominent industrialists from each ASEAN country, plus a chairman from Malaysia and a deputy from Indonesia.

Regarding intra-ASEAN trade, the most important policy is the ASEAN Preferential Trading Arrangement (PTA), which was initiated in 1977. Progress, however, has been slow. At present the over 20,000 products listed only account for about five per cent of intra-ASEAN trade.

ASEAN has concentrated its main efforts towards promoting ASEAN trade and investment with trading partners outside the region. At present ASEAN has six dialogue partners - the United States, Canada, Japan, Australia, New Zealand and the European Community (EC). The EC is ASEAN's most important dialogue partner, and the only regional organization with which ASEAN is affiliated. The remainder of this paper will therefore be devoted to outlining the development of, and future for, this relationship.

4. ASEAN - EC Relations

ASEAN-EC relations date to the 1972 establishment of the Special Coordinating Committee for ASEAN Nations (SCCAN), the purpose of which was to explore possibilities for closer EC-ASEAN ties. In 1974 a Joint Study Group (JSG) of ASEAN and EC officials was formed to discuss possible linkages. In February 1977, West German Foreign Minister, Hans Dietrich Genscher, proposed a joint EC-ASEAN Foreign Ministers meeting, and the first such meeting was held in November 1978 in Brussels. Since then there have been six further EC-ASEAN Foreign Ministers meetings. Additionally, an EC-ASEAN meeting of Economic Ministers was held in Bangkok in October 1985, where a working group to promote EC economic activities in ASEAN was created.

The latest EC-ASEAN Foreign Ministers meeting was held in Duesseldorf in May 1988. Points raised in the joint declaration are a useful summary of future trends in EC-ASEAN relations.

At the Duesseldorf meeting, the Ministers singled out future cooperation in the commercial and economic fields for special emphasis. To this end, a Joint Investment Committee has been set up in each of the ASEAN capitals, and a European Investment Consultant has been appointed. Steps have also been taken to establish a Partner Research Network to facilitate business cooperation and joint ventures, the improvement of information on investment opportunities in the ASEAN region, and initiatives aimed at promoting increased European investment. In keeping with intra-regional developments, emphasis has been placed on supporting private sector investment, particularly industrial joint ventures. The Ministers also stressed the continued importance they attach to the promotion of EC-ASEAN industrial cooperation and agreed that it should be accorded high priority.

With regard to trade prospects, the ASEAN Ministers acknowledged the role of the Community's GSP in contributing to the expansion of their exports, in particular in manufactured goods which constitute 50 % of ASEAN total exports to the EC.

The EC and its member states are the second most important source of bilateral development assistance to ASEAN countries. This development aid has primarily been in the fields of Human Resources Development, Science and Technology, and Energy Cooperation, where many projects have been undertaken.

In keeping with this interest in Human Resources Development, in Duesseldorf there was in principle ministerial agreement that an ASEAN-EC Management Centre be established in ASEAN. The Ministers were of the view that the Centre would effectively enhance the Community's long-term presence in the region. The Ministers requested the ASEAN-EC JCC to consider the operational details on the establishment of such a Centre and took note of ASEAN's intention to locate it in Brunei Darussalam.

In sum, the future of ASEAN-EC relations, judging by the progress made over the past decade, looks relatively bright. The network of relationships established between the two regional organizations certainly seems to have developed in the spirit of the "ASEAN way" mentioned earlier. Through discussion (*mesyuarat*), consensus (*muafakat*) has been reached on how cooperation (*gotong-royong*) can be enhanced in the decades to come.

NIE-JAPANESE STRATEGIC INTERDEPENDENCE AND THE PACIFIC BASIN

Henri-Claude de Bettignies
Professor
Institut Européen d'Administration des Affaires (INSEAD)
Boulevard de Constance
F 77305 Fontainebleau

An international round table of this kind should have taken place a long time ago: it addresses a set of issues of **critical, long-term** importance for Japan, the NIEs and their Pacific environment, and the dynamics it attempts to elucidate are strategic both for the US and for Europe. Twenty years ago, economists were too busy developing their **dependency** theory with its gloomy outlook for the North-South relationship; they missed Japan's take-off and failed to see the emergence of the Pacific region. The dependency paradigm (still cultivated by some) is today being superseded by the interdependence model which, however, is more frequently used in the rhetoric of policymakers and discussed among scholars than fully understood in its implications. We must hope that during the last decade of this century researchers will effectively elucidate some of the critical strategic issues and complex processes which will affect the next one. Interdependence and cooperation should indeed be among them.

In its current process of globalization, Japan is strengthening its interdependence, not only with the NIEs of Asia, but with the whole Pacific region. What are the characteristics of this growing interdependence? How is it evolving? What are the medium-term implications for the Pacific basin and for the rest of the world?

The NIE-Japanese Interdependence

As the globalization of the Japanese economy gains momentum, its

Europe-Asia-Pacific Studies in Economy and Technology
Kulessa (Ed.)
The Newly Industrializing Economies of Asia

interface with the NIEs and LDCs of the Pacific region, and with North America and Europe becomes more complex, and more difficult to manage, requiring both skills and vision, which many see as being in short supply. Whether the Japanese power is an "enigma" - as an attentive European observer recently suggested in a very provocative reassessment of the mechanisms underlying Japan's techno-financial power[1] - or if today Japan confronts the world as a "power without a purpose"[2], one can legitimately be concerned about the consequences of Japan's growing interdependence, not only with the Asian NIEs but also with the Pacific region as a whole and with the rest of the world.

Over the last two decades, the outward looking, market oriented economies of the Asian NICs have contributed significantly to the rapid development of intra-Asian trade, which grew twice as fast as Asian-North American trade whilst remaining modest in volume (US $ 189 billion vs. US $ 258 billion in 1987). In terms of world trade, over the last two decades the Asian NIEs' share has grown more than that of their regional partners; from 1.6 % to 6.5 % for exports, and from 2.1 % to 5.6 % for imports (see Table 1). The tremendous growth in the NIEs' exports (increasingly led by manufactured goods), reflecting the pragmatism of the countries' leaders in adjusting to change and in learning from the success of others, has accelerated the interdependence of Japan and the NIEs. The Japanese-South Korean pattern of interdependence illustrates this process better than any other. Japan has functioned as an efficient source of capital goods and technology for South Korea while propping up Korean industrial production and export capability. The appreciation of the yen has acceler-

----

1 van Wolferen K. (1989) The Enigma of the Japanese Power. New York, Knopf, p. 496.

2 Taggart M. R. (1989) Power without a Purpose: The Crisis of Japan's Global Financial Dominance. Harvard Business Review, 2, pp. 71-83

ated Japan's interdependence with its neighbors, increasing dramatically Japan's (traditionally "modest") imports of manufactured goods, and fostering its foreign direct investment in the region. The loss of international competitiveness of South Korea's low value-added products, and its export achievement (e.g. in Japan) illustrates how policymakers and corporate strategists have effectively assessed the implications of shifting comparative advantages, e.g. in the growing interdependence of the NIEs and ASEAN. The progressive liberalization (under "external" pressure) of imports in South Korea, as had been the case in Japan, has facilitated the NIEs manufactured exports boom (see Table 2) and eased tensions in regulating bilateral patterns of trade. Today, after the US, Japan is South Korea's most important trading partner. The significant (but decreasing) trade deficit with Japan is expected to be progressively reduced as local manufacturing of parts previously purchased in Japan, the diversification of sourcing (e.g. from the US, the EEC), and the growth of (competitive, adjusted and "quality") exports to Japan contribute to improved terms of interdependence between the two nations. The Korean case illustrates, even more clearly than that of Taiwan, how trade patterns, technology transfer and industrial cooperation can develop in spite of lingering cultural resentment.

Besides Asian NIEs, ASEAN countries are also stepping up their efforts to expand exports to Japan in response to the abolition of preferential tariffs granted by the US and the slowdown of Western economies. Thailand in particular is increasing its pressure upon Japan, its leverage being the fast-growing presence of Japanese FDI in the country. Trading houses in Japan are trying to become more effective importers of ASEAN (and Pacific-Asian in general) products, while manufacturers are active in enlarging the volume of their investment in the region, thus strengthening regional interdependence. Although besides Singapore, other ASEAN countries are in the process of joining the ranks of Asian NIEs (e.g. Thailand today, Malaysia tomorrow), ASEAN interdependence is not gaining much momentum. Throughout its short history (22 years) the successive failures of projects such as AIP (ASEAN Industrial Projects), the AIC (ASEAN Industrial Complementation), and the AIJV (ASEAN Industrial Joint Ventures) has demonstrated the difficulties of industrial cooperation in the region. In terms of trade, encouraging results are on the way, but intraregional economic cooperation is not progressing very quickly (less than 20 % of total ASEAN foreign trade takes place among the six members). The business community in the ASEAN region is now convinced that increased cooperation through market-sharing and resource-pooling will strengthen national economies and increase resilience in the region, but progress is very slow. Perhaps the absence of an external threat (in contrast to each of the four Asian NIEs) and economic structural issues fosters a certain attitude of complacency.

Though ASEAN cooperation in trade (and even more in industry where economies of **scope** and of **scale** would be particularly beneficial) is slow in coming, as international transactions become more active - with more FDI, more capital flows, the emergence and development of new Southeast Asian MNCs (stemming often from the dynamism of overseas Chinese entrepreneurs) - the potential efficiency gains from more integration will become more compelling among governments and policymakers.

Japan, NIEs and the Pacific Basin

The dynamism of the economic interdependence of Japan, the NIEs and the quasi-NIEs in manufactured goods is both a cause and a consequence of their rapid economic growth, while the horizontal division of labor among them has induced (somewhat "painful") change in industrial structure and a shift in comparative advantage. As the Japanese economy is the locomotive of the region, and will remain so for some time, the rapid appreciation of the yen has greatly accelerated these changes.

Will the acceleration of change in the regional division of labor, associated with the process of catching up which is bound to intensify, nurture the emergence of a Pacific **bloc** or a **Pacific community**? It is in this context that Japan, now the world's largest ODA donor, is now giving priority to its Pacific basin neighbors. As K. Matsuura, Director General of the Economic Bureau (Ministry of Foreign Affairs), says explicitly: "Japan offers aid with two goals in mind. The first is to foster economic and social development in the Third World and the second is to promote the relations between developing countries and Japan ... we shouldn't simply throw money around in random directions. Aid must be steered to places where it will bring long-term benefits back to its donor ... Sub-Saharan Africa is undoubtedly one of the poorest areas in the world today, and it receives a major share of North American and European aid. But this does not mean that Japan should concentrate on this area ... **As an Asian country, Japan's ties with its neighbors are naturally of central importance. Our foreign aid policy reflects this reality, the bulk of Japanese aid being channeled to other Asian countries.** There is no pressing reason to alter that policy now ...[3]. The target of the latest fourth ODA plan (1988-1992) is to raise cumulative ODA spending to $ 50 billion or more over the five year period, thereby doubling the amount of foreign aid. However, current ODA represents a mere 0.3 % of GNP, ranking Japan only 19th in terms of ODA as a share of GNP. Furthermore, "Japan has the lowest grant share among the DAC nations indicating that a major part of its aid comes in the form of concessionary loans"[4] and the government hopes to untie many of the strings attached to loans and

---

3 Matsuura K. (Spring 1989) Administering Foreign Aid: the View from the Top. Economic Eye, pp. 12-13.

4 Ibid. p. 15

to expand bilateral grants, technical assistance and contributions to multilateral agencies.

Taking the example of the ASEAN region, although Japan is the largest contributor of ODA, the biggest foreign investor, and the most important trading partner, it is still not much liked, and attitudes toward Japan remain "ambivalent"[5]. Its growing dependency (Japan buys 21 % of ASEAN's exports, provides 61 % of all non-military aid and owns between 20 and 50 % of foreign investments in four of the six countries)[6] and its memories of Japanese behavior 40 years ago (the Greater East Asia Coprosperity Sphere) cannot but influence ASEAN's attitudes towards Japan, in spite of its outstanding contemporary achievement. Will Japan's very large ODA effort - recently announced by the Japanese government to be fully "untied" by 1990 (for Malaysia, Thailand, the Philippines, Korea and Papua New Guinea) improve Japan's image in the Pacific region while strengthening regional linkages towards the development of a Pacific basin community? Will the intensity of Japan's links with its neighbors and the ASEAN countries - through increased FDI, bilateral trade, transfer of technology - create more tension and resentment in the delicate Japanese-regional interface, or will it alleviate them, soothe feelings and strengthen the buildup of a Pacific community?

The answer is unclear. Japan is only one of the partners in a complex regional system. The NIEs' foreign investment in Southeast Asia will develop, bringing mutual benefits, and will increase FDI diversification in host countries. The pace of the NIEs' economic growth, and of that of the region as a whole, will slow down, competition among NIEs will grow, while protectionism

---

5 Erlanger S., In Southeast Asia, Japan Dominates in Aid, Trade and Old Resentments. The New York Times, July 2, 1989, p. 2E.

6 The exceptions being the Philippines and Brunei.

(or "organized" trade), associated with lower growth in OECD countries, may curb imports from the Pacific region. Economic performance will also be affected by changes in wage structures (e.g. Singapore), land cost and infrastructure availability (e.g. Thailand), social tensions (e.g. South Korea), skills shortages (e.g. Hong Kong). Foreign investment will be increasingly perceived as a **mixed blessing**, transfer of (high) technology may become more **cautious** or **protected** (e.g. learning from the steel or shipbuilding industries in Japan).

After 20 years of academic and political debate on the Pacific economic **community**, there is still no institutionalized framework for organizing the Pacific through government cooperation. "Regional leadership", "coprosperity sphere", "hegemonic coordination" arouse fears of a Pacific regional organization. And, as the concept of a **Pacific community** is still somewhat conceptually loose, it is unlikely that the growing interdependence of the region will be organized on a governmental basis in the near future. The many networks currently in existence will develop, some will be more effective than others, and interdependence will progressively multiply them, while the further strengthening of the Japanese-American linkage may develop into a new geopolitical order. New NIEs will then exist in the Pacific Asian region, and dialogue among more interdependent partners will require many skills still to be learnt today.

Technological change has turned interdependence into a global process which means that the dynamics of the Japan-NIEs-Pacific basin complex have an immediate impact upon our European competitive environment. In trying to understand the logic of our different Asian partners we can possibly identify a different way to define our own European problems. A good example can be found in the way Japanese have reacted to the NIEs' interdependence, e.g., learning from the steel industry with its dramatic reduction of the workforce (from 65,000 to 27,000 employees in a decade), from industry's "wild" diversification (with its mixed results), from the government's vision and role (as a "coach") in facilitating the consequences of interdependence up- and down-stream - or in the way Koreans have selectively learnt from Japan.

Beyond **learning**, interdependence should invite us to **monitor effectively the changes** taking place in Japan and the NIEs. For example, in Korea a wage hike (+22 % in 1988) along with a labor productivity of +7 % and pressure to appreciate the won will push towards more capital- and technology-intensive industries and "limit" economic growth to 7 % for the next decade. With these changes Japan will continue to have a surplus with both South Korea and Taiwan - in 1988 Korea exported US $ 12 billion to Japan (19.8 % of its total exports) while it imported US $ 15.9 billion (or 30 % of its imports), and Taiwan exported US $ 8.7 billion to Japan (14.5 % of its exports) and imported US $ 14.8 billion (or 29.9 % of its imports). In both cases forthcoming change will modify interdependence, but at a pace which can and should be monitored, as the NIEs' products are likely to be increasingly present on the Japanese market and to affect Japan's plan for globalization.

NIE-Japanese dynamics in a Pacific basin still in the making, with its "late-comer", "catch-up", "boomerang" effects, is a "laboratory" for all of us: an experiment in sustained fast growth is successfully taking place which is changing the distribution of power around the globe and inviting policy- and decision-makers constantly to review their knowledge, to challenge their understanding and to quickly learn to anticipate the **mutation** our societies will have to experience in order to survive in the face of global competition and technological war.

Table 1

The Share of Western Pacific Nations in World Trade

		1965	1970	1975	1980	1985	1986
Exports	Asian NICs	1.6	2.2	2.6	4.0	6.2	6.5
	ASEAN-4	1.9	1.6	1.9	2.5	2.5	2.1
	Japan	4.9	6.6	6.7	6.8	9.7	10.4
	US	15.8	14.8	13.1	11.5	11.7	10.7
Imports	Asian NICs	2.1	2.9	3.3	4.5	5.6	5.6
	ASEAN-4	1.9	1.6	1.8	2.0	1.9	1.7
	Japan	4.5	6.2	6.9	7.2	6.8	6.1
	US	12.7	14.0	12.5	13.1	18.9	18.5

Notes: 1. The Asian NICs are South Korea, Taiwan, Hong Kong and Singapore.
2. The ASEAN-4 are Thailand, Malaysia, Indonesia and the Philippines. The other two ASEAN members, Brunei (which joined in 1984) and Singapore, are excluded.

Source: Yearbook of International Trade Statistics, United Nations

Table 2

Index of the Horizontal Division of Labor Between Japan and Other Asian Countries

	Consumer nondurables		Consumer durables		Capital goods	
	1980	1986	1980	1986	1980	1986
South Korea	0.28	0.31	0.42	0.50	0.19	0.08
Taiwan	0.29	0.33	0.39	0.38	0.11	0.19
Hong Kong	0.39	0.32	0.39	0.36	0.02	0.10
Singapore	0.09	0.11	0.25	0.20	0.14	0.16
Malaysia	0.09	0.19	0.13	0.19	0.06	0.09
Thailand	0.13	0.27	0.04	0.14	0.00	0.03
Indonesia	0.27	0.27	0.04	0.15	0.03	0.00
Philippines	0.31	0.19	0.18	0.16	0.04	0.02

Note: Index numbers are calculated as 1 minus the ratio of the absolute value of the difference between bilateral exports and imports to the total two-way trade for each category of goods.

THE EAST ASIAN NICs AND THE SOUTH ASIA REALITY

Ponna Wignaraja
Co-ordinator
South Asian Perspectives Project
Participatory Institute for Development Alternatives (PIDA)
The United Nations University (UNU)
75, Kynsey Road
Colombo 8
Sri Lanka

Introduction

The success of South Korea, Taiwan, Singapore and Hong Kong, popularly known as the "East Asian NICs", with rapid economic growth and industrialization over the last two decades, is widely known. During the period 1965-85, GNP per capita in all four countries grew at over 6 percent per annum. These rates far exceed those achieved by the world's most developed countries over the same period - Japan grew the fastest at 4.1 percent per annum and is followed by West Germany (2.4 percent), France (2.1 percent), the United Kingdom (2.1 percent) and the United States (1.8 percent). The outcome of twenty years of consistently rapid growth has been the attainment of high levels of per capita income by the East Asian NICs.

Many analysts have rightly highlighted the remarkable development record of the East Asian NICs. They would also generally attribute the industrial success of these countries to the adoption of an outward-looking strategy. The consensus view can be briefly summarized:

> Many developing countries influenced by the export pessimism of the 1950s and 1960s and by the supposed merits of Import Substituting Industrialization (ISI) adopted inward-looking trade strategies aimed at developing a modern industrial sector through protectionism, government planning and other di-

Europe-Asia-Pacific Studies in Economy and Technology
Kulessa (Ed.)
The Newly Industrializing Economies of Asia

rect incentives whose combined effect was a strong anti-export bias. At the same time, the ISI policies helped create a sizeable industrial sector in the countries. But, the easy phase of ISI (namely the production of consumer goods) ended in the 1960s, and many countries faced serious problems, including inefficient industries, foreign exchange shortages and a bias against agriculture. A few countries - notably South Korea, Taiwan and Singapore - "wisely switched" to outward-looking strategies, while others stubbornly and unwisely stuck to inward-looking ISI. The former group have shown themselves to be markedly more successful in terms of growth, industrialization, balance of payments, income distribution and employment. The opening to trade provided an important engine of growth at a vital juncture of the economic development of the East Asian NICs.

International scholars and practitioners alike have extolled the virtues of the East Asian NICs and urged the replication of the outward-looking strategy for model in South Asia as well. Pakistan and Sri Lanka adopted the strategy in 1977. More recently, India, Nepal and Bangladesh have started to liberalize their economies to trade.

Despite over a decade's experience with the outward-looking strategy the expected economic take-off has not occurred in Sri Lanka and Pakistan. In fact, both countries are characterized by limited industrialization and mass poverty, which continues to reproduce itself. Rising frustration among under-privileged groups in Pakistani and Sri Lankan society have fueled political instability. Today, more resources are devoted to defense-related expenditure than to development.

The question that emerges is why did the NICs succeed while two emulators - Sri Lanka and Pakistan - did not achieve the same results?

1. The world historical framework in which the East Asian NICs were incorporated fully into the global system has changed with most industrialized countries not playing to the rules of the game (e.g. protection against developing country exports) or being able to manage their internal economies effectively (e.g. the deepening recession in the West).

2. The NICs (particularly South Korea and Singapore), delinked for a sufficient period from their colonial past and built up an industrial base and internal technological capability - before they opened their economy to world market forces. This was also premised on a restructured agricultural system, with agrarian reform preceding the industrial push. Technological change in the form of a green revolution, redistributive land reform, cheap credit and technical advice were all part of the agrarian reform programme.

3. The sum total was the practice of "capitalism under non-classical conditions", i.e. land reform, a strong co-operative movement, attention to basic needs, with a safety net under the poor or other strategies to prevent polarisation. This is very different from the cruder versions of "open economy" and "structural adjustment" being forced on South Asian Countries today.

4. The East Asian countries had highly authoritarian regimes, effective central planning and control and a population that was culturally conditioned to this kind of authoritarianism.

5. Massive flow of external assistance and capital for countries with a population and with no responsibility for defence also helped.

These conditions taken together permitted these countries to be incorporated into the global system under the most favourable conditions. Now there are internal and external contradictions beginning to emerge. These have to be understood afresh and cannot be explained through simplistic paradigms and single discipline analysis.

South Asian scholars are now trying to understand their reality and the multifaceted crisis that is facing them. The attached paper summarises some of the thinking that has emerged from the efforts of one such group of scholars working under the auspices of the United Nations University and their response to the challenge of development, democracy and regional co-operation in South Asia. This response is directed not only to a new generation of South Asian scholars, but also to those in industrialised countries who wish to be "rational" and are themselves willing to change from outmoded paradigms and action in the light of pressing global problems and the changing world historical framework.

They are also trying to identify some damage limitation strategies and strategic entry points towards an alternative approach to eradication of mass poverty in South Asia.

Genesis of the Intellectual Quest : An Overview

In the late 1940s and 1950s, amidst the process of decolonisation in South Asia, a number of ideas caught the imagination of South Asian scholars and ruling elites. These included the "instant" creation of new nation states (with the illusion of transference of political power), the grand vision of progress through development with modernisation and industrialisation, and the notion of a single interdependent economic system (known as "One World"). Taken together these ideas appeared to provide a coherent paradigm that was to mould the destiny of the South Asian region for the next half century. Few hard critical reviews were made of the processes - economic, social and political - that followed the adoption of this paradigm. This uncritical acceptance was also extended to the more specific economic development intervention that was an integral part of the paradigm.

The partial success of India's early planning and efforts at industrialisation, the Green Revolution in Pakistan and later in India, the aid flows and foreign "expert" advice that accompanied it mesmerised all concerned and reinforced the belief that a rapid social transformation was underway and that the world economy would be managed for the betterment of all people.

Whatever criticism there was of the process as it unfolded, came mainly from a minority of conventional Marxist intellectuals who understood some of the dangers of incorporation of South Asia into the global capitalist framework. However, the limited categories in their early analytical framework did not permit them to either understand the complexity of the reality or to see many of the contradictions that were to emerge subsequently. Mahatma Gandhi with his now famous dictum "*The World has enough for everyone's needs, but not for everyone's greed*", provided an alternative vision for development, but with his death soon after Indian independence, neither the theoretical nor practical implications of his vision for South Asia were fully worked out.

As the warning signals began to emerge in the 1970s, under the auspices of the United Nations Asian Development Institute (UNADI), one of the earliest attempts by South Asian scholars to understand the reality, question the "development" intervention that had taken place and systematically conceptualize a possible alternative on a somewhat broader framework of political economy was reflected in a trilogy of separate studies, recently republished in one book under the title "Towards a Theory of Rural Development"[1].

---

1 De Silva G. V. S., Haque W., Mehta N., Rahman Md A. and Wignaraja P. (1988) Towards a Theory of Rural Development. Progressive Publishers, Lahore, Pakistan.

This alternative approach was based not on a priori theorizing or borrowed thinking from western social sciences. It was based on looking at the South Asian reality and formulating a more rationale intellectual framework for eradication of rural mass poverty, rooted in a "scientific" approach to South Asian history and culture. The material basis for their generalizations on alternatives was provided both by the negative impact of a quarter century of development on large numbers of people in South Asia, as well as by the first generation of positive experiments at the micro grassroots level. This analysis demonstrated the possibilities of incorporating social justice and participations, into a process of accumulation and economic growth which would involve and benefit the poor and the vulnerable in the all round development of their lives. In particular, there was increasing evidence that such processes were sustainable at the micro-level. At that time, the UNADI scholars also had the lessons of China's post-war development experience of "socialism under non-classical conditions" and South Korea's "capitalism under non-classical conditions" to draw from[2].

In the 1980s the countries comprising South Asia began to face an even more critical crisis of development. With the global system itself in disarray and the structures and institutions of the South Asian nation states, unable to cope with the twin crises in development and democracy, another intellectual effort was crystallised. A larger network of South Asian scholars, under the auspices of the United Nations University South Asian Perspectives Project (UNUSAPP), came together to understand the steady slide of these societies into anarchy and destabilisation, despite the rhetoric of development, democracy and regional cooperation. Breaking out of the conventional paradigms and transcending the cruder versions of neo-classical and Marxist thinking,

---

2 Wignaraja P. (1984) Towards a Theory and Practice of Rural Development. Development (Journal of the Society of International Development) 2.

UNUSAPP scholars also took a deeper look at the emerging reality and articulate issues for an alternative, within an interdisciplinary framework. The aim of the exercise was not only to examine the available alternatives, but to focus on those which were sustainable in the present South Asian context. The results of this research and reflection were embodied in a book titled "The Challenge in South Asia: Development, Democracy and Regional Cooperation"[3].

A part of this United Nations University network was also concerned with the Gender and Equity crisis - another facet of South Asia's growing economic, social and political problems. Here again there was an increasing body of positive evidence which indicated that:

a) poor women contributed significantly to development, particularly in the informal sector, and that
b) they could overcome their double burden of being women and poor through better organization and using local resources and knowledge and their own creativity.

Moreover, where they had support from sensitive macro institutions, the small development actions initiated could also go to scale and be sustainable. A study entitled "Women, Poverty and Resources"[4] attempted to draw the lessons from these experiences for poverty alleviation among women and further refine the concepts and methodology of the alternative approach for South Asia.

These three books have now paved the way for a further probing of

---

[3] Wignaraja P. and Hussain A. (eds.) (1989) The Challenge of South Asia: Development, Democracy and Regional Cooperation. Sage Publications, New Delhi, Newbury Park and London.

[4] Wignaraja P. (1989) Women, Poverty and Resources. Sage Publications, New Delhi, Newbury Park and London.

the South Asian reality at both the macro and micro levels. Building on a number of positive fresh development experiments at the micro-level, the new study entitled "Participatory Development: Learning from South Asia"[5] not only highlights the deepening multifaceted crises that are confronting South Asia, but also provides a harder and systematic critique of the dominant development framework which has guided a major intervention into the lives of the people of South Asia. The impact of the dominant development framework for South Asia is examined at a theoretical and empirical level, using some of the most recent literature and quantitative data available. From this analysis, deeper insights into an alternative methodology for reversing these processes have been identified. A number of peoples' movements and experiments in South Asia which have matured in the 1980s have also provided the further basis for the generalisations. These movements and experiments demonstrate both the potential for damage limitation and reversing past processes, as well as possibilities for initiating positive sustainable development actions with the participation of the poor and vulnerable.

The four studies taken together make an important contribution to understanding the larger crises in South Asia, particularly mass poverty and marginalisation of unacceptably large numbers of people. They also provide operationalisable elements for initiating a reversal of these processes.

Participatory Development: Learning from South Asia

The United Nations University network of South Asian scholars has attempted to deepen the critique of the dominant development paradigm, and their understanding of South Asian reality. From

---

5 Wignaraja P., Hussain A., Sethi H. and Wignaraja G. (1990) Participatory Development: Learning from South Asia. Oxford University Press, Karachi and Oxford.

this, they have attempted to refine further the methodology for not only partially reversing past processes, but also to initiating the transition to a new strategy of development. The approach taken builds on the positive lessons of the innovative participatory development experiences on the ground, which have matured and are proving to be sustainable in South Asia.

This book will serve a fourfold purpose. First, it will highlight the multifaceted crisis that is already upon South Asia, albeit in varying degrees of intensity and inter-relatedness in the different countries which makes it imperative for these countries to adopt a different development pathway. Secondly, it will provide a critique of the dominant development paradigm that has been adopted and show that neither in its own narrow ideological and socio-economic terms nor as a response to the wider crisis is it sufficient. Thirdly, it will articulate in an unambiguous manner elements in an alternative strategy based on participatory development at the micro level which can both limit some of the damage of past strategies, as well as go a long way towards alleviating the worst forms of poverty and de-humanisation in South Asia. This process at the same time, once initiated at the micro-level, can provide a transition to sustainable development. Finally, it will help refine some of the methodological and analytical tools which are indispensable for reinforcing these alternative processes already underway.

The crises that South Asian countries face, is no longer merely the poverty crisis, but is now taking the form of the ecological crisis, ethnic violence, gender conflict, militarisation and external destabilisation. These are not isolated phenomena, but are interrelated both to each other and to the fundamental developmental intervention that was initiated after de-colonisation. Taken together they have deep consequences for the fragile democratic processes at work and the task of nation building.

Fundamental to the new methodology is the epistemological proposition that the development of development theory and practice itself occurs in a dialectic relationship with each other and at each stage the lessons of practice will form the basis for further theory, just as a deeper theory will feed back into deeper practice. For this reason the formulation of the alternative theory must be rudimentary. However, specific elements of the process in place can be clearly identified, and inform a variety of micro-level actions. As actions are taken through praxis, more explicit theorising can follow. The nature of the alternative theory is that it develops not through a priori formulation, but through the comprehension of its application to practice at each stage of praxis.

Thus the rudimentary state of the alternative theory should not be taken to be a reflection of the rudimentary state of understanding of either the South Asian reality or the alternative process which is emerging and cannot be stopped.

THAILAND AND THE SO-CALLED "NEWLY INDUSTRIALIZING ECONOMIES (NIEs)"

Suchat Prachimdhit
Counsellor
Department of Economic Affairs
Ministry of Foreign Affairs
Saranrom Palace
Bangkok

1. Overview of the Thai Economy

1.1 Traditionally, Thailand is an agricultural country with over half of the country's population engaged in farming activities and agriculture presently accounting for 20.9 per cent of gross domestic product.

1.2 Today, agricultural trends in Thailand are changing and the country is now moving progressively towards industrialization with an emphasis on agro-based industry and on diversified natural resources and export markets.

1.3 In the process of its economic and social development, Thailand has adopted the Buddhist precept of the middle path policy as the guiding philosophy for economic management. The said policy, which depends on reducing inequality, has indeed helped Thailand to balance its three economic objectives of growth, long-term economic stability and a fair income distribution.

Thailand's Economic Growth

1.4 With regard to Thailand's economic growth, it is to be noted that over the last three decades Thailand has earned a reputation as one of the fastest growing and most successful de-

Europe-Asia-Pacific Studies in Economy and Technology
Kulessa (Ed.)
The Newly Industrializing Economies of Asia

veloping countries in the world. It maintained an average high growth rate of 7 to 8 per cent per year in real terms during the 60s and 70s. In the 80s, facing a declining global economic situation, Thailand still achieved an annual growth rate about 2 per cent higher than the average for the middle-income developing countries.

1.5 Most recently in 1988, Thailand's economic growth recorded one of the highest growth rates in the ESCAP region, with GDP (gross domestic product) growth of 11 per cent. It is also expected that in 1989 Thailand's economic growth will continue to be strong, with the rate of increase estimated at between 7 per cent and 10 per cent. This figure compares favourably with those of other countries in the region as the average GDP growth rate for ASEAN members is estimated at 6.3 per cent. It is therefore expected that, if that pace is sustained for another generation, Thailand will be able to lift itself from being an underdeveloped country to join the middle-echelon countries.

Development Strategy

1.6 Currently, under the Sixth National Economic and Social Development Plan (1987-1991), Thailand is undergoing many structural changes and its economic growth is continuing along with stabilization through monetary and fiscal policies, industrial development, greater diversification in the agricultural sector, decentralisation and closer cooperation between the public and private sectors.

1.7 The Seventh Economic and Social Development Plan (1992-1996), which is now under preparation, will provide more opportunities for Thailand to implement its development strategy towards industrialization and to improve the living conditions of the Thai people. In the light of the Seventh Plan, emphasis will be placed on two important policy objectives:

- Firstly, the Thai Government will continue to maintain the economic growth by internationalising the economy and boosting the country's competitiveness in the industrial market-place.

- Secondly, the Seventh Plan will dictate the Government to further improve the well-being of the Thai people, and to strengthen the income redistribution effort by restructuring mechanisms and regulations currently controlling economic expansion and income distribution.

The Seventh Plan includes four guidelines recently endorsed by the Joint Committee for Industrial Development.

- First, the Government must restructure monetary, fiscal and investment promotion mechanisms to stimulate efficient and fair competition in the economic system. This will enable the internationalization of the Thai economy.

- Second, the private sector will be encouraged to play a greater role in commerce and industry. The Government will improve existing regulations and remove barriers.

- Third, there will be guidelines to further improve infrastructure, human resources and other facilities with emphasis on a greater private sector role.

- Fourth, there will be guidelines to develop industries to suit geographic conditions in the provinces.

2. Thailand and the NIEs Issue

2.1 As a result of its continued high growth, its successful economic performance and its bright prospects for the future, Thailand is now moving towards industrialization and, according to international organizations (including the OECD), it will emerge as a newly industrializing economy (NIE) and join the club of the other four Asian NIEs, namely South Korea, Singapore, Taiwan and Hong Kong.

2.2 This prospect is good enough for Thailand. However, in recognising the role to be played by the NIEs in their cooperation with the developed and the developing countries, Thailand is not, at this stage, in a position to become a NIE and is not yet qualified to assume this status.

2.3 As a matter of fact, there are now encouraging signs that Thailand will become a NIE, providing that, in comparison with other NIEs, its economic growth exceeds a satisfactory level in many key sectors. In this connection, Dr. Kongkiat Opawongkan, Chief Representative of Baring Research Ltd. (a subsidiary of Baring Securities Ltd.) presented the following facts during the Euromoney Conference recently held in Bangkok:

(1) Thai production of industrial goods has already exceeded 20 per cent of GDP to reach 22.6 per cent last year, compared to 27 per cent in Singapore, 29 per cent in South Korea and 40.8 per cent in Taiwan.

(2) Exports of industrial goods have surpassed 50 per cent of total exports. The country's exports of manufactured goods last year represented 66 per cent of total exports while Singapore, South Korea and Taiwan were able to achieve 66 per cent, 93 per cent and 95 per cent respectively.

(3) The proportion of the labour force in the industrial sector has been steadily increasing. In this respect, Thailand has been doing fine, since the employment rate in industry is expected to rise from a current 12 per cent to 19 per cent at the beginning of the next century, while that of the service-related industries will step up from 24 per cent in 1989 to 32 per cent in the year 2001.

2.4 Despite these encouraging trends, Thailand will not in the near future emerge as a NIE. In order to become a NIE, Thailand must at least eradicate poverty and raise its per capita income to the required level.

2.5 Currently, the majority of Thai people still lives in poverty, and Thailand's per capita income remains surprisingly low at US $ 1,022, compared with the well-accepted NIC or NIE per capita income base rate of US $ 2,000. Singapore, in fact, has a per capita income of US $ 9,462 while Taiwan's is US $ 5,864. In this regard, Thailand has to improve the conditions of its poor majority, mostly people living in rural areas, to encourage the equitable distribution of income and to narrow the income gap between the rich and the poor majority.

2.6 Moreover, in order to keep up the pace of its economic and social development and its rapid industrialization, Thailand has to create a better economic environment and a favourable investment climate by:

- Improving infrastructure and overcoming shortage of qualified manpower (noting that rapid economic growth has caused structural change in the economy and has a few bottlenecks in infrastructure and manpower).

- Appropriately modifying the education system (in order to

cater for the changing demands of industry).

3. The NIEs Viewed by the Thai Leaders

3.1 In his statement before the World Economic Forum's First Annual National Meeting on Thailand, held in Bangkok in May 1989, the Thai Prime Minister, General Chatichai Choonhavan, made the following remarks on Thailand's becoming a NIC (or NIE):

- It is no longer a question of whether Thailand is economically backward or not. The very fact that many people from abroad are talking about Thailand as the next NIC (or NIE) is sufficient proof that the Kingdom has made great strides in economic and technological development. Rather, the problem is how to manage the direction of Thailand's economic development, not only to ensure continued growth, but also to bring benefits to all, to create social justice for all, and to allow for a life of quality to be led by all.

- For these reasons, since August last year (1988), the Thai Government has endeavoured to initiate and to accelerate many projects, particularly those connected with infrastructure and technology which form the basis of Thailand's future economic performance.

3.2 On the question of the dialogue between the OECD and the NIEs, Deputy Prime Minister Pong Sarasin, during the same session of the World Economic Forum, stated that:

- Thailand also welcomes a dialogue between the OECD and the so-called "NIEs". Thailand is, however, neither a NIE, nor in a position to assume responsibilities on the same scale as the NIEs as called for by certain developed countries.

- Thailand has responsibilities. However, as a member of the developing world, sharing much of its common problems and interests, Thailand's potential for shouldering responsibilities remains somewhat limited.

- Thailand needs the support (even if only in moral, political and/or diplomatic terms) and solidarity of this majority group of members of the United Nations, or the so-called "Group of 77", to promote self-reliance, and mutual benefit, and a bargaining leverage with the economically much more powerful industrialized countries in various international fora.

- South-South cooperation forms a very important part of Thailand's foreign policy. And, in implementing this policy, Thailand has offered innumerable economic and technical assistance programmes to the less developed members of the Group of 77. However, because of resource constraints and political, geographical, cultural and other considerations, Thailand has given more assistance to its Asian-Pacific neighbours, including the Indo-Chinese countries. Nevertheless, cooperation with Thailand's closest non-socialist neighbours (ASEAN), which share similar views on democracy and the free-market economy, remains the central core of Thailand's foreign policy. ASEAN has continued and must continue to be a moderating influence in North-South and South-South relations.

STATE INTERVENTION, STATE INVOLVEMENT AND MARKET FORCES - SINGAPORE AND SOUTH KOREA

Hans Christoph Rieger and Wolfgang Veit
Südasien Institut der
Universität Heidelberg
Im Neuenheimer Feld 330
D-6900 Heidelberg

1. Introduction

Singapore and South Korea have been frequently cited as examples of how developing nations can emerge as newly industrializing economies by placing emphasis on market forces and the private sector as a major motor for economic growth. Addressing an international conference on aid to the Philippines recently, US Secretary of State James Baker advised President Corazon Aquino to draw on the experience of Singapore and South Korea, two Asian nations which have joined the industrial democracies as donors for the first time (20).

While there can be no doubt regarding the economic success of the two NIEs cited, it would be incorrect to attribute it entirely to the emphasis given to the private sector and to ignore the important role that government has played in both countries in bringing about and stimulating economic development. The examples of Singapore and South Korea suggest that the textbook dichotomy of planning versus the market is too simplistic and that economic planning by government and the use of market forces to determine the allocation of resources are not necessarily mutually exclusive.

The present paper focuses on the way in which the governments in Singapore and South Korea have intervened in their respective economies by setting the market conditions and have become involved by taking up economic activities beside (and sometimes in

Europe-Asia-Pacific Studies in Economy and Technology
Kulessa (Ed.)
The Newly Industrializing Economies of Asia

lieu of) the private sector.

Table 1 presents a number of measures of the role of government in the economies of Singapore and South Korea in 1984. Taiwan has been added by way of comparison. It is clear that in all three cases government plays an important and in some respects overwhelming role in the economy. The perception that a free market economy based on private sector initiative is the prime reason for the phenomenal economic success of these NIEs is obviously a myth.

In fact, the impact of government actions on the economies of Singapore and South Korea respectively is both complex and pervasive. In this paper we can only deal with selected examples out of the complex system of interrelated government policies. An important conclusion emerges: it is not the fact of government activity per se which is crucial, but the way in which it is geared to the operation of the domestic and international market.

In the following sections we intend to briefly present the development of government economic policies in Singapore and South Korea. In spite of the undoubted successes achieved in the economic field we will also indicate a number of problems that have become apparent. Finally, we will try to draw a number of conclusions from the analysis.

2. Economic Policies in Singapore

2.1 Historical background

Singapore achieved full independence from Great Britain as part of Malaysia in 1963, and separated from Malaysia in 1965. In 1971 the British gave up their naval base under the British Far East Command in Singapore. Singapore's government was confronted with the question of survival. It no longer had a hinterland, yet the basic needs of its population of about two million had to be met. Food and other consumption items had to be imported, so the foreign exchange to pay for them had to be earned. There was an acute housing problem. The level of education of the population was low, and health services were inadequate. In the absence of family planning the population was growing at an alarming 3.2 per cent per annum. The unemployment rate of 13.5 per cent required the immediate creation of additional jobs.

The gravity of the situation was compounded by the fight against communism, both at the political level domestically and with regard to guerilla activity in the jungles of Malaysia.

The architects of Singapore's economic system after independence and separation from Malaysia were pragmatic in their approach, and their initially socialist ideology quickly changed to a more market-oriented approach in recognition of the fact that Singapore could not achieve economic viability outside the international trading system and that the solution of the pressing social problems required fast economic growth.

Four basic questions regarding the economic system had to be addressed: first, what role should be given to direct government control of the economy on the one hand and to market forces on the other? Second, how should industrial relations between employers and employees be regulated? Third, how should foreign economic relations be arranged? And fourth, should the government operate economic enterprises or leave such direct economic activities to the private sector? The answers to these questions were provided by the prime minister, Lee Kuan Yew, a lawyer by training, and by Goh Keng Swee, an economist, who became the main architect of Singapore's economic development.

2.2 Government control versus market forces

In the light of the experience of other developing countries with attempts at complete control of the economy through central planning, the first question was decided in favour of a market-oriented approach. In a special lecture before the 26th World Congress of the International Chamber of Commerce in 1978, Lee Kuan Yew put the rhetorical question: "Did I ever contemplate nationalization, socialist planning for industrialization and economic transformation?" and answered: "Frankly, no. ... I had before me, by 1965, the salutary lessons of U Nu's Burma, Bandaranaike's Ceylon and Sukarno's Indonesia" (12).

Nevertheless, market forces were not accepted unconditionally as a matter of dogma. They were regarded as a means to achieve economic development, and not an end in themselves. For this reason, there has never been any hesitation on the part of the Singapore government to intervene in the market place whenever this appeared necessary for pragmatic reasons. However, the form of intervention has generally been of a "market compatible" type, influencing decisions via the price mechanism rather than using outright restrictions or licensing systems.

In particular, Singapore has not made use of market-distorting subsidies to reallocate resources, with the exception of three strategic areas: housing, health and education, all areas in which the productivity of the labour force could not otherwise be effectively raised.

2.3 Industrial relations

With regard to the relations between workers and employers, the architects of Singapore's economic system regarded strikes and other confrontational means of wage bargaining, as witnessed in the industrialized countries, as a waste of resources that the small island economy could not afford. Although trade unions already existed at independence, they were primarily organizations to achieve political aims. The Singapore government, by a combination of threats and promises and by infiltrating them with its own officials, systematically turned the unions into instruments for furthering its own objectives. The present trend favours the establishment of firm or house unions that are more easily kept under control. Although the strategy used by the government was not accorded wholehearted approval by those concerned, the undoubted international success of the Singapore economy has led to a widespread feeling of solidarity and loyalty and has led to the recognition among workers that industrial confrontation over distribution issues merely serves to reduce the pie to be distributed.

Each year, the National Wages Council (NWC), comprising representatives of management, employees and the government and presided over by an economist from Singapore's university, makes recommendations regarding pay increases. These recommendations have come to be widely accepted in all spheres of the economy. The instrument of the NWC has not only been used with micro-economic goals of viability and distribution of individual firms in view, but has also been employed to achieve macro-economic objectives such as stabilization during business cycles and the maintenance of Singapore's competitiveness in the international market.

At the end of the 70s and the beginning of the 80s the government used the instrument of the NWC to restructure the economy in favour of more capital-intensive industrial production. After successfully conquering unemployment, further increases in per capita income were only possible through greater productivity, and this required more capital input per worker employed. By deliberately increasing wages through NWC recommendations, the Singapore government forced numerous firms either to modernize and to automate or to shift their production out of Singapore to Malaysia or elsewhere or to close down. Concurrent efforts to increase the skills of workers ensured that the scheme was largely successful.

2.4 Foreign economic relations

The third basic economic question concerned the economic relations with the outside world. Given the constraints of the city state, it permitted only one answer. Self-reliance in a closed system was unthinkable. There was practically no alternative to opening the economy to foreign competition and to integrating it with the international market. Nevertheless, the consistency and hard-headedness with which the earlier strategy of import substitution was replaced by export diversification was remarkable. The Singapore government was strong and purposeful enough to resist the pressures of individual and group interests that called for "special treatment" and "exceptions" from economic policy decisions. Practically all tariffs and import restrictions were removed. The result was a reduction of consumer goods prices as well as a reduction of input costs for the export industries. At the same time the removal of customs formalities made Singapore an attractive location for foreign businesses serving the region.

In addition to the opening of the Singapore economy to foreign trade, foreign direct investment was welcomed in Singapore. While recognizing the truism that investors seek to make profits rather than to further the development objectives of the host country, the kind of restrictions on foreign investment common in many other developing countries were removed in Singapore. Control over foreign investments is not obtained by such restrictions, but rather by the competition between foreign investors and potential investors in a relatively unrestricted market place.

Finally, the Singapore government had no inhibitions about bringing in qualified personnel from abroad. About 20 per cent of the work force in the categories of managers, engineers and technicians in 1978 were foreigners. They and their enterprises in manufacturing, services and commerce helped to employ 30 per cent of the total work force. At the same time, Singapore remains restrictive regarding the immigration of unskilled workers from neighbouring countries.

2.5 Government enterprises

The fourth basic economic question concerns the involvement of the government in direct economic activities. To be sure, there are areas in all economies that cannot be left to the private sector: public utilities, and the provision of infrastructure, and so on. The Singapore government provides these essential public (and even private) goods and services through numerous statutory boards operating as natural monopolies.

However, over and above this function, the Singapore government has had no compunction to get involved in the economy by establishing government enterprises in many areas which compete with the private sector - domestically or abroad. The Singapore government has, either on its own or jointly with local or foreign private entrepreneurs, amassed some 490 government-owned companies in many sectors: manufacturing, petrochemicals, shipbuilding and ship repairing, transportation, construction, banking and finance, trading and other services sectors (13).

Official releases and information on the extent and magnitude of government involvement in public enterprises in Singapore are scarce. According to one source, "the Singapore public enterprise system appears to be the largest compared to those in other Asian countries" (13). The latest official disclosure in 1985 gives 70 first-level companies comprising three holding companies and their main subsidiaries in 1983. But if all companies in which the government has either a direct or indirect share are included, such as subsidiaries of subsidiaries, the number jumps to 450 companies involving $ 2.4 billion in paid-up capital and $ 18.2 billion in fixed assets. To these 450 companies can be added another 40 subsidiaries of statutory boards (13). According to 1983 statistics (Straits Times, 6 April 1985, quoted by Linda Low) the 450 companies employed 58,000 workers or 5 per cent of the total labour force. Their total (cumulative) fixed assets at $ 18.2 billion was 16.5 per cent of cumulative gross domestic capital formation (1961-1983). Total sales of these companies at $ 8 billion in 1983 made up 21.4 per cent of sales in the manufacturing sector.

Pervasive government influence in the economy is often the main reason for mal-allocations of resources and inefficiencies that prevent developing countries from achieving faster economic growth. However, despite the strong involvement of government enterprises in the Singapore economy, they do not manifest the symptoms of overbureaucratization and inefficiency so prevalent in many other developing countries of the region. This is because they are run with the express intention of generating profits, and not as social institutions for employing the otherwise unemployed (or unemployable). The majority of them have to compete in the international market and cannot afford inefficient practices. Unprofitable companies are wound up, inefficient managers fired.

In recent years, especially after the recession of 1985, the Singapore government has followed a policy of gradual privatization of government enterprises.

2.6 Problem of the mid-80s

The picture of economic policy in Singapore that emerges from this description would be incomplete without reference to some of the shortcomings that became evident during the recession of the mid-80s. The wage increases generated by the NWC over the years, the high levels of forced savings through a fully paid-up pension system along with the generally high rates of corporate taxation had reduced the international competitiveness of the Singapore economy to such an extent, that it took a severe beating in 1985. The Singapore economy contracted for the first time in two decades.

However, once again the Singapore government showed its pragmatism and flexibility in dealing with crisis situations. The Economic Committee set up under the chairmanship of the prime minister's son and minister of trade and industry, Lee Hsien Loong, undertook a searching analysis of the plight of the economy and within a very short time the necessary action was taken: reduction of central provident fund rates, lower corporate taxes, temporary wage freeze. Because of its successes in the past and because of its efficiency in decision-making and in communicating with its people, the government was able to convince all sections of the population of the need for common action and austerity measures. The recession was overcome in a surprisingly short time span, and double-digit growth rates have once more been achieved.

2.7 Summary

Perhaps nothing sums up better the economic success of the judicious mix of government intervention and involvement on the one hand and market forces and free enterprise on the other as practiced in Singapore, than the evaluation by two Swiss groups of the competitiveness of ten NIEs and potential NIEs in their

"World Competitiveness Report 1989". The rankings are presented in Table 2 (21). They show that, while Singapore is ranked last in terms of natural endowments, it is first with regard to dynamism of the economy, industrial efficiency, financial dynamism, human resources, outward orientation and socio-political stability. In spite of the massive involvement of the Singapore government in the economy as described earlier, "state interference" actually perceived by businessmen is in fact low, as indicated by the second ranking on this dimension in the table - second only to Hong Kong.

3. Economic Policies in South Korea

3.1 Historical background

For more than 500 years, i.e. from 1392 until 1910, Korea was ruled by the YI-dynasty. Isolated from its ambitious and rivaling neighbours, this resulted in a homogeneous, but static social structure which, due to Confucian tradition, restricted economic and technological progress (19). This situation of a "recluse-kingdom" was changed radically in 1910 when Japanese colonial rule led to increased investment in infrastructure, agriculture, and mining.

Korean rule of the country in a true sense and a Korean political system were established only after the economic and political shocks of the war had been overcome. The internal structure of military dictatorship, installed by Park Chung Hee in 1961, was of a Confucian type: power was transferred to the one person at the centre, who was supported by a bureaucracy consisting of the social elite. While the century-old structures were restored with relatively few changes, the military now filled the posts that had been occupied by civilians before 1910. "Militarization of the Confucian system" (19) had a considerable impact on both political stability and economic progress. For example, in 1982 about one third of the population of working age and probably two thirds of those employed in industry had passed through military service (19). Not only did this contribute to sound technical training (4) but also to the spreading of virtues and values such as discipline, responsibility for the social collective, and abstention from consumption.[1] Thus, Confucian tradition was combined with the requirements of industrialization and integration into world markets: political stability and low wages contributed to international competitiveness.

The government's raison d'être resulted from both a traditional system of power and the accomplishment of economic goals; it was independent of democratic procedures.

Changes of economic strategy were initiated by the government. Two eras of economic reform can be identified: during the 60s tariffs, non-tariff barriers, exchange rates, interest rates, capital imports and prices were liberalized to some extent. In the late 70s and early 80s, further liberalization took place in the fields of foreign trade, financial markets, and prices (24).

Amongst others, the set of major instruments for export-promotion contained selectively liberalized capital imports, including foreign direct investment[2], selective tax- and tariff-exemptions, support for joint ventures, and subsidized loans for exporters.

---

[1] Dee (4) mentions six categories of Korean values: "fatalism (including the desire to avoid risk), familism, authoritarianism, emotional humanism (where maintaining continuous active relations with others becomes an end in itself, not a means to achieve cooperative goals), ritualism and anti-materialism (placing more emphasis on honour, prestige, integrity and virtue than on material reward)".

[2] Foreign investors were offered the opportunity of repatriation of the original dollar investment, i.e. without exchange-rate risk (2). This policy led to the development of a capital market denominated in a parallel currency. All negative aspects of the dollar debt were left with domestic borrowers, because repatriation ought to be legally guaranteed. Chelminsky, however, does not give detailed information here. See also (6).

The economic structure as well as export performance were mainly affected by government intervention in factor markets rather than product markets (e.g. tariff and price control). Within factor markets, financial markets were a major target (11;24;9). It is for this reason that we will concentrate on the pervasive effect that government intervention in the financial markets had on South Korea's economic development.

In particular it was credit policy and the resulting regulation of interest rates which contributed to close ties between export-oriented industry and government. In addition to rather informal personal relationships, influence via general economic planning, and specific instructions for investment in state-owned enterprises (2), substantial relationships of economic dependence also appeared. Typically, the South Korean export-industry was under-capitalized. Low-interest loans led to the sector's heavy indebtedness with the government-controlled banking system. In the end, cheap finance resulted in increased government influence in private industry.

3.2 Economic planning, and the role of the public enterprises

First steps toward formalized economic planning were taken in the late forties. However, it was Park Chung Hee who strengthened the influence of the institutions responsible for designing economic strategies. He incorporated the tasks of the Bureau of Statistics and the Bureau of the Budget in the Economic Planning Board, thus concentrating control and decision-making in the same institution. Equally important was the upgrading of the head of the EPB: he was given the rank of deputy prime minister. So one important condition for successful planning, i.e. persons and functions of economic planning being anchored firmly within the top political sphere, was fulfilled.

Participation of people concerned is another important prerequisite to successful planning. This was achieved by periodically holding meetings (18), sometimes on an informal basis, of politicians, administration staff, and representatives of industry and economics. These meetings constituted a kind of privatization of plan implementation in that they linked private industry to political decision-making. In the first Five Year Plan this type of economic policy was called "guided capitalism".

Economic growth via the promotion of exports rather than employment or social equality was the one outstanding target of economic planning (1), and it was pursued in a very pragmatic way. The importance of macro-economic modelling seems to have declined over time in favour of a "particularistic" approach, involving discretionary intervention by government in specific industries or companies, whenever market forces failed to comply with planning targets.

The number of public enterprises rose from 52 in 1963 to 108 in 1972, then, as a result of privatization, falling again to 90 in 1984 (23). The IMF listed 37 public enterprises plus 117 local government enterprises in 1987 (7). Between 1963 and 1981 the share of public enterprises in gross domestic capital formation (GDCF) was at 30 %, compared with the private sector's share fluctuating between 31 % and 42 % (7).

3.3 A supply-side view of export performance

Cost efficiency seems to have been the major intermediate target on the way to export-led growth. It was achieved by deliberately manipulating the markets for production factors, i.e. labour, capital, and technical progress.

Labour: Wages were kept relatively low by both natural factors and government policies. From 1955 to 1987 the population of South Korea doubled from 21 million to 42 million (8). From 1971 to 1981 the number of low paid female employees increased by 47 %, while the number of higher paid male employees increased by 37 % (1). The substitution of well trained male workers by untrained females enhanced the cheap supply of qualified personnel to the technically more advanced sectors of the economy. This was supported by the government in two ways: first by the restriction of free trade unions and the introduction of a social security system reducing the bargaining power of workers. Second, by a kind of "wage repression" which prevented companies from raising prices to meet costs caused by higher wages. Here, again, the particularistic type of intervention becomes apparent.

The restrictive labour policies allowed market forces to work in the product markets. But given the high degree of corporate concentration, market structures increasingly favoured capital owners. This has to be borne in mind when labelling the South Korean economy as a "free market" economy.

Capital: Both mobilization and allocation of capital via domestic financial markets was at the centre of South Korean economic policy. Therefore it will be discussed in a separate section.

With regard to foreign direct investment, there was no legislation (FDI) until 1960. Since then, the inflow of capital has been under tight control. FDI during the period 1973-1980 had to meet rather restrictive conditions which were designed to protect domestic industry from competing foreign investments, while at the same time attracting capital-intensive and high-tech investment. Before 1973 and after 1980 FDI was handled more liberally. This is reflected in the volume of FDI during the respective periods (in million US $: 1966:13, 1974:105, 1980:-7, 1985:200,

1987:418).[3]

Technical progress: The introduction of technical progress was promoted by several means. First, besides the regulations covering FDI, high-tech imports were attracted by the Foreign Capital Inducement Law and the Engineering Export Promotion Service Law. Second, domestic development of technologies was supported by setting up specific institutes which merged into the Korea Advanced Institute of Science and Technology (KAIST) in 1980. R & D is granted subsidized finance, a typical instrument of economic policy in South Korea. However, the government did not manage to link public research institutes and private industry effectively. Since 1981 private R & D expenditure has exceeded public R & D expenditure (1).

3.4 South Korea's financial markets since the mid-60s

Until 1965, only a rudimentary and heavily regulated financial market existed. In 1973 McKinnon, calling the South Korean financial markets "financially repressed" (14) showed that real return on time deposits was mostly negative and heavily fluctuating, from +5.3 % to -14.6 %. However, the period of 1977-1986 showed even stronger fluctuations (-24.1 % in 1980, +8.2 % in 1986), without being given the same attribute of financial repression. As a matter of fact, in the mid-seventies the South Korean government permitted a certain orientation of formal, regulated markets towards the informal and unregulated markets. At the same time new unregulated operations were allowed or at least tolerated. Thus, erratic movements of the real interest rate were accompanied by institutional liberalization. However, the informal rate was about twice the official rate.

----

[3] (8) The economic crisis of the early 80s has certainly been responsible for part of the negative FDI in 1980.

The 1965 change in monetary policy was a decisive moment in the history of the South Korean financial markets. It brought about a substantial increase in deposit rates and temporary abolition of ceilings on loan rates. Activity of banks grew depending on the difference between their capital cost and their return on lending business.

Increasing promotion of export industries meant a return of interest ceilings in the 70s. According to Virmani, 80 % of total lending was "forced lending". The results of this policy were typical for regulated credit markets: at the micro-level the bank's evaluation of borrowers concentrated on the amount of real security pledged, at the macro-level there occurred a considerable expansion of the monetary base (15), which accelerated inflation. Five years after the reform, the following was typical of the financial markets:

- all major financial enterprises were publicly owned;
- slightly less direct control of credit compared with that of the time before the reform, but still widespread regulation of interest rates which, together with inflation, punished savers;
- banks suffering from low margins and returns;
- preferential treatment of exporters who showed a high present value of real security, whereas the innovative potential of those producers that might show a high future value of securities or high returns on investment was ignored.

As regulation was confined to the official financial markets, the importance of informal ways of finance increased. Large industries took advantage of this and created segmented markets for the financing of their (medium-scale) suppliers, who therefore became even more dependent. This is another example of how the government created market imbalances in order to support final exporters.

Until the mid-eighties the government's attitude towards financial market policy shifted several times, one reason, amongst others, certainly being the oil-price shocks. However, a coherent concept for financial market policy like that in 1965 was not discernible.

Concurrence of government intervention, external shocks, and underdeveloped financial markets contributed to the economic crisis of the early eighties. Switching several times from monetary expansion to contraction and back again, the government at the same time made more use of forced lending to priority sectors like heavy and chemical industry.

In addition to this, worldwide recession was detrimental to exporting companies, some of which faced bankruptcy and resorted to extremely risky operations: the problem of Moral Hazard on the part of the borrowers worsened the banks' situation, driving some of them close to illiquidity. In the end the government had to come to the rescue by channeling money into the economy via the banking system.

The Effects of Financial Market Policy on Economic Structure

First success of the South Korean export-oriented development strategy coincided with stringent measures for a reform of the financial sector in the mid-60s. As a matter of fact the government made extensive use of financial institutions in order to promote exporting industries, in particular improving general conditions for large, export-oriented industrial groups. The burden of this strategy was carried mainly by middle-scale industries and banks with the following results:

- middle-scale industries saw their independence reduced;
- disincentives to innovative sectors, again especially middle-

scale industries, were created;

- banks were not allowed to engage in business activities that would have led them to develop efficient methods of intermediation.

Altogether, the South Korean government has handled incentives and direct interventions in a way that was in line with the goal of export promotion. At the same time considerable costs in terms of domestic economic imbalances were incurred. Market power was deliberately distributed in an uneven manner, freeing exporters in particular from burdens as far as possible (22).

3.5 Outlook

South Korea is discussing to become a member of the OECD within the next decade. This requires a considerable change in domestic financial markets towards a higher degree of liberalization and technical skills. First steps seem to have been taken by allowing foreign banks to operate within certain limits in South Korea. However, "administrative guidance" (reflected in the tug-of-war between the central bank and the finance ministry) seems to be a continuing feature of South Korea's financial markets (17).

Similar problems are found by the government in the restructuring of ailing industries. Here the political changes seem to have ended the period of relatively undisputed decision-making by the government. As an illustration, one may compare the way in which the government successfully restructured shipping lines in 1984 (by a kind of economic blackmail) with its attempts to restructure dockyards in 1989, as yet without success because of considerable resistance by workers and owners (1;3).

With the 30-year old social and political basis gradually sliding away, political decision-making and implementation may have to look for a new approach.

4. Conclusion

It seems that our overly simplistic classification of market economies, planned economies and "mixed" economies along a market-planning continuum as depicted in Figure 1 needs refinement in order to take account of the more subtle differences encountered in reality. After all, if all economies of the real world turn out to be "mixed" to some degree or other, the traditional classification is not of much help.

The textbook dichotomy of "market" on the one hand and "planning" on the other turns out to be false in that planned economies are increasingly making use of market mechanisms to bring about the allocation of resources while many economies that at first sight appear to warrant the classification as market economies (such as Singapore and South Korea) turn out to be objects of quite tight government control. Furthermore, the dichotomy implies that a reduction of planning automatically entails an expansion in the operation of market forces, and vice versa. This is clearly wrong. Experience shows that market restrictions are frequently introduced without additional planning in the sense of looking ahead and coordinating in a rational manner, or that planning endeavours are reduced without a concomitant liberalization of the market.

We therefore suggest that it would be better to replace the fallacious market planning dichotomy with a three-dimensional system as in Figure 2, within which reality can be more usefully encompassed.[4] The dimensions are characterized as follows:

---

[4] We are grateful for fruitful discussions with Achim Piechottka regarding the following distinctions.

Figure 1

Traditional Classification of economies

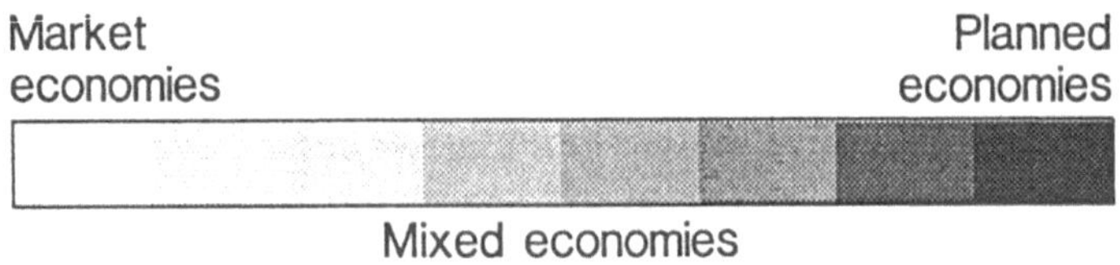

Figure 2

Suggested Classification of economies

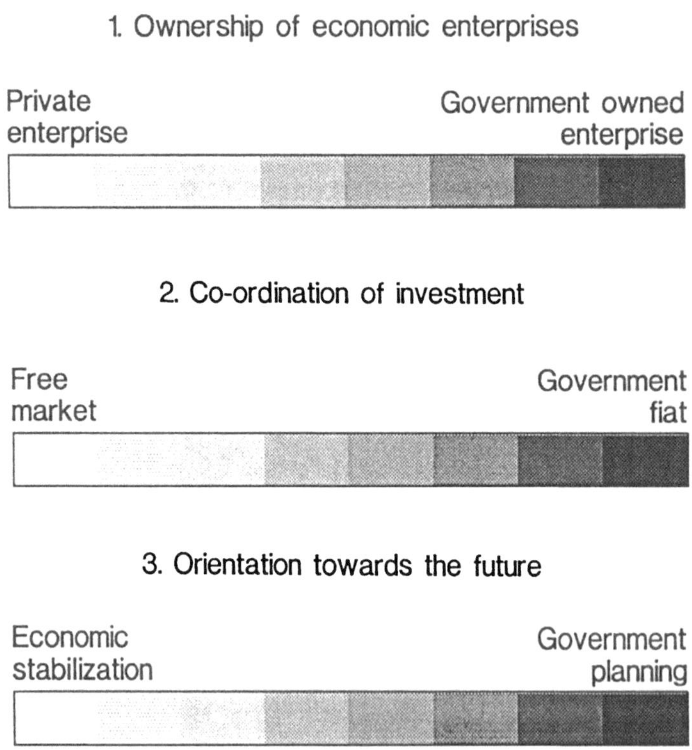

1. Ownership of economic enterprise. The continuum along this dimension runs from complete state ownership through a mix of government enterprises and private enterprises to complete private ownership of enterprises. It could be measured in terms of contribution to GDP.

2. Coordination of investment. Investment decisions and the allocation of investable resources can be controlled by government in many ways, for example by mopping up private and corporate savings, by extending credit for particular purposes or, in the extreme, by fiat. At one end of the continuum is complete government control and at the other the pure operation of market forces in the allocation of investment. It should be noted that this dimension is largely independent of the ownership dimension: Private firms can be strongly influenced by government measures (for example in South Korea) while conversely, government enterprises can operate according to market principles (as, for example, in Singapore).

3. Future orientation. Planning is surely more than the control by government of allocation decisions in an economy. Many governments in developing countries have been encouraged to set up long- and medium-term plans to coordinate investment decisions and to steer them towards the attainment of specific growth targets in given time frames. Others, and among them are the more successful ones, have found it sufficient to stabilize the economy in the face of external shocks and to let the path of growth find its own course. This does not mean that planning in a narrow sense is absent in the latter economies, since government actions to stabilize or influence the economy need to be "planned" or rationalized in one way or the other, but it does mean that planning in the sense of elaborating multi-year plans is. The continuum encompasses complete planning of all economic activities in a medium- or long-term time frame at the one end, and reliance on stabi-

lization decisions to keep the economy on an even keel on the other.

It is clear that the three dimensions suggested above are not entirely independent of each other. Thus long-term planning is obviously not very meaningful in a system characterized by private ownership of enterprises and reliance on the market mechanism for investment allocations. Nevertheless, the unraveling of the traditional market-planning dichotomy appears to be useful in analyzing the relative success and failure of various real life economies and thus for drawing conclusions for future strategy.

Singapore and South Korea thus exhibit interesting similarities and differences. Singapore has a large government enterprise sector, whereas this is smaller in South Korea. But in both countries the government makes use of market mechanisms to stabilize the economy, rather than to rely on direct fiat. Where government has tried to influence investment decisions more strongly, as in South Korea, stresses and strains within the economy have tended to develop suggesting that government is not always the best judge of the direction industrialization should take. Economic planning with medium or long-term planning horizons was given up early on in both countries in favour of short term stabilization type control of economic development. On this dimension both countries are nearer to the system prevalent in western industrial economies than to that of most developing countries.

Table 1
Measurements of the Role of Government in the Economy of Singapore, South Korea and Taiwan in 1984
(Current prices, in per cent)

Classification	Singapore	South Korea	Taiwan
1. Government revenue plus current surpluses of government enterprises/GNP	43.5[a]	18.4	22.9
2. Government revenue/GNP	29.4	17.1	18.0
3. Government expenditure/GNP	20.8	17.3[b]	22.7
4. Current government expenditures/GNP	15.2	10.0	16.6
5. Government development expenditures/GNP	5.6	7.3	6.1
6. Public sector gross saving/ gross national saving	64.0[c]	28.8	12.7
7. Public gross domestic fixed capital formation/total gross domestic fixed capital formation	33.4[d]	17.6	42.7
8. Government consumption/total consumption	19.9	14.8	24.4

[a] Government revenues plus current surpluses of seven major statutory boards, but excludes undistributed profits of public enterprises.
[b] Excludes other special accounts separately funded, which amounted to 3.7 % of GNP in 1984.
[c] Current surplus of government plus current surpluses of seven major statutory boards, but excludes undistributed profits of public enterprises.
[d] If measured in 1968 prices it would be 22.6 %.

Sources: (10) drawn from Ministry of Trade and Industry, Economic Survey of Singapore 1985, Major Statistics of Korean Economy 1985, and Taiwan Statistical Data Book 1985.

References

1. Bagchi A. K. (1987) Public Intervention and Industrial Restructuring in China, India and Republic of Korea. ILO, New Delhi.

2. Chelminsky V. (1986) Economic Failure in Latin America and Prosperity in Asia. Journal of Economic Growth, Vol. 1, No.2.

3. Clifford M. (1989) Breaking Up Is Hard to Do. Far Eastern Economic Review, 11 May, 1989.

4. Dee P. S. (1986) Financial Markets and Economic Reform. The Economics and Politics of Korean Financial Reform. Tübingen.

5. Gesellschaft für Umweltforschung und Entwicklungsplanung, ed. (1989) Planung und Entwicklung. Saarbrücken/Fort Lauderdale.

6. IMF (1986) Foreign Direct Investment in Developing Countries. Washington.

7. IMF (1988a) Government Finance Statistics Yearbook.

8. IMF (1988b) International Financial Statistics Yearbook.

9. Jung W. S., Gyu Lee. The Effectiveness of Export Promotion Policies: The Case of Korea. Weltwirtschaftliches Archiv, Vol. 72.

10. Krause L. B., Koh Ai Tee, Lee (Tsao) Yuan (1987) The Singapore Economy Reconsidered. Institute of Southeast Asian Studies, Singapore.

11. Krueger A. O. (1983) Trade and Employment in Developing Countries. Vol. 3, Chicago.

12. Lee Kuan Yew (1978) Extrapolating from the Singapore Experience. Special Lecture at the 26th World Congress of the International Chamber of Commerce, Orlando, Florida, USA, 5 October, 1978.

13. Low L.(1985) Privatisation Policies and Issues in Singapore. National University of Singapore, Department of Economics and Statistics, Staff Seminar Paper No. 7.

14. McKinnon R. I. (1973) Money and Capital in Economic Development. Brookings Institution, Washington.

15. McKinnon R. I. (1976) Saving Propensities and the Korean Monetary Reform in Retrospect. In: McKinnon R. I., ed. (1976)

16. McKinnon R. I., ed. (1976) Money and Finance in Economic Growth and Development. Marcel Dekker, Basel.

17. Neue Zürcher Zeitung (1988) Südkoreas Finanzmärkte vor der Liberalisierung. 17 November, 1988.

18. Piechottka A. (1989) Einige Gründe des koreanischen Planungserfolges. Gesellschaft für Umweltforschung und Entwicklungsplanung, ed., 1989.

19. Schulz P. W. (1981) Südkorea. Bonn.

20. Singapore and Seoul Held up as Models for Developing Nations. The Straits Times Weekly Overseas Edition, 8 July, 1989.

21. S'pore Topples HK as Most Competitive NIE. The Straits Times Weekly Overseas Edition, 15 July, 1989.

22. Veit W. (1989) Entwicklungspolitik im Lichte des Property-Rights Ansatzes: Die Finanzmärkte in Südkorea und Nepal. Gesellschaft für Umweltforschung und Entwicklungsplanung.

23. Whan In-Joung (1987). The Role of Government in Economic Development: The Korean Experience. Asian Development Review, Vol. 5, No. 2.

24. World Bank (1987) World Development Report.

THE DEVELOPMENT OF SMALL AND MEDIUM-SIZED ENTERPRISES IN THE ASIAN NIEs
Business opportunities for Western Europe?

Philippe Régnier
Research Coordinator
Modern Asia Research Centre
63, rue de Lausanne
CH-1202 Genève

1. Small versus Big Scale Business Activity: a World Outlook

For a long time and especially since World War II, most economists have strongly argued that world production and employment were just condemned to go big scale and that small and medium-sized business was just a kind of necessary but transitory stage in industrial development. Large companies have attracted most attention from social scientists and policy decision-makers till recent years, with a widely and often unquestioned belief that business concentration and integration would be the long-term natural outcome of universal economic development: in this perspective small and even medium-sized business would gradually stagnate, decline or disappear because of poor efficiency and management, backward technologies, lack of capital and marketing ability. Looking back at the golden years of rapid economic growth in the OECD countries (at least up to the mid-70s) or reading today's newspaper headlines dealing with daily mergers of big companies throughout the world may lead to similar conclusions, especially among those who might advocate or fear the emergence of major "fortress" economic zones under American, Japanese or EEC leadership.

However, since the early 80s, there have been mounting voices and increasing scientific evidence which underline or rediscover the important role played by SMEs[1] in industrialization as in post-

---

[1] SMEs in the text (Small and Medium-sized Enterprises)

Europe-Asia-Pacific Studies in Economy and Technology
Kulessa (Ed.)
The Newly Industrializing Economies of Asia

industrialization development processes. Small business has actually retained statistical importance in most industrialized economies, with an even obvious revival since the late 70s, and it has also drawn some growing attention in most newly industrialized economies and less developed countries. During the last 15 years marked by slower economic growth, recession and/or restructuring in most OECD countries, and by enormous difficulties in planned economies and less developed countries, it may be said in very general terms that small business has been increasingly associated with the concept of better production adaptability and flexible specialization.

2. Development and Internationalization Process of SMEs in the Far East: Japan and the Asian NIEs

Big business accounts for only a small part of all companies in Japan: SMEs have been a decisive contributing factor in the overall Japanese economic growth, consistently accounting for over 80 % of all secondary and tertiary sector businesses. As reported again by JETRO in 1987-88, the Japanese business structure is made of a small club of conglomerates at the top and of a large number of SMEs at the bottom, acting very often as subcontractors and suppliers. This economic integration and the vitality of local SMEs are certainly an essential explanation of Japanese rapid postwar expansion. The Japanese economy can be compared to one single factory with all kinds of specialists in manufacturing and services: these specialists are SMEs having the operational scale and technical expertise needed to contribute to the total activity of the "national" factory. Taking full advantage of their small size and flexibility, the Japanese SMEs have been able to grow by responding both to big companies and to all types of demand which is beyond big business capacity. This global "system" of business activity might be one major reason why the Japanese economy has been able to survive two oil crises and remain vigorously competitive despite sharp appreciations of the yen since the late 70s.

Because of economic proximity and interaction between Japan and its Asian neighbours, there is no doubt that both the Japanese industrial experience at home and its economic performance overseas have a continuous and great influence on the rapid industrialization process in the Asian NIEs: SMEs have also played a decisive role in the development of both Taiwan and Hong Kong, with a more recent but significant role in Korea and a more modest one in Singapore.

Since the 60s and 70s, the Japanese big manufacturing conglomerates and trading houses have increasingly come to Western Europe. These moves have certainly accelerated considering some major industrial, trading and financial changes taking place worldwide since the early 80s. Because of rapid currency appreciation and increasing trade pressures during the last three years, a lot of Japanese SMEs have massively begun to expand overseas, including to Western Europe. As described by the business community of some major commercial cities in Western Europe like Hamburg, London or Rotterdam, more and more Japanese SMEs have first been using the know-how and networks of the Japanese big companies already heavily represented in Western Europe. Then, they have rapidly tried to develop more direct and autonomous activities of their own in relation with Western European clients, suppliers or partners. In 1989, they are expected to account for about one third of total Japanese manufacturing investment and partnership in the EEC countries!

Some similar moves should be expected from the Asian NIEs in the very next years, especially from Korea and Taiwan, and this should contribute to some new types of business relations with Western Europe. Because of similar currency and trade pressures from the USA and the new perspective of an EEC integrated market beyond 1992, the Asian NIEs want to diversify their overseas markets and partners in order to secure further development and growth at home. This new business strategy is also related to their growing financial capacity as export surplus economies and to some domestic factors affecting local production costs (like wage increases, labour unrest or scarcity of labour).

Some big industrial and trading conglomerates from Korea and Taiwan have already started to invest worldwide and also in Europe (including Eastern Europe) and many SMEs of the four Asian NIEs (which have already vast interests all over Northeast and Southeast Asia) are now considering imitating them and/or Japanese SME counterparts.

No doubt, as observed during two research surveys conducted by our research centre in 1988 and 1989, that the Asian NIEs and their SMEs in particular are looking for much closer relations with Western Europe in trade, technology cooperation and even financial venturing. Compared with their high level of market knowledge about Japan and the USA, they still lack detailed information on how to establish various types of business links with some very diversified potential counterparts in Western Europe. If there was some similar interest on the European side, this could inaugurate some new business opportunities (perhaps less conflictual as well) between Western Europe and the Far East.

3. The Global Role of SMEs in the Four Asian NIEs

The development of SMEs in the Asian NIEs has followed either the "Japanese model", with very close and integrated links between big industry and small business (like Korea), or the "Hong Kong model", with local SMEs reacting to domestic and regional/international demand. The unique examples of Taiwan (where the role of local SMEs prevails) and Singapore (where it is quite modest) are somehow between these two "models". This very short introduction to the local SMEs is another example of the well-cut similarities and differences among the four Asian NIEs.

Statistical data shows the relative or important contribution of SMEs to the global economic performance of the Asian NIEs. There are about 1.65 million SMEs in South Korea, 730 000 in Taiwan, 90 000 in Hong Kong and 70 000 in Singapore, in both industry and services. The definition of SMEs differs in each case, but it can be said that SMEs represent on average 91 to 98 % of total existing companies, 46 to 70 % (Taiwan) of total work force, 31 % to 55 % (Taiwan) of total value added, and 17 % to 66 % (Taiwan) of total direct exports.

The two first indicators show little difference between the Asian NIEs: only Singapore ranks behind the three others because of the dominating role of multinational corporations and big public holdings in the economy of the small island republic. According to the two other indicators, Hong Kong and Taiwan come first because of the SMEs' important role in these two economies. Korean and moreover Taiwanese SMEs are extremely dynamic in terms of their contribution to total direct exports (32 and 55 % respectively). Based on a strong tradition of Chinese small entrepreneurship, SMEs are today an essential pillar of Taiwanese business activities and also a strong element of the Hong Kong economy.

In Taiwan in particular but also in the other NIEs, several factors can explain the vitality of local SMEs: the professional background of local entrepreneurs and the type of family business, the valorization of all human resources (education and training), the increasing availability of capital and low taxation, the flexibility of production and capacity of finding niches of specialization, the good infrastructures and highly efficient marketing facilities (including through big conglomerates and trading houses), and the selective but strong hand of government or semi-public schemes (with the relative exception of Hong Kong).

SMEs in Taiwan

730 000 SMEs in Taiwan compared with a population of 19 million: most local Chinese dream about being their own boss and the density of entrepreneurship is very high with one or several entrepreneurs per family!

Although occupied by the Japanese like Korea in the past, Taiwan has not copied everything from Japan. A sound land reform and a reorganization of former Japanese agro-industrial companies, a necessary balance in Kuomintang's politics and economic rule between migrant Chinese from Mainland China and native Taiwanese have sustained Taiwan's own strategy for rapid industrialization after 1949. This strategy has relied on both state intervention in most areas of heavy and strategic industry (especially in sectors where the domestic market was much too small for potential private infant industry) and on the private sector with a few big companies and a very dense network of SMEs in light industry, subcontracting and services. Manufacturing SMEs (160 000 out of a total number of 730 000 SMEs, average size below 50 employees) play a key role in textiles and clothing, footwear, plastics, chemicals, precision machinery, metal work and publishing. They have become one major agent of Taiwan's trade surpluses since the mid-80s.

Compared with the Korean SMEs in particular, local SMEs in Taiwan are far less related to a comprehensive and satellite system of production controlled rather exclusively by big business. Of course, subcontracting is very active but also very diversified in terms of demand and supply. Like in Hong Kong, free reaction to both domestic and international orders has much contributed to the dynamics of SMEs, which have also benefited from very efficient export promotion services provided by the government and the private sector (trading companies). Looking at the Korean and Japanese experiences, the question was raised again in 1985-86, at the top government level, whether much more business concentration was needed in order to maintain future Taiwanese competitiveness. But it has been felt so far that a pragmatic balance between a few key big companies and a myriad of SMEs is well suited to finding some good niches of specialization on world markets, also with the very supportive business network of the overseas Chinese all over the Pacific Region and beyond.

SMEs in Korea

Unlike Taiwan and Hong Kong, the development of Korean SMEs during the last 30 years has largely followed the "Japanese model" with very close subcontracting activities between small and big firms. In Korea in particular, very little room was left to small autonomous entrepreneurship: under Presidents Park and Chun, the role of SMEs was recognized on paper (in 1960-62 already), but most domestic resources and massive international borrowings were allocated for the very rapid development of big conglomerates or so-called Korean chaebols, especially in the heavy industry and electronic sectors. This big scale industrial policy under obvious strong and even military guidance led to the relative decline of SMEs in the global economy up to the mid-70s; this trend was then reversed because of increasing subcontracting demands from big conglomerates and a steady diversification process of Korean manufacturing. However, 2 % of all existing Korean firms are still responsible today for 62 % of total value added.

The official definition of a SME ranges from 1 to 1000 employees, but it is 1 to 20 only for services except in the transport sector; the average size of Korean SMEs is below 300 employees and there is no systematic classification yet by company declared capital and corporate assets. Most Korean manufacturing SMEs concentrate today in textiles and clothing (the number one sector), metal products, heavy and mechanical machinery, chemicals, plastics, food processing and footwear. Following the big scale industrial options of the last 30 years, they have shifted more and more from light to heavy industrial activities and this probably explains why they are able today to contribute, directly or through big trading houses, to nearly 35 to 40 % of total Korean exports.

SMEs in Hong Kong

Like Taiwan, SMEs are a strong element of the Hong Kong economy, but with less than 50 workers on average their size is to be compared with the Singaporean SMEs; 62 % of all manufacturing establishments have fewer than 10 employees. With the initial immigration of experienced Chinese entrepreneurs in 1949 and after, SMEs have rapidly flourished and played an essential role in entrepôt Hong Kong from early industrialization during the 50s to industrial take off during the 60s and 70s and to further diversification till today. In the manufacturing sector, they have progressively shifted, like the big companies, from labour-intensive manufacturing (textiles and clothing as number one) to more capital- and technology-oriented production (electronics as number one) and they are very dependent on a nearly 100 % foreign trade oriented economy, in most cases through foreign and local multinationals and big trading houses. Since the economic reforms in China, they have also increasingly contributed to the delocalisation of labour-intensive and low-tech activities from Hong Kong to the nearby region of the Pearl Delta River and Guangdong Province in South China.

Compared with the other NIEs, the proximity of China, which is much less developed but also unstable, raises some difficult questions about the future: a large number of Hong Kong SMEs tend to remain in rather traditional sectors of business activity and to answer the enormous but yet "basic needs" oriented demand of their huge neighbour. This trend, coming in addition to Cantonese Chinese entrepreneurs who are too often interested in maximum profit for minimum investment, could maintain local SMEs in light consumer production and low-tech business. Political uncertainty, brain drain and poor local government support could widen the performance gap between Hong Kong SMEs and their counterparts in the other NIEs, especially in neighbouring Taiwan.

SMEs in Singapore

The figures available about SMEs in Singapore show that they play a significant role in the economy in terms of number of companies (mainly in commerce and services) and employment. But manufacturing SMEs in particular have a rather low profile in terms of their contribution to total value added or total exports.

Until independence in 1965, Singapore was mainly an entrepôt and service economy and, contrary to the situation in Hong Kong, there were very few local entrepreneurs in the industrial sector. This factor was one obvious reason why the government decided to rely on vast inflows of foreign investment and on the creation of large firms serving both international and regional markets, especially after the sudden separation and independence from Malaysia. During the first two decades as a sovereign island city-state, top priority for rapid industrialization has been given to local operations by foreign multinationals partly counterbalanced by state intervention in public services, in a few key secondary and tertiary sectors and in the global management of the national economy. Local and private entrepreneurship was not much encouraged and even after the new and second stage industrial policy adopted in 1978-79, the Economic Development Board did not pay much attention to the existing SMEs because of the assumption that they were all low-tech oriented, not efficient and innovative, and ready to disappear or merge with bigger companies sooner or later.

Nevertheless, some SMEs have survived and developed pretty well even in Singapore, probably because of the small size of the domestic market but mainly because of the spillover effect of sustained high growth of the global economy and a good regional and international market environment. In 1984-86, the first economic recession ever experienced by Singapore since independence (with a clear slowdown of big business activities, the multinationals in particular) has underlined the vulnerability of the city-state and, among other factors of explanation, its much too small cushion of flexible SMEs, especially in manufacturing. This has led the government to recognize in 1986 the need to promote the role of SMEs for a more balanced development of the economy in the future.

4. Domestic Promotion and Internationalization of SMEs in the Asian NIEs: the Case of South Korea

In both Northeast Asian and Western European economies, SMEs play a very significant role: today and on both sides, the SMEs have to adapt to new types of world business competition and to look for new avenues for international trading, technological and financial partnership, but they still know extremely little about each other.

With the semi-exception of Hong Kong, where the government is supposed to be non-interventionist, the local authorities in the other Asian NIEs have initiated substantial assistance programmes/and supporting schemes in favour of their most promising SMEs.

The Case of South Korea

Even if still outpaced by the economy as a whole, Korean SMEs found 1988 to be another year of steady growth with manufacturing production of SMEs growing by 10.6 %. Statistical data as shown above gives some evidence of the SMEs' important role in the Korean economy, although it remains far behind that of Japan or Taiwan especially.

The Korean government began to initiate some assistance schemes in favour of local SMEs from 1975-78 onwards. Since 1986-88, as Korea moved to open domestic markets and to decrease public support for big conglomerates, much emphasis has been put on strengthening SMEs and helping them to cope with international competition. Also looking quite enviously at Taiwan's myriad of SMEs and their performance, the Korean authorities have given high but also concrete priority to the promotion of SMEs in the Economic Development Plan 1987-91. With 650 million US dollars of direct government support and 7.8 billion of loans from the national and provincial banking community, Korean SMEs are expected to contribute about one half of total manufacturing value added and exports by the mid-1990s.

Government support for SMEs is combined with increasing promotion provided by business associations, cooperatives, banks and private firms, especially in the fields of manpower training, technology development, finance and venture capital. There are five major agencies promoting SMEs in Korea:

- *The Small and Medium Industry Bureau*, a division of the Ministry of Trade and Technology, is responsible for the overall coordination and implementation of government policies for SMEs.

- *The Korea Federation of Small Business* (established in 1962) is responsible for SME cooperatives throughout the country. It federates about 25 000 SMEs, and it offers government subsidized grants, loans and tax exemptions.

- *The Industrial Bank of Korea* (one European representative office in London) and *Citizen's Bank* are two major banks providing SMEs with specific credit facilities at the national level. They are particularly responsible for implementing government guidelines which require commercial lending institutions to supply a minimum percentage of loans or guarantees to SMEs during the year: 35 % and 80 % of total corporate loans for commercial and local banks respectively, 35 % of total discounted bills for finance companies, 25 % of leasing contract amounts for merchant banks. Total outstanding loans to SMEs reached 25.43 billion US dollars in 1988 (7 billion by IBK alone), accounting for 48.3 % of total loans provided to Korean enterprises throughout the country.

- *The Korea Credit Guarantee Fund* (set up in 1976) extends credit guarantee support to sound firms which lack financial collateral. With a total of about 1 billion US dollars, the outstanding balance of guarantees issued to SMEs reached 3.96 billion in 1987 or 97 % of the total.

- *The Small and Medium Industry Promotion Corporation* (established in 1979, one European representative office in Frankfurt), has become the central agency for the development of SMEs. It carries out a wide range of very concrete financial and technical assistance programs for SMEs. SMIPC is also responsible for promoting the internationalization of SMEs through joint ventures and overseas technology transfer.

SMIPC Centre for Foreign Investment Services is in charge of foreign joint ventures with SMEs in Korea and has implemented so far two special investment programs with European counterparts, one with the West German Agency for Technical Cooperation and GOPA Consultants (50 projects realized since 1979), one with the French Industry Promotion Association APRODI (44 projects so far), and one similar program should start with British partners in 1989-90.

SMIPC Centre for Overseas Investment Services advises Korean SMEs looking for investment abroad and it provides various tax incentives and overseas investment insurance schemes in association with the Korean Exim Bank. Considering the very rapid increase in the number of Korean SMEs investing overseas (about one half of total Korean investment overseas in 1988), COIS supported more than 80 projects in 1987-88 against 62 only between 1980 and 1986.

There is little doubt, then, that the very next years should be a period of increasing business matching opportunities between Korean and Western European SMEs.

Looking at the Korean SMEs' performance in 1986-89, the most attractive sectors should be in the heavy industry: fabricated metals, equipment machinery, building materials, non-metallic minerals, chemicals and plastics, electrical appliances and automotive components in particular.

As another very interesting indicator, potential foreign investors and partners should attentively look at the annual selection of the most promising SMEs by the Korean Ministry of Trade and Industry:

- for the sixth consecutive year, the Korean MTI selected in 1988 the most promising SMEs (731 in total) and the growing medium-sized export firms (42), which received 673 and 165 million US dollars respectively of so-called government strategic support for future development.

- 337 large firms and 2200 most promising SMEs have also been selected as primary and sub-contractors in some 40 various industrial subsectors. In the near future, some industrial subsectors like consumer electronics, automotive components, fine chemicals, precision electrical machinery, synthetics, toys, footwear, wood and paper, furniture and food processing should be reserved by government decision and more or less exclusively for SMEs' development.

Table: The Global Role of SMEs in the Four Asian NIEs

SMEs	in % of total number of companies	in % of total work force	in % of total value added	in % of total direct exports
Hong Kong	98	62	57	17
Singapore	91	46	31	18
South Korea	98	66	38	34
Taiwan	97	70	55	66

Source: Government Statistics, 1986-88
SMEs defined according to local sources
- Hong Kong: 1 to 200 employees
- Singapore: corporate assets below S $ 8 M (US $ 3.7 M)
- South Korea: 1 to 1000 employees (1 to 20 for services)
- Taiwan: declared capital below NT $ 40 (US $ 1 M) and corporate assets below NT $ 120 (US $ 3 M)

Part Two

The Relations between the Asian NIEs and Europe
in a Worldwide Perspective

A WORLD SCENARIO: THE EMERGENCE OF THREE MAIN TRADING ZONES THE EUROPEAN COMMUNITY / JAPAN - EAST ASIA - PACIFIC / USA - CANADA

Theodor Leuenberger
Director
Institute for Technology Management (ITEM)
University of St. Gall
Unterstrasse 22
CH-9000 St. Gallen

I. Transformation of Power on a World Scale

If we speak of the emergence of regional world zones

the USA - Pacific zone
the Japan - NIEs zone
the Europe 1992 zone

- including the reform dynamics of Eastern Europe -

we must speak of the changing world power structure. It is no longer the bi-polarity of the fifties and sixties but a plurality of centres.

The world economy is not a neat pattern of five powers which can arrange everything among themselves. Rather, it is a fluid field. We might describe it as a process, as a gradual replacement of one pattern by another.

The approach of this analysis is this:
Periods of history are dominated by specific themes and specific patterns of conflict.

The two patterns that are familiar as conflicts are the East-West conflict, which may be the war of the past, and the North-South conflict and the South-South relations, which will remain and

Europe-Asia-Pacific Studies in Economy and Technology
Kulessa (Ed.)
The Newly Industrializing Economies of Asia

possibly intensify. The theme has become economic/technological and in this conflict/cooperation pattern there is a plurality of influence, power centres, nations, regimes, coalitions and so on.

These transformations of power have also affected the nature of the international hierarchy. There is no longer one hierarchy based on military power. There are separate hierarchies and one can no longer speak of a clear main power (see Hoffmann S. (1978) Primacy of World Order, New York).

Of course, there is still the strategic-diplomatic system. The same actors, however, participate in other systems or games. There are non-strategic games of economic interaction between East and West, North and South and South and South.

Modern power games are very complex. The possible use of power has changed. With the internationalization of economies, with the world-wide spread of technology and entrepreneurship and with the growing international economic transactions, the rules of the game have changed. The interdependence of all actors is both an opportunity and a restraint for each of them. It is a chance to exert influence on a global scale. But it is a restraint also on a hostile use of one's own power. The level of interdependence is often such that one state cannot reach its goal unless others achieve their own development. Thus a joint gain is in everybody's interest. A very aggressive use of one's power may well backfire. Thus the new interactions are quite different from traditional interactions: "You can harm me, and I you, but neither one of us can retaliate fully without harming himself." (Even if I try to increase my share of the pie, I should not destroy it; otherwise my share is gone). Or: "I need you, but you need me, even if you are much stronger than I am." In the present power-game: "I could use my advantages at your expense on a given issue, but must refrain from doing so because I need your support on an-other issue." Thus, the capacity of the strong to exploit their own power advantage is very limited. The United States may be at the top of every hierarchy of technological and economic power. But she is not a master with free hands. The "stronger" has always to expect the revenge of the "weaker" if she demands too much.

We see the present international system no longer in neat formulas: the classical balance-of-power diplomacy cannot cope with the global or regional management of interdependence. The same is true for the trilateral concept: it has little to say about global management (trilateralism: USA, Western Europe, Japan).

The trilateralists' basic theme is to replace balance-of-power politics with world-order politics. But both a triangular and trilateral policy is not enough. The drama of world order lies in the interconnection. There is no simplifying formula. There are different partial ways for coping with each one of them. The potential for ordering a complex world is minimal. There is no unity in the world system. Of course, the players participate in a common set of games. But they belong to different patterns of world politics. There is a mix of differences in economic levels, degree of development, degrees of independence and interdependence. It is a potpourri of conflict and cooperation.

Future Scenarios and Their Implications

a) *Pax Americana* to be restored

According to this scenario, the United States would restore its economic hegemony that was effectively sustained from the end of World War II to the first half of the 1960s. This particular future image is often reflected in the statements of those Americans who call for a "strong America".

b) *Pax Nipponica*

Japan would replace the United States as the hegemonic power in the world economy. Regardless of whether Japan could actually establish *Pax Nipponica*, it would not be conducive to a smooth, cooperative relationship with the United States and other trading partners if influential Japanese policymakers and business leaders held on to this scenario. American efforts to prevent the Japanese hegemony might only stir up reactive Japanese nationalism.

c) Competing trading blocs

If both countries sought to achieve economic hegemony and failed, they might try to create their own exclusive trading blocs, as we saw in the 1930s. According to one analyst, the United States might create a bloc consisting of Canada, Mexico, and Central American and Caribbean nations, while Japan might create a bloc composed of ASEAN (Association of Southeast Asian Nations) countries, Australia and New Zealand. Putting aside the question of which countries might belong to which blocs, the emergence of such competing economic blocs would lead to a very unstable situation.

d) Creation of a joint leadership system

Americans and Japanese would realise that neither country could unilaterally retain or achieve economic leadership hereafter and would create a joint leadership system to maintain a basically free economic order, along with other advanced industrial countries. They would consolidate a policy-coordinating mechanism to minimise negative effects of economic interdependence, while encouraging transnational industrial collaboration among Japanese, American and European companies as well as multinational corporations based in other countries.

Four Scenarios for the World Economy

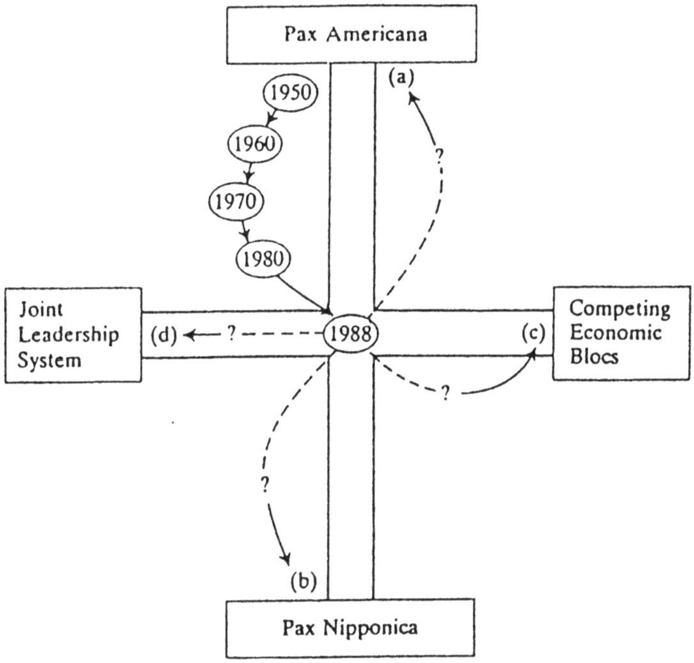

(a) Pax Americana
(b) Pax Nipponica
(c) Competing Economic Blocs
(d) Joint Leadership System

Source: Adapted in a modified form from R. Drobnick, 'The International Economy at a Crossroads: Implications for the Pacific Rim', (mimeo), University of Southern California, 1985, p. 2.

Let me elaborate on the scenario "*Pax Nipponica*". I am convinced that we are experiencing a shift in the balance of economic and technological power.

I do not mean the decline of the United States and the rise of Japan; it is not a question of Japan arriving on the global scene as a major industrial power and the United States leaving the scene.

It is a fact that the United States will remain a strategic industrial superpower at the beginning of the next century.

The shift in power is relative. Relative to the United States, Japan is rising, and current trends, whether financial, industrial commercial or technological, show that the shift in the global balance of power will be sustained.

At the same time, it must also be recognized that the trend is reversible.

In the Herald Tribune of Sept. 16/17 1989 we read:

> " The Japanese Century is ending, almost before it began, according to a small minority of economists and foreign policy experts inside Japan and abroad who believe that the Japanese economy has peaked and is entering an age of decline.
> "We have come to a peak in our history", said Kenichi Ito, a former Japanese diplomat who heads the Japan Forum of International Relations. "The more we pursue expansion, the more we have to lose".
> Mr. Ito and other scholars point to many factors that could fasten a Japanese decline: the rapid aging of its society, a hollowing-out of its industry, the sclerosis of its once flexible ruling elite.
> They also suggest that an easing of Cold War tensions will work

against Japan by making the western world less tolerant of Japanese economic expansion.

"To the extent the Cold War was alive, the United States was willing to turn a blind eye to Japan's nuisance as an economic animal", said Johsen Takahashi, an economist at the Mitsubishi Research Institute.

"Now, Japan clearly is losing its raison d'être in the global scene, its significance as guardian of the frontier of the free world", he said. "What Japan can do in this situation is extremely limited."

Neither Mr. Ito nor the other pessimists argue that Japan is headed for a sudden fall. Hiroshi Mitsuzuka said recently that Japan needed "revolutionary change."

Japan and Asia

Japan has proved to be a very powerful economic model. There is a lot to learn from the innovative ways in which the Japanese have managed every aspect of economic activity. Again, one should not exaggerate. Japan is not an industrial utopia. There are ups and downs also in Japan's relations with East and Southeast Asia. There are war memories. There are antipathies etc.

But, in many respects the Asian economies, including Australia, are witnessing a dynamic vertical integration, with Japan at the apex, in trade, manufacturing, technology and services. It has become a cliché to say that whereas the Japanese failed to establish the Greater East Asia Coprosperity Sphere militarily in the forties, they have succeeded economically in the eighties.

It is natural that all countries, but especially neighbouring ones, should turn to Japan, whether for investments, loans, technology, etc. At the same time as the "pull" forces are exerting their powers, turning to Tokyo is all the more necessary because

Asian countries are being "pushed away" from Europe and North America. The perception in Seoul, Taipei, Beijing, Bangkok, Kuala Lumpur, Canberra, etc. is that Fortress Europe and Free Trade Zone America/Canada leave Asians no choice but to get together.

In other words: we are observing the emergence of a regional zone. A new economic order is forming within the region: the probable outcome will be the creation of an informal Asian trading region (not a bloc) with Japan as "avant-garde" including "Greater East Asia": Korea, the People's Republic of China, Taiwan and Hong Kong, with active participation by the ASEAN countries and Australasia. This transformation will be characterized by a rapid expansion of Japan's economic and political power; fast-growing economic links with Korean, Taiwanese, and Hong Kong neighbours; an ascendant Thailand; and a resurgence in ASEAN states touched off by capital flows from Japan and the newly industrialized countries.

According to the Medium-Term Economic Outlook of the Nomura Research Institute (June 1989) we will see a sustained dynamism in the Asia-Pacific economies.

Rising intraregional trade and investment are changing the economic relations among countries in the Pacific region. For example, in addition to being a key supplier of capital goods to the Asian NIEs, Japan is also emerging as a major export destination for these countries. The relations between the Asian NIEs and ASEAN and China are also moving in this direction. This multilayer catching-up process has been, and will remain, the core of dynamism in this region. As income rises and regional integration gathers pace, a West Pacific economic region comparable to the EC will take shape by the turn of this century.

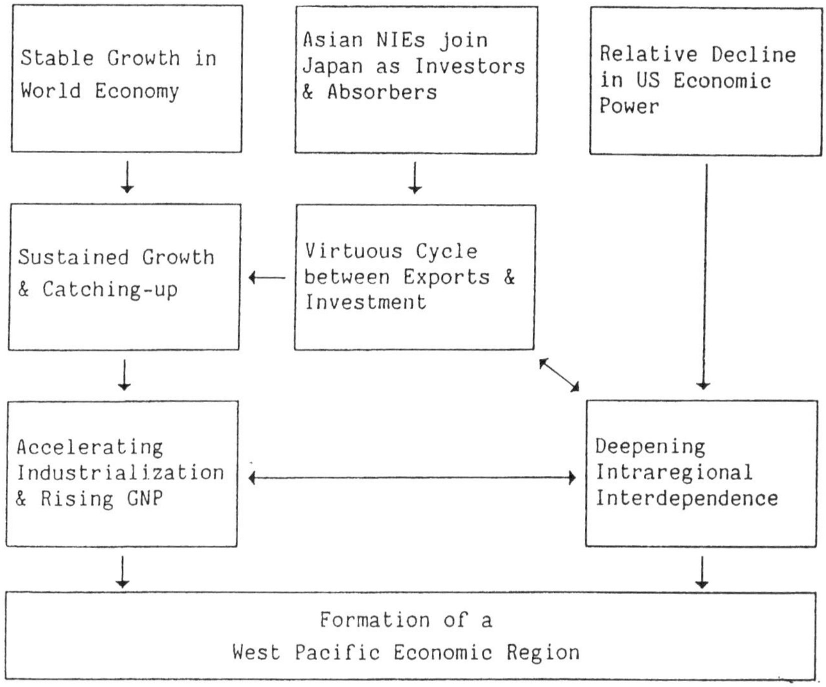
Stable Growth in World Economy
Asian NIEs join Japan as Investors & Absorbers
Relative Decline in US Economic Power
Sustained Growth & Catching-up
Virtuous Cycle between Exports & Investment
Accelerating Industrialization & Rising GNP
Deepening Intraregional Interdependence
Formation of a West Pacific Economic Region

Asian nations are becoming increasingly interdependent in the trading arena; Japan, Korea, Taiwan, and Hong Kong are importing more from the rest of Asia/Pacific. The region as a whole already sells more to itself than to the US - the top single market for a majority of Asian/Pacific countries. Japanese, Taiwanese, and Korean companies are boosting intraregional investment.

Influenced by the strong yen, protectionism, and tightening competition, Japanese investors will continue to move production facilities abroad and invest heavily in financial services and real estate - at a growth rate of 25-35 % p.a. A report released last year by Japan's Ministry of International Trade and Industry (MITI) suggests that automotive, computer, office machinery, and machine-tool industries will move 30-50 % of their production abroad within the next 5 to 10 years.

Japan's International Role

Japan has become a world economic power, but it has yet to develop truly international attitudes and policies. This is not to say that Japanese foreign policy has remained static.

Japan is moving towards more active responsibilities and higher visibility in regional and international affairs. The domestic debate centres upon the pace of developments and the precise mix of economic, political policies.

USA - Japan

In all of Japan's regional activities the USA remains a key element.

The Japan-US alliance is the single most important bilateral relation held by two nations today. It is a combination of economic interdependence and strategic dependence. Certainly the future of Japan-US relations will be marked by a mix of competition and co-operation.

I am sure that the American-Japanese relationship will survive present and future crises. In its competitive and its cooperative aspects it will force economic reforms in each society.

Relations between Japan and China

Deng Xiaoping spoke of these relations. He remarked they had not been better this century.

Japan expects to be the principle force behind China's modernization in the coming decades.

Both the Japanese government and the private sector are preparing for this task.

Japan, unlike the USA, has no emotional need to stand for democratization. The whole package of Confucian culture and authoritarian power is also a part of Japanese culture. Only if the political environment in China was damaging for Japanese business would they withdraw.

The Chinese have their own reservations. They are concerned by signs of Japanese nationalism.

They are irritated at Japan's strong ties with Taiwan and the network of unofficial political ties. Japan is following a de facto one China, one Taiwan policy in China's view.

What might be the consequences of these trends? One message seems clear: the socialist bloc in Asia is now lagging behind. Even radical reforms in the command economies will not reestablish the standing of socialism as a plausible development model in the region. There is the desire of the Soviet Union to develop closer links with the Pacific economy, particularly from the Soviet Far East.

The question still is, both for the USSR and China, how to turn a planned economy into a market economy without pushing it over the brink of disaster. It can be done, but only with a comprehensive strategy that takes into account the peculiar conditions of an economy ravaged by shortages, dominated by monopolies and distorted by black markets.

The Soviet and Chinese governments have no such comprehensive strategies as yet.

Thus, I do not see the emergence of a socialist Pacific economy centering around Mainland China. But the rise of the Asian Pacific societies does not mark the triumph of western capitalism either. What does the Asia-Pacific area mean for western policies? In policy terms, a new modus operandi needs to be developed - no longer fashioned in the North Atlantic image.

The games have changed. We are no longer in an area of Western/American hegemony but of a new world interdependence in which regional arrangements have their own right. The challenge is not to get the NIEs into the Euro-American system. It is more a question of strengthening an Euro-Asian network/dialogue covering the key areas - i.e. foreign policy, monetary policy, trade policy, technology policy. As we have a regular political and sectoral dialogue between the United States and the European Community and a dense cooperation network, we must aim at a similar intense dialogue, both formal and informal. It will be a topic of our discussions here whether the existing arrangements are sufficient. I do not think they are. We have not yet reached the necessary frequency of contacts, information exchange and consultation.

I think we should consider the kinds of institutional links that have long characterized transatlantic cooperation.

To promote closer Pacific ties we envisage a consultative body along the lines of the Organization for Economic Cooperation and Development (OECD). The question of closer ties was among the main themes at the annual meeting of the Association of Southeast Asian Nations in Brunei this year. There is - as we know - already one institution along this line: the Pacific Economic Cooperation Conference which brings together government, business and private sector traders.

Although it has remained a loose organization to accommodate the diversity of its members, this body could well become the agency for deeper cooperation that we have in mind.

The dialogue is an intercultural venture which brings new patterns into the present North Atlantic - Western European social and political institutions. The whole postwar setup of GATT, OECD, IMF etc. and the foundation of transnational and international agreements and institutions have been dominated by the values of western civilisation. Both the East and Southeast Asian civilisations produced different, sophisticated traditions of government.

For successful, more integrated development, such ideas need to be harmonized with the demands of regional and supraregional interdependence.

Literature

1. Miyohei Shinohara, Fu-chen Lo (ed.) (1989) Global Adjustment and the Future of Asian-Pacific Economy. Institute of Developing Economies, Japan/Asian and Pacific Development Centre, Kuala Lumpur.

2. Cotton J. (1988) The Pacific Century: The Political Impact? The Pacific Review, Oxford University Press, Vol. 1, No. 2, p. 145.

3. Cotton J. (1989) Continued High Growth in Sight for the Asian NIEs (Summary). Fuji Economic Review, March-April 1989.

4. Teruhiko, Ishizaki (1989) Les blocs économiques: une évolution préoccupante. Cahiers du Japon, No. 39, printemps 1989, p. 33.

5. Teruhiko, Ishizaki (1989) New Moves to Economic Bloc Formation. Kanagawa University Economic Review, No. 1, March 1989, p. 13

6. Iwao Nakatani (1989) Une zone de libre échange nippo-américaine. Cahiers du Japon, No. 39, printemps 1989, p. 38.

7. Iwao Nakatani (1989) Medium-Term Economic Outlook. Sustained Dynamism in the Asia-Pacific Economies. Nomura Asia Focus, June 1989, p. 1

8. Lehmann J.-P. (1989) Japan and a New World Order: Implications and an Agenda for Europe. European Affairs, No. 1, spring 1989, p. 41

THE CONCEPT OF THE INTERNATIONAL DIVISION OF LABOUR AND PRINCIPLES OF COOPERATION

Ulrich Hiemenz
Director
Section for Developing Countries and World Economy
Kiel Institute of World Economics
P.O.Box 43 09
D-2300 Kiel 1

1. The Concept

The international division of labour theory is essentially based upon two elements: the "Theorem of Comparative Cost Advantages", which originates from Ricardo, and the "Factor Proportion Theorem" founded by Heckscher and Ohlin. The reason why international trade takes place and profits result for all participants in the process, can be deduced from the theorem of comparative cost advantages. The factor proportion theorem, which is considerably younger than the theorem of comparative cost advantages, attributes comparative cost advantages to differences between countries in the way they are endowed with factors of production. World trade and division of labour can be said to be optimal, in terms of economic welfare, when they offer each participating country a national welfare maximum - assuming a given distribution of factors. This optimum would then be achieved if each country produces those goods, the factor absorption of which - in the course of the production process - comes closest to the country's factor distribution. Each country participating in international trade thus achieves the maximum national product possible with its given supply of factors of production. National and international distribution of income is, at the same time, also optimal, in the sense that full employment of all production factors prevails.

An essential task of empirical economic research today consists

Europe-Asia-Pacific Studies in Economy and Technology
Kulessa (Ed.)
The Newly Industrializing Economies of Asia

in identifying factors that can establish comparative cost advantages and explain the trade structure. In this context, dynamic aspects have increasingly come to the fore. There are two basic categories here: on the one hand, there are changes in factor distribution and factor prices that take place in the course of a country's development process and replace conventional comparative advantages with new ones; on the other hand, there are shifts in the advantages in the production of certain goods, based upon the maturing process that these goods go through (product cycle goods).

The first category of dynamic changes results from the fact that, in the course of the development process - i.e. the rise in per capita income - capital becomes more plentiful in comparison to labour. At the same time, the labour force's level of qualifications also rises as a result of learning processes during production ("learning by doing") and training. Both can establish comparative cost advantages in manufacturing processes that require more capital inputs than before and make higher demands on labour's qualifications. This triggers off a permanent process of structural change. The question as to which individual manufacturing processes hold the advantages cannot, of course, be determined mechanically by means of the per capita income, but rather depends upon previous economic developments, the specific production experience gained during this time, and the qualification trends of the labour force.

The second category of dynamic effects comprises changes resulting from the fact that products go through a maturing cycle. The early stages of developing and producing a product usually require a large amount of investment in research and development, as well as highly qualified labour, in order to make the product fit for the market and to produce it. The longer the product has been manufactured, the more the product itself and the necessary production processes are standardized, and the greater the advantages of developing countries in the manufacture of these goods. As yet, it is not possible to estimate empirically more closely the extent to which such product cycles determine changes in the international division of labour and promote growth in developing countries.

The international division of labour theory sketched here has both a positive and a normative character. As a positive theory, it describes why international trade exists and with which products it takes place between countries. As a normative theory, it specifies how an international division of labour should be constituted so that world economic, and thereby national economic welfare can be maximised. In awareness of the potential for increasing economic prosperity through an international division of labour, the architects of the international trading system, which was to emerge from the ashes of World War II, envisaged a framework of rules leading to, and securing, open markets. The General Agreement on Tariffs and Trade (GATT), which came into being in 1948, laid down such trade rules, basically the principles of non-discrimination and multilateralism in world trade. The aim was *not* to establish free trade, without any government intervention. What was meant is liberal trade, in which governments may interfere, but using price measures which are transparent and do not rule out competition (i.e. non-prohibitive tariffs rather than quantitative restrictions or subsidies). Adherence by the member countries to the principles of multilateralism and non-discrimination was expected to give rise to the production of an international public good: stability and predictability of trade rules.

2. Theory and Practice

The international trading system worked reasonably well up to the early seventies. Tariffs were reduced substantially in successive rounds of multilateral trade policy negotiations, especially with regard to manufactured goods. The stimulus to world trade was, by any historical standards, remarkable indeed: In the period 1955-73, world exports of manufactures expanded in real terms at an average annual rate of 9.2 per cent, as compared to an annual rate of growth of world manufacturing output of 6.6 per cent.[1] This pace of integration not only allowed the advanced countries to further increase real income. It also permitted other countries, most spectacularly Japan and various Asian and Latin American newly industrializing countries, to progress up the scale of economic development.

This contrasts sharply with the deterioration which the global framework for trade has been undergoing during the last fifteen years or so. Parallel to the 1973-79 Tokyo Round of trade policy negotiations under the GATT, which was supposed to substantially reduce tariff and non-tariff barriers to international trade and to make the fundamental rules of the world trading system clearer and more predictable, protectionism has increased. Even worse, protectionism has become more discriminatory among countries and more selectively tailored to individual goods or sectors, bypassing GATT's trade rules. By now, more than one fifth of world trade in manufactures is subjected to non-tariff restrictions, in some cases covering industrial branches as a whole (textiles and clothing, iron and steel, shipbuilding, automobiles, consumer electronics, for instance). World trade in agriculture is still heavily interfered with (about three-fifths of the trade value). Not surprisingly, the rate of growth of world exports in real terms, has been declining in recent years and became negative in 1982 (which had occurred hitherto only in 1958 and 1975). World exports of manufactures increased by only 4.5 per cent per annum in the period 1980-87.

----

1 The data reported here and below have been calculated from GATT, International Trade, various issues.

This current trend of events is discouraging for at least two reasons: One is that it describes developments which make for serious policy-induced uncertainty, adversely affecting long-term investments and retarding the revitalization of the world economy. The other reason for being concerned is that political frictions between countries, which lead to formal disputes and uncontrollable resentments, are generated; the current controversies within the European Community (EC), between the EC and the United States, between these two and Japan, and between old industrial and newly industrializing countries are rooted to some degree in a competitive process of government protection (including subsidies).

3. Causes of Increasing Protectionism and its Effects on the International Division of Labour

When talking about the causes of increased protectionism the focus is on western industrialized countries. However distorting trade policies of developing countries (and for that matter, of the socialist countries) may be, the functioning of an open and multilateral world trading system is much more affected by the policies of the industrial countries, in particular those of the United States, the EC and, increasingly, Japan. Increasing structural rigidities, in connection with the widespread belief in the omnicompetence of governments, have been major forces behind the trend towards bilateralism and sectoralism in trade policies of western industrialized countries. Old-fashioned tariffs are no longer important means of keeping imports at bay. As a result of the tariff reductions achieved in the Tokyo Round, the average level of nominal tariffs on manufactured imports amounts to 4.4 per cent in the United States, 4.7 per cent in the EC and 2.8 per cent in Japan (January 1987). Nowadays, non-tariff trade barriers have become a tool of structural policy. Therefore, they are designed to regulate trade in specific items by non-price measures and they deliberately discriminate against the most competitive suppliers from abroad. The policy variants which seem to best meet the needs of sunset domestic branches or firms are the bilaterally negotiated "voluntary" export restraints, the orderly marketing agreements and the concession of direct financial aids (mainly subsidies). They all are incompatible with GATT rules and the Tokyo Round failed to settle them.

At a conceptual level, there are a number of dangerous misconceptions involved in the ongoing debate in the industrial countries about the need for protection. To begin with, governments of industrialized countries often consider imports as a source of serious market disruption. In a fundamental sense all imports which are not complementary to local production disturb the market position of individual firms and jobs. This is in the nature of competitive, market-oriented economies, of which international trade is only one dimension. It is analogous to the flow of goods from one region to another within a particular country. That is, international trade is commonly the means by which comparative advantages and disadvantages are transmitted between countries just as countries or regions can export best what they can produce cheapest, they will import goods that are cheaper than domestic output. When foreign supplies are cheaper, the exporters normally do not exert "abnormal" or "unfair" competition, as is so often argued, but just exploit their comparative advantage. This comparative advantage often derives from lower wage costs than those prevailing in the importing countries. If, for instance, our workers in the textile and clothing industry or in shipbuilding are to be paid wages amounting to, or exceeding, the national average, whereas productivity in these industries is lower than the national average, and if wage costs are several times higher than abroad as a result, then international competitiveness cannot be maintained in these industries.

The contention that increased manufactured imports from Japan and the NICs have led to increasing levels of unemployment, especially in Western Europe, does not hold either. In a growing economy, import competition - or for that matter competition from within - is only one of various sources of change in employment opportunities. The other sources are shifts in domestic and foreign demand (exports) as well as the increase in labour productivity. As a matter of fact, the latter has been by far the most important source of labour displacement in Western manufacturing industry. To conclude that productivity should not have increased would be incorrect. Correct would be to conclude that if productivity had not increased so much employment would have decreased even more at given real wages. This even holds for branches such as textiles, clothing, footwear and leather products where import penetration from the NICs (and from other developing countries) has risen sharply in recent years. When firms have been driven out of the market, it was often by the more efficient domestic competitors rather than by imports (whatever their country of origin).

That import competition initially leads to a loss of the least viable jobs and industrial capacities, or slows down their expansion, is only one side of the coin. The counterpart of this pressure to adjust is the creation of new jobs and productive capacities in higher productivity lines which embody more skilled labour and more sophisticated machinery, including the manufacture of goods being exported to countries from which the competitive imports originate. It is fallacious to think that foreign countries (in particular Japan and some NICs) can supply everything more cheaply than Western European or North American countries can (taking due account of quality differentials) because in this case they would not export at all. In fact, most of the industrial countries' foreign trade in manufactures is of an intra-industry type, i.e. the countries export and import very similar goods. In trade relations with developing countries (as well as with the centrally-planned economies) inter-industry specialization predominates so that trade-induced job displacement and job creation takes place in quite different branches and regions. Yet, even within declining industries, firms which are not able to compete with imports co-exist with those which actually do (or could by reducing costs if it were a matter of survival). Textiles and clothing, in which product variety was substantially reduced and production was sharply upgraded, constitute one example; another is shipbuilding, in which several medium-sized firms have specialized on technology-intensive vessels and marine equipment and given up the production of oil tankers and bulk carriers.

Another misconception lies behind the widespread concern in the United States and the EC about the persistent and growing deficit in trade with Japan, South Korea and Taiwan. This has given rise in the United States to feelings about the need of a new, "aggressive reciprocity" in bilateral trading arrangements, in the sense that new import barriers are imposed against a country which is considered to be protectionist itself. However, in a multilateral trading system bilateral trade balances are of no economic significance. Moreover, it is doubtful to assume, as the advocates of the aggressive reciprocity do, that the Japanese market is more or less closed for foreign suppliers of manufactures. Indeed, import tariffs in Japan are lower than in the United States or in the EC and there is in Japan nowadays much less use of non-tariff measures than ten years ago. It is possible that the internal retailing system in Japan favours domestic products in accordance with the customs and attitudes of the population much more than is the case in the United States and Western Europe. But there are examples of North American and European firms making the determined marketing effort which is required to sell in Japan - and those are successful.

A final example of misconception relates to the quest for protection or subsidies in order to counteract foreign subsidized competition. The point here is that if a foreign country subsidizes the export of products in which it has a comparative disadvantage, the latter will be better off in welfare terms than it would in the absence of subsidized foreign supplies, at least as long as the currency of the subsidizing country does not appreciate. It should also be noted that the subsidies which foreign governments grant to their export industries do not necessarily provide a competitive edge on the world market. Frequently, and most prominently in developing countries, these subsidies are intended to neutralize a competitive disadvantage which derives from the domestic system of import protection or an overvalued currency.

The advocates of protection usually claim that government support allows domestic industries to adjust to import competition more easily. The evidence does not support this notion. If anything, experience with industry-specific protection has shown that such "breathing spaces" reduce the incentives to adjust in an efficient manner. Sooner or later, firms adhering to a mere survival-by-protection strategy encounter serious problems, in some cases (particularly in textiles, clothing, consumer electronics, steel, shipbuilding) ending in bankruptcy. Evidently it is an illusion to believe that protection by itself transforms underlying comparative cost disadvantages into advantages. This explains why so many protectionist measures which are announced as temporary have endured over time.

By the same token, there is no reason to expect that protective assistance granted to certain industries which are supposed to have a considerable growth potential (i.e. technology-intensive industries) could be easily phased out after some time. If the investment in these industries is a success, governments of other countries may be prone to emulate, providing vigorous support now for their own industries. Attempts by the fore-runners to keep their lead in the so-called growth industries may founder in retaliatory escalation or competitive subsidization. If, on the contrary, the industries chosen for encouragement fail, the government will be made liable for protecting the capital invested and the jobs created and, therefore, continue the assistance, which then becomes indefinite support for survival.

4. Future Perspectives for the EC

The preceding section has shown that protectionistic trade policies are the least appropriate means to solve the underlying structural problems industrialized countries are facing. The essence of protection, as standard economic theory shows and empirical evidence confirms, is the distortion in the allocation of resources, both in a static and a dynamic sense, and nationally as well as worldwide. Selective protectionism has particularly high costs since it delinks economic development from market conditions and reduces progressively the structural adaptability of the economy to internal or external unpredictable opportunities and setbacks. The protectionist policies serve to favour more or less systematically the comparatively less efficient and less essential industries.

Turning from the past and present to the future, further changes of the international trading order are hard to predict since a number of conflicting forces will remain at work, particularly with respect to the EC.[2] First, EC member countries have agreed to establish a "Common Internal Market" by 1992. this is a political decision which would require an enormous amount of harmonization among widely differing national standards and norms,

---

2 For details, see e.g. Ulrich Hiemenz and Rolf J. Langhammer, (1988) ASEAN and the EC - Institutions and Structural Change in the European Community. Singapore: ISEAS, VIII.

common rules for national subsidy schemes, and a dismantling of non-tariff trade barriers. Observers tend to agree that the necessary negotiations and legal procedures will not be completed until the envisaged date, in particular since the southern enlargement of the EC has complicated the matter substantially. Nonetheless, there are many proponents of deregulating trade within the EC who expect a common market to create new trade opportunities and to enforce a harmonization of economic policymaking among EC member countries. Whatever the final impact on trade policies will be, there is a justified concern that a common market is likely to be achieved only at the expense of more discrimination against suppliers from non-EC countries, including newly industrializing countries in Asia.

Secondly, the EC budget is in a financial crunch which has to be resolved before a common market can be established. In the past, disputes over financial matters have been settled by increasing contributions to the EC and simultaneously shifting some cost-intensive regulations back to the national level. As it looks now, both remedies will again be applied to solve the present financial crisis. Renationalization of sector policies regarding, for example, agriculture or steel runs counter to the harmonization and deregulation envisaged establishing a common market. The experience particularly in agriculture shows that national support schemes differ widely among EC member countries and can be sustained only when intra-EC trade is severely restricted. The EC steel cartel represents the result of a similar basic situation. Therefore, renationalization of EC competences and the establishment of a common market are mutually incompatible.

And finally, there is an increasing pressure on EC institutions and member governments to open EC markets to non-EC suppliers which is not likely to abate. Mainly the United States, but also some highly indebted NICs, demand a reduction of EC trade barriers in agriculture and fewer subsidies for sunset industries. The

United States is also pushing the issue of free trade in services. Most of these topics are on the agenda of the current GATT Round, and the US appears to be determined to win some concessions from the EC.

The ultimate outcome of this struggle between countervailing political and economic forces is hard to predict with some accuracy. The writing on the wall is, however, that institutional intervention in the functioning of EC markets is going to increase rather than diminish over the next 10 or so years. These interventions will continue to aim at slowing down structural adjustment with the underlying intention of preserving existing jobs. In addition, they will attempt to enhance technological progress based on a concept of strategic industrial policies.

More interventions will in any case mean slower growth of imports from non-EC countries, but may have different implications for intra-EC trade. In agriculture and such sunset industries as steel and shipbuilding the signs clearly point to a renationalization of interventions with the necessary consequence of less extra- and intra-EC trade. Trade in textiles and clothing is subject to renewed international negotiations between sellers and buyers in 1991. Little change is expected for these industries since the EC cannot act independently without fear of retaliation. However, trade liberalization does not seem to be in store either. Concerning sunrise industries, budget constraints and politico-economic considerations will contribute to an enlargement of supranational competences at the EC level and hence, the establishment of a common market is likely to make headway in this area, albeit again at the expense of non-EC suppliers. The only exception from this gloomy picture could develop in the area of services. The collusion of interests among consumers, producers and non-EC governments suggests at least some degree of trade liberalization in services.

TECHNOLOGY AND GLOBAL COMPETITION: THE CHALLENGE AHEAD FOR NEWLY INDUSTRIALIZING ECONOMIES

Dieter Ernst
Senior Advisor
Research Programme "New Technologies, Industry and Trade"
Organisation for Economic Cooperation and Development (OECD)
Development Centre
94, rue Chardon-Lagache
F-75016 Paris

Introduction

This paper deals with the role of technology in the worldwide restructuring of industrial manufacturing and trade, and its impact on international competitiveness in a number of Asian and Latin American Newly Industrializing Economies (NIEs). It is based on a study undertaken for the OECD Development Centre which is just about to appear.

Apart from presenting a "state-of-the-art" review of what we know about this complex issue, this study analyses how the above basic transformations affect industrial and trade policy options for NIEs, and what this implies for economic rivalries and industrial co-operation between OECD member countries and NIEs. An important message of this study is that technological change affects developing countries mainly through its impact on global competition between the United States, Japan and Western Europe. Developing countries, including even the most successful first-tier Asian NIEs, find themselves to be marginal players in such games, unable to influence the rules of competition.

The post-war recovery of Japan and Western Europe led to a world where trade was dominated by three major trading blocs. This triangular relationship will be strengthened by the continuing success of Japan in international markets, the new alliance linking the United States and Canada, and the planned EC integration in

Europe-Asia-Pacific Studies in Economy and Technology
Kulessa (Ed.)
The Newly Industrializing Economies of Asia

1992. New technologies, particularly those that are knowledge-intensive and that lead to highly integrated production systems, have worked principally to the benefit of this charmed circle of countries. Other nations have succeeded in achieving rapid economic growth only by entering the markets and production networks of one or more of the dominant groups. This applies in particular to first-tier and second-tier Asian NIEs. So far, such export-oriented industrial growth has, however, remained heavily dependent on imports of generic technologies and product standards from OECD countries, and the same applies to most of the machinery and the critical parts and components used.

By the late 1970s, some of the countries, in particular South Korea and Taiwan, had in place effective strategies to utilise foreign technology acquisition as an important instrument of latecomer transformation. Based on strong monitoring capacities for international technology flows and sophisticated negotiation strategies, some of these countries were also starting to implement ambitious strategies to diversify their technology imports and to speed up the absorption of productivity - enhancing generic technologies. But just as the first benefits of such strategies were materialising, access to international technology became increasingly restricted. While international technology flows to China, India, South Korea, Taiwan and a small number of Asian nations continued to increase, they began to stagnate and sometimes even to dry up for a growing number of other developing countries. This applies in particular to imports of capital goods and to foreign direct investment flows. But even South Korea, the archetypical success story of export-led industrialization, is finding it increasingly difficult today to gain access to those products and process technologies which it needs for an upgrading of its industrial structure and product portfolio. In short, while new technologies contain a huge, and still largely untapped potential for unlocking new technology combinations and thus for increasing productivity, the blunt fact remains that most of the world appears to be locked out of significant options for productivity growth. Barring something to break the trend, the gap separating rich and poor nations is likely to increase.

Are there any realistic options for re-establishing international transfer of technology as an instrument for promoting global economic security? And more specifically, is there sufficient scope for establishing viable forms of international technological cooperation which would include rather than exclude developing countries, and which would reap the mutual benefits of complementarity? Much depends on future development of the international technology system. Will it become more closed and restrictive or will the barriers to entry for latecomers be reduced?

In what follows I will discuss two alternative scenarios for the future development of the international technology system.

The *pessimistic* scenario is one in which current trends towards a more restrictive system continue or even accelerate, and barriers to entry for latecomers become more severe. Its results will be devastating for global economic security. Yet, in the absence of major changes in our prevailing policy doctrine, it is quite plausible that it will become reality. Some would even argue that the die has already been cast, and that we are well on our way to an increasingly restrictive and balkanised international technology system. The *optimistic* scenario is one where the international technology system becomes more open and accessible to latecomers. While there are some factors which make the more optimistic scenario at least remotely possible, substantial modification of the OECD government policies and corporate strategies would be an essential prerequisite for such a scenario to materialise. From a long-term perspective, such changes would bring sizeable benefits both to OECD countries and to the NIEs. Nevertheless, policymakers and firms in the former may behave on the basis of shortsighted assessments of their interests, even at the expense of jeopardising those longer-term gains.

In discussing each of the scenarios, I will focus on the implications of the degree of openness of the technology system for three areas of economic interaction between OECD countries and NIEs. These are:

i) The prospects for NIE manufactured exports;

ii) The prospects for the NIEs' import capacity; and

iii) The implications for cross-investment links and international technology diffusion.

2. Scenario I: Intensifying Technological Protectionism

2.1 Key features

This scenario rests on two assumptions:

First, in industry after industry, we will witness a shift from US hegemony to a heterogeneous and consequently highly unstable global oligopoly, with American, Japanese and European companies fighting to position themselves in the lead. Their relative strengths differ, of course, depending on the sector and technology we are talking about.

Second, we assume that at least some other actors, in particular a few NIEs in Asia and Latin America, are finally able to enter this global oligopoly, at least in a few select industrial sectors and technology fields. In terms of industrial sectors, this would go well beyond clothing and toys and would include shipbuilding, steel, cars and components, consumer electronics (including VCRs), computer peripherals and (with some question marks) PCs, and semiconductor commodities (in particular D-RAMs) - to mention but a few in a long list of possible candidates.

In terms of technology, excellence in manufacturing engineering, as practiced for instance in South Korea and Taiwan, is certainly an area open to dedicated latecomer entry strategies. But even in such sophisticated areas as software engineering and circuit design, it cannot be excluded that some of these NIEs will accumulate sufficient technological capabilities, say within the next five years.

One could in fact argue that the relative success of latecomers to industrialisation is a reflection of the aforementioned intra-OECD rivalry and the concomitant destabilisation of existing global oligopolies. In a number of cases, growing intra-OECD rivalry may have improved considerably the scope for latecomer strategies. In principle, intensified competition among American, Japanese and European companies can drive down the cost of technology and of some of the capital equipment and final products which embody such technology. A case in point is the drastic long-term price decline for semiconductor commodities, in particular D-RAMs, and simple micro-controllers and - processors which, depending on market structures and competitive pressures, can lead to equally drastic price falls in a number of electronic consumer devices and computer-based machinery. In the latter case, a vast potential for productivity gains would be opened up, at least for those countries that have sufficient resources (both in terms of finance and technological capabilities) to buy and absorb such technologies. To a certain degree, growing intra-OECD rivalry has also increased the diversification of the sources of international technology flows, thereby expanding considerably the options open to technology importers. In addition, latecomers can compare and learn from, the experience of the leading oligopolists, particularly their failures, in reducing costs and adapting products and the distribution system to buyer needs.

Through judicious strategies of "creative imitation", latecomers can avoid being trapped into huge R & D cost burdens. Finally, at least in areas where incremental technological change prevails, latecomers have the great advantage of being able to set clear targets for development and engineering activities.

Yet this is by no means the full story to be told. Global oligopolies are not only intrinsically unstable and tend towards self-destruction, but they are also challenged from outside. In such a situation of extreme volatility and unpredictable risks, it is not at all clear to what degree latecomers can reap the potential benefits of increasing intra-OECD rivalries. It might be argued in fact that under conditions of "destructive" oligopolistic competition, all major actors involved in the global oligopoly will try to raise the barriers to entry by almost any means. An impressive arsenal of policy instruments is currently being assembled by governments in nearly all major OECD countries, and in some NIEs, to implement an increasingly aggressive "high-tech neo-mercantilism". At the same time, corporate management in the United States, as much as in Japan and Western Europe, is experimenting with new strategies for sustaining technological leadership which would allow for strengthening of the "appropriability regime" of new technologies and, at the same time, raising the threshold level for their implementation. The following strategies should be mentioned in this context:

i) Internalising sources of technological change, that is, aggressive strategies of worldwide sourcing for technological building blocs, and increasingly also for applied and even fundamental research.

ii) Establishing absolute cost or differentiation advantages in technology development activities:

- Economies of scale and learning economies involved

in R & D give large and experienced firms an absolute cost advantage;

- Due to the high fixed cost burden of R & D, the firm with the largest market share can realise the lowest unit costs of R & D;

- Particularly for the main building blocs of advanced electronics (that is, 32-bit microprocessors), investment thresholds for product development are dramatically increasing, which for all practical purposes, precludes the entry of latecomers;

- Large and vertically integrated companies have a superior capacity to exploit technological interrelationships (cost sharing of R & D) through cross-subsidisation; transfer of skills from one activity to another; etc.); and, finally,

- Incremental product and process refinements are often much more scale-sensitive than basic innovations.

iii) Broadening the firm's skill basis, in particular through the worldwide relocation of at least some elements of the research / development / engineering chain to areas where skilled labour is available cheaply.

iv) Restricting the rate of technology diffusion, by means of aggressive strategies on intellectual property rights, and through a policy of "pervasive secrecy", treating all contacts with outsiders, even buyers, as a threat to proprietary know-how.

v) Increasing the threshold barriers to the implementation of new technologies. It has been argued for instance that threatened market and technology leaders may consider huge, very costly and highly centralised systems of factory automation as a convenient weapon to prevent new competitors from gaining a market share or even entering the market. Unable to shoulder such huge capital burdens and risks, less powerful companies are expected to rapidly lose market shares, to end up in small market niches, or to be driven out of the market altogether.

Such strategies do not always meet with unalloyed success and often produce quite contradictory results. Nevertheless, assuming that OECD firms and governments are capable of learning-by-doing, it can be expected that the international technology system will become less accessible to all but a privileged few NIE firms with sufficient muscle to stay in the bout. In fact, much of this has already become reality. This applies in particular to technology flows from the OECD region to developing countries, with the exception of a few NIEs in East and Southeast Asia and China. Since the early 1980s, the main indicators of the volume of international technology flows - foreign direct investment, capital goods imports, payments for licenses and know-how, and official technical assistance - show an unprecedented shrinkage of technology flows to developing countries.

2.2 Implications for trade and investment links between the OECD region and NIEs

If the international technology system becomes more restrictive, what will be the implications for trade and investment links between the OECD region and NIEs, and how will this affect international technology diffusion?

2.2.1 Prospects for NIE manufactured exports

The first and most obvious consequence would be an erosion of the competitiveness of NIE manufactured exports in OECD markets. Without continued access to new product and process technologies, NIE firms would not be able to keep abreast of rapid shifts to new generations of products, nor would they be able to upgrade their production capabilities to compete with the advanced manufacturing technologies being diffused in the OECD countries. To the extent that the growth of certain NIEs is driven by manufactured exports, their economies would slow down substantially and perhaps even stagnate. Nor would the more advanced NIEs be able to recover their competitive advantage in traditional labour-intensive manufactures like shoes, garments, toys, etc., since there are already a number of other less developed countries which have become highly competitive in these areas. Thus their export prospects would be far dimmer than in the past.

Anticipating such a scenario - which to an extent is already being played out - the NIEs have been trying to take countermeasures. Most importantly, they are more actively searching out all opportunities to gain access to the technologies they need. They have been forced to experiment with new forms of technology co-operation. A "window of opportunity" opened, for example, to South Korean chaebol a few years ago when they were able to trade low cost manufacturing capacity and quick plant start-up capabilities in semiconductors for design expertise of US semiconductor firms searching for ways to staunch the flow of Japanese chips into the US market. As the South Korean firms have become more sophisticated technologically, however, their erstwhile US partners are beginning to view them as a competitive threat, and are more reluctant to transfer their advanced technologies.

The NIEs are also working hard at diversifying their export markets, to lessen their dependence on the US market where a rising tide of non-tariff restrictions is making market access more difficult. In this scenario, such restrictions become more extensive in the future. In addition, the European Community after 1992 is likely to become much more highly protected from manufactured imports from the NIEs, with the exception of a few countries in the European periphery with close links to one or another European economy (something like Mexico's relationship to the United States). Large European technology-based oligopolists will continue to forge closer co-operative links in R & D, but to the exclusion of non-EC firms. Thus the European market does not offer much promise of compensating, even in small measure, for the reduction in US market penetration.

Third, it is assumed that the Japanese market will continue to open up under pressure of intensifying trade conflicts with the United States and the EC. In this scenario, however, the process is painfully slow and highly selective. In short, the Japanese government, faced with the prospect of growing domestic opposition to drastic liberalisation, might seek to manage it in such a way that trade concessions are made bilaterally with Japan's major trading partners - the United States and the EC - in exchange for continued market access. At the same time, the NIEs - which for Japan are a less strategic market at present - would bear the brunt of efforts by Japan to restrict liberalisation to levels that are politically acceptable to powerful interest groups. Thus NIE exports would have only limited access to the Japanese market, and then only for less sophisticated products.

With no OECD market able to compensate adequately, then, for declining export growth to the United States, the NIEs would have to look towards developing country markets, but increased OECD protectionism is certain to slow the growth of the developing world and thus impair import capacities.

2.2.2 Prospects for NIE import capacity

The debt-induced crises of many Latin American NIEs since the beginning of the 1980s have dramatically demonstrated the impact of impaired NIE import capacity on US export performance. If the import capacity of other NIEs is similarly impaired by a steep decline in their export growth, there would be severe repercussions for the export performance especially of the capital and intermediate goods industries of OECD countries. For example, almost two-thirds of Japan's textile machinery exports are to other Asian countries, with South Korea, Taiwan and China being the three largest markets. A major decline in their textile industries would adversely affect not only Japanese but also Swiss, German, Italian and other textile machinery producers. Similarly, some NIEs have become major markets for electronics industry-related production equipment, the bulk of which is still made by OECD firms. A serious retrenchment in South Korea's semiconductor industry would have a strong negative impact on US and Japanese semiconductor equipment manufacturers. Likewise, the stagnation of the South Korean or Mexican or other NIE automobile industries would hurt Swedish, German, Japanese, United States, and other sophisticated machine tools manufacturers.

2.2.3 Implications for cross-investment links and technology diffusion

This scenario involves a worsening of the environment for collaboration of all kinds between OECD and NIE firms. An atmosphere of hostility and suspicion toward the NIEs prevails in the OECD region. OECD firms become more guarded in their contacts with NIE firms, which they perceive primarily as potential competitors. To the extent that OECD firms continue to invest in the NIEs, they insist, wherever possible, on 100 per cent ownership as a way of safeguarding proprietary technology. Appointing expatriates to key technical posts also becomes a major concern. Licensing agreements are linked to rather "peripheral" or mature technologies. Under such conditions, collaboration with NIE firms is aimed principally at securing low cost manufacturing capacity or at gaining access to a potentially large NIE market. Technology flows are minimised by every available means. In addition, governments of OECD member countries would also escalate bilateral pressures on major NIE exporters to tighten their protection of intellectual property.

Because in such a scenario NIE technology development would be stunted by the restrictive practices of OECD firms and governments, NIE firms would not have much scope for developing complementary assets which could make them attractive partners for OECD companies. In this restrictive scenario, technology exports from NIE firms to OECD firms, by definition, would remain insignificant. NIE firms seeking to gain access to those technologies by investing in OECD countries, would face drastically tighter restrictions on their ability to acquire equity stakes in high technology firms.

The repeated frustration of NIE firms' efforts to gain access to foreign technologies would make them more isolationist in their technology policies, with more countries finding the traditional path of "self-reliance" pursued by India and China the "lesser of two evils". As a result, the prospects for OECD firms to export capital goods and in general to have access to NIE markets would become increasingly dim.

3 Scenario II: Barriers to International Technology Diffusion Decline

3.1 Key features

This alternative (more optimistic) scenario is much less likely to materialise than the previous one, although it would certainly have much more positive implications for global economic security. Major changes are required, both in government policies and in company strategies, and this applies to all actors involved in the international economy. As a matter of fact, in nearly all major OECD countries the proliferation of high-tech neo-mercantilism has gathered such momentum that it will be very difficult to reverse it. Important and often quite far-reaching changes have taken place in the industrial and trade policy doctrine, as well as in the relevant institutional set-up. Examples include the considerable softening of anti-cartel policies, both in the United States and Western Europe, and institutional innovations such as Sematech, the HDTV consortium, ESPRIT and EUREKA which, on a so far unprecedented scale allow firms and governments to merge their increasingly aggressive competitive strategies.

Nevertheless, there are at least some chances that a break will occur in the current trend towards increasing barriers to international technology diffusion, which in turn could open up new possibilities for industrial co-operation between OECD member countries and NIEs.

Two main assumptions underlie this scenario:

i) fundamental shifts in the international demand structure, particularly for manufactured exports, will open up new possibilities for redirecting not only international trade flows, but also international investment and technology flows. In particular, we assume that Japan's role in compensating for a decline of US demand for manufactured exports will materialise earlier and on a larger scale than foreseen in our first scenario.

ii) It is possible to imagine that states and firms

> would come to realise in time that current trends towards an increasingly restrictive international technology system, if allowed to continue, would have damaging (even disastrous) consequences for all concerned. As a result, the policy debate would shift from an exclusive concern with the "NIEs' competitive threat" to a more balanced view, where competition would not necessarily exclude co-operation with NIEs. Under such circumstances, it might not be impossible any longer to see the emergence of broader and increasingly complementary forms of technological co-operation between OECD member countries and NIEs.

This second scenario must be distinguished sharply from the neo-liberal dream of a free market world economy. The invisible hand of market forces will certainly not produce the fundamental changes required for reducing barriers to international technology diffusion. Rather, for this scenario to materialise, we need the visible hand of substantially modified company strategies and government policies.

I also do not intend to promote unrealistic expectations: a restructuring of the world trading and technology system in a way which would substantially redistribute power away from the technology-based oligopolists is unlikely to materialise any time soon. The scenario suggested here is unlikely to reduce substantially the huge gap in wealth and economic power between the OECD region and even the most successful NIEs. Rather, it is an attempt to identify the limits of the possible, given the severe constraints imposed by global competition. It is worth stressing that in some instances the leading oligopolists themselves may be in the best position to anticipate and benefit from movements in new directions which would reduce the barriers to international technology diffusion. At the same time, it would be a serious mistake to ascribe omnipotence to the IBMs, NECs and Philips of this world and other "high tech" potentates. Not only do they leave quite considerable markets uncovered, but even those they do cover they do not always cover well. Moreover, even they need a network of suppliers and subcontractors to maintain their pre-eminence in the main growth markets of the future.

3.2 Shifts in the international demand structure for manufactured exports

In what follows, I will present some hypotheses on how the international demand structure for manufactured exports could change and what this could imply for international technology diffusion.

So far, the United States has been, by far, the main market for manufactured exports, and this applies in particular to those originating from developing countries. Between 1981 and 1984, US imports of manufactured goods from developing countries more than doubled, from $ 34 billion to $ 70 billion, while Japanese imports rose by only $ 2 billion and European imports actually declined. And in 1985, 62 per cent of the developing countries' exports of manufactured products to OECD countries went to the United States. "... During the first half of the 1980s, when demand declined and then stagnated in the other developed countries, the US became the buyer of last resort and was a major impetus to growth for the developing countries", that is, basically for the first-tier Asian NIEs.

In the future, the importance of the US economy for manufactured exports is bound to decline. This is a simple reflection of three fundamental structural imbalances which have accumulated in the US economy since the late 1970s: a record debt (more than $ 400 billion by the end of 1987); a booming US trade deficit (more than $ 140 billion by the end of 1987); and, finally, a towering US federal budget deficit (more than $ 150 billion at the end of fiscal year 1987). As a result of such major imbalances, drastic changes are bound to occur in the integration of the US economy to world markets. Given the limitations to an expansion of US exports, whether manufactured or services, most of this adjustment has to come from a drastic reduction of US imports, whether recession-induced or via selective import substitution, as part of a deliberate industrial policy. In other words, the heavy concentration of world industrial exports on the US economy has become an anachronism which cannot be sustained for long.

i) Currently, the US absorbs about 70 per cent of the manufacturing exports of the developing world, while Japan absorbs only about 8 per cent. With an economy roughly two-thirds to three-quarters as large as the American economy, that is obviously a situation that must change. On the one hand, any US administration must lower the balance of payments deficit, and thus will try to reduce import penetration. On the other hand, Japan is coming under increasing pressure from practically everybody else, to internationalise its economy, that is, to open it to imports and foreign investment.

ii) Japan's extremely biased integration into world trade flows of industrial products is unlikely to continue. Today, Japan's dominant position in world industrial exports goes hand in hand with its low profile as an importer of manufactured products. In the early 1980s, Japan's imports of manufactured goods were about the same as those of Switzerland, a country with about 5 per cent of Japan's population. Of all major OECD countries, Japan is the only country where large exports in key industrial sectors are not matched by large imports. In fact, whenever Japan had a strong export industry, imports in that industry were likely to be close to zero. Finally, between 1975 and 1983, while the average import-penetration ratio for manufactured goods rose from 7 per cent to 10.3 per cent in the United States, and from 24 per cent to 35 per cent in Germany, and also in France and Italy, in Japan it only rose from 4.9 to 5.3 per cent.

In the future, however, imports of manufactured goods are likely to increase substantially in Japan. One reason is the yen appreciation which has acted as a catalyst for Japanese firms to drastically expand their global sourcing strategies. Historical experience tells us that global sourcing strategies are bound to lead to growing import penetration, because they increase intra-industry trade. This may also induce Japanese companies to reconsider their so far highly restrictive policies on technology transfer.

Of even greater importance, however, is that intensifying international trade conflicts will force the Japanese government, willy-nilly, to proceed with market liberalisation in a growing number of industrial sectors. And while the US administration makes the most noise, exporters from Asian first- and second-tier NIEs, and from some European countries, may well draw the greatest benefits from such market liberalisation. Between 1983 and 1988, for example, Japan's manufactured imports from the first-tier NIEs (South Korea, Taiwan, Hong Kong and Singapore) increased from 14 to 19 per cent of total manufactured imports.

In short, the Japanese economy will become more internationalised, and its importance as a market for world industrial exports will increase quite substantially. Among the first to realise this and to adopt aggressive market penetration strategies, have been South Korean and Taiwanese companies, particularly in the field of consumer devices.

However, it is difficult to see how Japan, even under the best of circumstances, could ever compensate Asian NIEs for their declining share of the US market which is "... simply too large to be replaced by any single country". This becomes clear when we compare the absolute figures involved. In 1985, the US market for NIEs' manufactured exports was nearly ten times larger than that of Japan, \$ 52.3 billion versus \$ 5.8 billion. And in 1987, Japan's imports from the Asian NIEs were only about one-third of US imports from those countries. In short, while Japan's market is likely to become more accessible to manufactured exports from NIEs, this will be a relatively slow process.

iii) Markets in NIEs are bound to become more important for world industrial exports. This applies in particular to exports of capital goods and of related services, where a huge demand potential exists not only in the quasi-continental economies of China, India and Brazil, but also in a number of first- and second-tier NIEs in Asia and Latin America. While in Asia, particularly in the first-tier NIEs, this potential is already being translated into concrete projects, in Latin America the current debt crisis is a major barrier.

A case in point are demand projections for first-tier Asian NIEs in one of the archetypical high-technology industries: semiconductors. Particularly for "hot growth" products like cMOS integrated circuits and microwave transistors, a massive shift of demand is under way from the US to Japan, and increasingly also to South Korea, Taiwan and Singapore. In 1985, the Japanese market share for these two crucial product groups was 46 and 37 per cent respectively, and thus had overtaken a combined US/Canadian share of 32 and 27 per cent. There are strong indications that this is a long-term, irreversible trend. In other words, the US market, which used to be the Mecca of worldwide semiconductor demand, is unlikely to retain much longer such a privileged position.

Of particular interest are recent projections by the Semiconductor Industry Association (SIA) that till 1990 the market volume in South Korea, Taiwan and Singapore will more than double from about $ 2 billion to $ 5.4 billion, and thus will reach or even surpass Europe's demand levels.

iv) A particularly interesting development takes place in the CMEA region, where new possibilities for technology co-operation with NIEs could materialise. Take for instance the Soviet Union. In order to proceed with its current "modernisation drive", this country will have to increase drastically its international trade and technology imports.

Given the still quite rigid position of the US administration on technology export controls, Europeans, Japanese and some NIEs are likely to play an increasingly important role in this context.

"Significant market opportunities in the Eastern bloc will thus develop, with the Europeans, the Japanese, and South Koreans expanding the scope of their linkages already in place. (Their) economic ties (with CMEA countries) will thus accelerate far ahead of the Americans, and as the military threat lessens for the Europeans, US efforts to restrict trade, in concert with COCOM partners, will face greater resistance."

Together with Asian NIEs, China, and India, markets in CMEA countries, and in particular the Soviet Union, will thus significantly increase their importance as future high growth markets.

In this context, I would like to underline the following important fact: both for CMEA countries and for China, trade requirements revolve primarily around low and moderately R&D-intensive products. Apart from the already predominant countries from the EC (in particular the FRG), this opens up new and quite substantial export possibilities for NIEs.

Finally, two major questions are hanging over this possible geographic decentralisation of demand for manufactured exports:

i) What will be the implications resulting from the establishment of a Common European Market in 1992? Will this increase the attractiveness of Europe as an export market and as a partner for technology cooperation, or rather, will it lead to a selective isolation of Europe from the world economy, and add further to the already quite strong trends towards regional economic power blocs with a minimum of mutual interconnection?

ii) Will it be possible to overcome the deep and fundamental crisis of the international financial system? After all, international technology co-operation is simply not feasible in the context of global financial turmoil and crisis. Particularly for Latin American NIEs, the spiralling debt crisis, combined with the growing instability of international financial markets, has drastically reduced their capacity to import capital goods.

3.3 From international transfer of technology to complementary technology co-operation

My second assumption takes as a starting point some of the more creative efforts at technical collaboration between OECD firms and NIE firms. It also encompasses more extensive and richer technical collaboration among NIE firms themselves. Of course, I am also referring to the ongoing development of technology exchanges between the large South Korean chaebol and large-scale enterprises in other NIEs and their counterparts in OECD countries. The mutual benefits from such exchanges increase over time, as the NIE firms become more adept at product and process innovation and thus have something more to offer than efficient manufacturing capacity or cash reserves. The relationship becomes more durable and even evolves to the point where technology development is a joint product of two or more firms. These cross-technology links also serve as avenues for assuring mutual market access.

Such co-operation need not - and ideally should not - be limited to links between the leading oligopolists in the OECD and the NIEs. One important source of technology for NIE firms in the past has been the highly dynamic start-up firms of Silicon Valley and their equivalents elsewhere. By taking small equity shares in, or buying technology, from such firms, the NIE firms could remain close to state-of-the-art. Such opportunities may be disappearing soon, as this sort of firm becomes a candidate for the "endangered species" register. In some cases large NIE firms have taken over such firms to internalise their know-how. Far more frequently, OECD oligopolists have been the predators. Many have come to recognise that in their eagerness to internalise knowledge, they may be "killing the goose that lays the golden egg". In our optimistic scenario, effective policy measures as well as changes in firms' strategies would ensure the renewed vigour of the archetypal "born-in-a-garage" firm. Policy changes would be needed not just in OECD countries themselves, but also in many NIEs to inject more dynamism into the entrepreneurial small and medium firm sector. One development which might help to strengthen such small- and medium-scale firms financially, both in the OECD and in the NIEs, would be the formation of networks of such firms in different countries that may then be able to interface with comparable networks elsewhere. For example, trade associations of machine tool builders in an OECD country and a NIE may establish communications channels which would facilitate technical collaboration between members of the two associations. Some such links already exist.

The possibility for establishing others are limitless. In some cases the interface between two networks could be mediated by "model" firms in each country that have themselves established broad-ranging technical collaboration. For example, a South Korean chaebol and a German conglomerate enter into a technical co-operation agreement which involves the mutual interaction of the two firms' subcontractor networks in the design and development of common parts and components, subsystems, etc.

Similar sorts of collaboration could be envisioned between different NIE firms. The technical co-operation accord between Argentina and Brazil covering a range of industries and technologies, while still at an early stage of implementation, at least suggests the possibilities that may exist.

Regional integration is also advancing in Southeast Asia, with growing intra-regional, intrafirm trade organised by large Japanese conglomerates and their supplier networks. Again the evidence does not yet exist to be able to assess what the implications of this development will be for the economies of the region and, more specifically, for their technological capabilities. If such regional integration is to be fruitful, it needs to be accompanied by a greater opening of the NIEs towards trade with their neighbours and, in the case of the Asian region, a much more dramatic opening of the Japanese market to the exports of its NIE neighbours.

3.3.1 Prospects for manufactured trade flows

Our optimistic scenario would allow much greater scope for continued expansion of NIE exports of a variety of manufacturers. By allowing the more advanced NIEs to scale down their production of certain more labour-intensive products without major social dislocations, it would also make it easier for other developing countries to step into the breach left by the first-tier NIEs. As a consequence, significant shifts in the composition of international trade flows would be likely.

First, complementarity of technologies and production structures between the more advanced NIEs and the OECD countries should increase. In other words, both may have advanced machine tool sectors, but they would produce complementary elements of a product set. Certain models might, for reasons of accumulated experience (skill availabilities, relative costs, etc.), be more suitably produced in one location, other models in another. Traditional "factor endowment" explanations of such patterns of specialisation would be of extremely limited usefulness.

Secondly, if this complementarity of production structures were to evolve, then intra-industry trade flows between the NIEs and the OECD countries would grow in importance relative to inter-industry trade. Trade would tend toward greater balance, as manufactured exports from OECD to the NIEs would grow simultaneously with exports in the other direction.

Thirdly, capital goods producers in the OECD countries would experience robust demand in the NIEs as the latter invest in upgrading production. Links between the capital goods suppliers of the NIEs and the OECD would enable each of them to serve the other's market better since user/producer links are especially crucial in this sector.

3.3.2 Prospects for cross-investment and technology diffusion

Both investment and technology would have to flow increasingly in two directions. The same "creative tension" between collaboration and competition which characterises relations among the OECD firms would come to characterise relations between OECD and their NIE counterparts. One would expect to observe a growing number of instances of OECD firms setting up R & D and design facilities in certain NIEs and vice versa. Cross-licensing agreements between OECD firms and NIE firms would proliferate as firms pooled technologies, production capabilities, and markets.

Those NIE firms which are not yet in a position to become technology suppliers, would at least be able to gain access to technologies on more favourable terms than under the pessimistic scenario. A growing number of NIE firms would become technology licensors in competition with OECD firms, giving buyers a broader range of options on more attractive terms. Increasing foreign investment flows from the more advanced NIEs into other developing countries would also broaden the foreign capital base. Yet whether technology diffusion via FDI by NIE firms is more effective than that occurring via FDI by OECD firms, cannot be known without more empirical evidence.

Other developing countries may be integrated more extensively into regional investment flows as the NIEs broaden their subcontracting networks and make more labour-intensive components and sub-assemblies in lower cost regional locations. The OECD firms with investment ties and technology exchanges with NIE firms would also make use of those supplier networks, while the NIE firms presumably would utilise them within or on the perimeter of the OECD markets, for example, in Spain or Portugal for the EC market, in Mexico or Canada for the US, in Southeast Asia for Japan.

4. Establishing Viable Forms of Industrial Co-Operation between OECD Countries and NIEs: Concluding Remarks

How can viable forms of international technological co-operation be established which would not be restricted to countries from the OECD and the CMEA, but would increasingly include NIEs and other, less developed Third World societies?

Obviously, established concepts of technological co-operation require some careful reconsideration. OECD countries still tend to subsume such arrangements under the heading of technical aid, where the non-OECD country remains a mere receiver. Yet, at least for NIEs, such concepts have become quite obsolete. The challenge today in fact is to ensure a transition towards a more complementary relationship, where both partners would bring in their respective strengths, and which would open up new possibilities for expanding mutual flows of trade, investment and technology.

North-South technological co-operation which does not allow for more complementary relationships would hardly be of interest to

NIEs. Viewed from an OECD country perspective, insisting on traditional concepts of "technical aid" would in fact be quite harmful; it would preclude reaping the benefits of increasing intra-industry trade and investment flows, and it would force member countries into increasingly tough rounds of mutually harmful neo-mercantilism. It is in the long-term interest of OECD countries to generate sufficient demand for new technologies and related capital goods in as many developing countries as possible. Strengthening the technological capabilities of developing countries should not be viewed as running counter to the interests of OECD countries. It could be an important mechanism for arresting the recessionary demand conditions that are likely to confront most of the OECD region's high-tech industries in the years to come. As a matter of fact, the growth of the major OECD economies increasingly depends on the growth of world demand for the output of their high-tech industries and related services. Promoting the international diffusion of new technologies should and can be done without endangering the competitive position of OECD economies. According to a recent study, commissioned by the Overseas Development Council "... the acceleration of technological development in the Third World will not undermine the US competitive position, because science-based development is a cumulative process in which the innovative capacity of US institutions and corporations will continue to support a technological edge, provided industrial growth keeps pace with scientific discovery". This, in turn, depends on whether or not demand growth is sufficiently large for US industrial exports which, it is argued, would not be possible without growing Third World markets. "Thus, the more rapid the adoption and diffusion of new microelectronics technologies in the world economy, the stronger the relative competitive position of the US is likely to be." Hopefully, such far-sighted concepts will gain in importance in future debates about industrial adjustment requirements of OECD member countries.

THE NEWLY INDUSTRIALIZING ECONOMIES AS MODELS FOR ESTABLISHING A HIGHLY COMPETITIVE INDUSTRIAL BASE - WHAT LESSONS TO LEARN?

Wolfgang Hillebrand
Senior Industrial Economist
German Development Institute (GDI)
Fraunhoferstrasse 33 - 36
D-1000 Berlin 10

1. Differing Perceptions of the Mechanisms Underlying Growth in Asian NIEs

The amazing success of the "Newly Industrializing Economies (NIEs)" in Asia as large-scale exporters of industrial goods has aroused the interest of both policymakers and academics from the outset. To date, however, their various attempts to explain the dynamics of export-oriented late industrialization in Southeast and East Asia have failed to produce a consensus as regards the key determinants and the links between them:

- One school of thought, which may be labelled the "liberal school", maintains that the success of Singapore, Hong Kong, Taiwan and Korea (Rep.) is mainly due to the fact that these economies have, by and large, "got their prices right", i.e. they maintained a competitive exchange rate, relied on low levels of effective protection, emphasized competition on domestic markets, implemented policies that did not, in aggregato, discriminate between broad groups of industrial activity, and reduced the role of government as the economy became more complex.[1]

- Another school of thought, which may be labelled the "structuralist school", feels that a broader view is needed to understand more fully the phenomenal rise of the first generation of Asian NIEs. While not denying the importance of

---
[1] World Bank, World Development Report 1987, p. 71

Europe-Asia-Pacific Studies in Economy and Technology
Kulessa (Ed.)
The Newly Industrializing Economies of Asia

"getting the prices broadly right" and the early emphasis on exports as favourable conditions for successful industrialization, this school advances additional key factors, namely the importance of a strong, capable government (including a strong national consensus on long-term economic goals), sound industrial targeting, selective industrial policies and infant industry protection, at least in the larger countries.[2]

A deeper understanding of the reasons underlying successful industrial restructuring is by no means of merely academic interest. If the basic message is that a free market economy, a competitive environment, free and unrestricted trade and a philosophy of economic management which relies on general rather than specific policies, together form a sufficient and sound base for establishing international competitive industries, export-oriented industrialization strategy might be a distinctly feasible proposition for any developing country provided that the markets are allowed "to do the job". If, however, the basic message is that a complex strategy of "managed economic and social change" is necessary for overcoming economic backwardness - such as has in fact been adopted by most of the Third World star performers, the lessons which can and should be learned from the Southeast and East Asian development models will differ radically from neoliberal prescriptions. In the following, an interpretation along the lines of the "structuralist school" will be presented.

2. The Role of Long-Range Visions

Planning concepts relevant to economic decision-making have never been based on the assumption of a stable external and internal

---

[2] A full account on the controversies over the different theories of allocation is given in Hillebrand W. (1990) Industrial and Technological Strategies of Newly Industrializing Countries. Controversies over Theories of Allocations and Conclusions Based on the Korean Experience. (Forthcoming) Berlin.

environment, full predictability of future events and the feasibility of designing optimal programmes for securing a given result once and for all. Instead, planning approaches in both developed and developing market economies have sought to facilitate decentralized decision-making as the various actors are confronted with a superabundance of data which make the selection of key data and information a difficult and extremely time-consuming process. In other words, planning must help transform the highly disparate *data* on internal resources, existing and emerging technologies, international market trends, international competitors, etc., into *information*, thereby facilitating the clarification of relevant issues from the corporate and public policymakers' perspective, and all this under heavy pressure of time.[3] It seems that Singapore, Taiwan and Korea (Rep.) have indeed established management systems and decision-making structures allowing for sufficient openness and flexibility at a fairly early stage of development; these are still of immediate relevance today, as is illustrated by a recent statement of the Korean Ministry of Science and Technology on the characteristics needed in the administration of science and technology in the future:

"First an overall administration is necessary to oversee the many complex fields. Second, we need a systematic organization to coordinate the extremely diversified policy measures. The third requirement is that the administration must be flexible due to the introduction of rapidly changing new technologies. In addition, the administration must be creative for the development of unprecedented ideas. The administration must also be a leading one. This will encourage researchers and industrialists to actively engage in R & D activities towards the national development. Finally, the administration must be future-oriented to forecast the

----

3 Weiss D. (1981) Some Reflections on Outward-Looking Economic Management in a Turbulent International Environment. L'Egypte Contemporaine, Revue Trimestrelle de la Société Egyptienne d'Economie Politique, de Statistique et de Législation, Cairo, No. 385.

Sagasti F. (1988) National Development Planning in Turbulent Times: New Approaches and Criteria for Institutional Design. World Development, 16:4, pp. 431-448.

long-term trends of this vastly complicated field".[4]

Consequently, it would be a misconception to believe that although more emphasis will be placed on decentralized decision-making in the 1990s, countries such as Korea (Rep.), Taiwan and Singapore will by and large abandon their basic philosophy of economic management which up to now has been based on a judicious mix of long-range visions and medium-term and short-term planning.

It seems that it has primarily been the long-term visions meant to probe future social and economic needs and identify the economic and social sectors and branches of science and technology which could help meet such needs which have been highly instrumental in framing national policies and supporting anticipatory decision-making in business; this becomes clear from a glance back to the 1960s and 1970s:

- In Korea (Rep.) various long-term visions of strategic importance have been developed: in *1967* envisaging the establishment of a fully integrated and coherent industrial structure by the end of the seventies; in *1976* the "Long-Term Prospect for Economic and Social Development 1977 - 1991", which prepared the ground for a transition from extensive to intensive (technology-based) industrialization and socially more equitable growth; *in the early 1980s* envisaging the establishment of a pluralist society and a welfare state by the mid-1990s and *in the mid-1980s* the vision of "Korea 2000", setting out the broad outlines of Korea as a future mature society.

- As for Singapore, the following can be seen as visions of overriding importance in guiding future economic and social change: The Winsemius Report drawn up in 1961, arguing, inter

----

4 Ministry of Science and Technology (1987) Introduction to Science and Technology, Republic of Korea, Seoul, p. 72.

alia, for a radical shift towards export-oriented industrialization, a strategy of "industrialization by invitation" (attraction of as much foreign capital as possible) and for strong public institutions to spearhead the industrial drive; the concept for a "New Industrial Policy" developed in the *early 1970s* and was implemented from the end of the same decade (second industrial revolution), calling for the full use of modern technology, the establishment of "high-tech industries", namely a fully integrated electronics complex (hardware/software), biotechnology, a service-oriented aircraft and aerospace industry; and "finally", the vision of the *late 1970s* becoming a "global city" by the year 2000, i.e. a regional and world centre for international trade and production-oriented services (banking, finance, insurance, communication).

- In Taiwan, too, the industrialization process was strategically planned, including the deliberate development of intermediate industries and capital goods industries from the *early 1970s* and an increasing emphasis on high-technology industries from the late 1970s. As a result, the industrial structure which has emerged by the end of the 1980s is not only a fairly diversified one but also a fairly integrated one.[5]

It is important to note that none of the "strategic blueprints" summarized above was prepared by "armchair strategists"; they resulted from careful analytical work carried out by numerous bodies and experts which took stock of the contemporary state of

----

[5] A detailed assessment of the Taiwanese approach to economic management is given by Taake H. H. (1973) Politische Planungs- und administrative Entscheidungsprozesse bei der Aufstellung und Durchführung von Entwicklungsplänen. Empirische Analyse einiger ostasiatischer Länder unter besonderer Herausstellung Taiwans, Berlin. See also Gälli A. (1988) Taiwan ROC: Eine chinesische Herausforderung. Von der Handelsmacht zum Technologiezentrum. München.

internal and external affairs, continuously scanned emerging trends in the world economy and thoroughly assessed the strategies being pursued by relevant competitors. It was only these broad-based and careful approaches to exploring the future which prepared the ground for "anticipatory decision-making" in government, business and intermediary institutions and hence the timely concentration of scarce resources in areas of critical importance.

3. The Relevance of Future-Oriented Value Systems, Homogeneous Social Structures, Pro-Industrial Elites and External Pressures

Planning is not a matter of drafting plans. Nor is planning which is based on critical reviews of past trends, the present situation and possible future trends at variance with decentralized decision-making; instead it can support and facilitate it. Consequently, the question which really matters has been why some countries are apparently better able than others to organize purposeful action guided by a judicious mix of flexible, long-term and medium-term planning and decentralized decision-making based on market signals. Theories of economic and social change have so far not produced a convincing answer to this question. Consequently, the explanation which follows is highly speculative in nature and largely based on "soft categories". On that basis the ability of the first generation of Asian NIEs (Hong Kong excepted) to adopt a managed approach to economic and social change may be attributed to

- the pragmatic future-oriented value system held by the respective society as a whole, in which Confucianism plays a dominant role;

- a high degree of cultural homogeneity which is seen to facilitate agreement on long-term goals and the necessary short- and medium-term action to achieve them;

- the limited range of relevant development options available in view of the fact that all the countries in question are poorly endowed with natural resources and have therefore had to concentrate on human resources development, a resource which proved to be extremely helpful in surviving a period of radical technological change;

- the existence of a powerful pro-industrial elite with a strong development commitment which was able not only to concentrate resources in areas of priority concern over long periods but also to suppress any opposition trying to implement an alternative approach to economic and social change;

- and the pressures emanating from the international environment, namely military threat and turbulent changes in the world economy which facilitated national consensus-building and broad-based purposeful action at all levels of society.

This "explanation" may of course be rejected on the grounds that it reflects merely naive "cultural and psychological mysticism".[6] Even so, better explanations of why the first generation of Asian NIEs was able to design and implement a strategy of managed economic and social change have yet to be advanced.

4. Proactive Measures to Create Dynamic Competitive Advantages

According to neoclassical trade theory, industrial competence and

---

6 For a discussion of cultural factors in development with respect to Japan see Wiliams D. (1985) Beyond Political Economy: A Critique of Issues Raised in Chalmers Johnson's MITI and the Japanese Miracle. East Asia, 3:231-247.

international competitiveness develop best when a "stages approach to comparative advantage" is adopted.[7] Under free trade and free market conditions, developing countries are recommended to specialize in labour-intensive production lines at the early stage of their industrialization process. Countries at the intermediate stage of development lose their competitive strength in the labour-intensive sectors and should henceforth phase out labour-intensive lines and concentrate on more capital-intensive industries. Countries approaching industrial maturity should move from capital-intensive to skill- and technology-intensive industries.

This approach of "marching through the sectors" - implying fairly specialized production structures at any stage of industrial development - has always been challenged by proponents of growth pole theory and a strategy of unbalanced growth, who emphasize the importance of inter-industrial linkages and industrial and technological networks as a more reliable base for building up industrial competence and achieving a strong competitive position.[8]

The concept of concentrating on "poles of competitiveness" within the production system rather than establishing functionally unrelated sectors (as implied by the "stages approach to comparative advantage") rests on the assumption that a strong commitment in certain "families of industries" facilitates:

- economizing on indirect production costs (communication costs), finer-tuned meshing of production at the several

----

7 Balassa B. (1977) A "Stages Approach to Comparative Advantage". Washington.

8 Commission of the European Communities (1980) Industrial Specialization in Twelve European Countries Before and After 1973. Series FAST, Brussels, No. 1.

stages, more effective quality control;

- the chronological up-grading and continuous learning within and among industries, and

- the timely provision of complex-related infrastructural facilities (physical, human).

Although the process of industrialization in all the NIEs in question started along the lines recommended by the "stages approach to comparative advantage", it deviated substantially from that approach at the later stages of industrial development. Rather than being based on a strategy of simply "marching through the sectors", industrial growth in Asian NIEs was characterized by the alternative approach of "marching within the sectors", which transformed the structure of production within the various branches of industry and "families of industries".[9] As a result the industrial structure which has emerged in Asian NIEs can aptly be described as a system of (partially overlapping) industrial complexes including the so-called traditional industries such as textiles/clothing as core industries (cf. Table 1).

Moreover, industrial transformation which took place over the decades in Singapore, Taiwan and Korea (Rep.) was supported by highly selective policies, namely infant industry protection (Singapore excepted), preferential access to credits and foreign exchange, large-scale localization programmes to support the evolution of industrial and technological networks, mission-oriented R & D and manpower development and the active promotion of exports.

Although the degree and forms of state intervention in all these

----

9 Kaplinsky R. (1988) Industrial Restructuring in LDCs: The Role of Information Technology. Brighton (mimeo), pp. 33 - 36.

Table 1 - Industrial Complexes (Core Industries) in Singapore, Hong Kong, Taiwan and Korea (Rep.) at the end of the 1980

Countries / Core-Industries	Singapore	Hong Kong	Taiwan	Korea (Rep.)
<u>resource-based industries</u>				
- agro-industries	(x)		x(x)	
- chemical and petrochemical industries	xx		x(x)	xx
<u>labour-intensive industries</u>				
- clothing, textiles, shoe, leather	x	xx	xx	xx
<u>engineering industries</u>				
- shipbuilding/repair marine engineering	xx	(x)	(x)	xx
- automotive industry/parts			x	xx
- (other) non-electrical machinery			(x)	xx
- electrical machinery/ electronics	xx	xx	xx	xx

KEY: x = medium overall importance
xx = key industrial complex

Table 2 - Promotion of Key Industries in Korea (Rep.)

	Stage I (-1974)	Stage II (1975-80)	Stage III (1981-)
Benefiting industries	• Key industries receiving preferential treatment: shipbuilding, iron and steel, chemical fertilizer, power generation plant, synthetic fibres, motor vehicles, machinery, electronics, petroleum refining, industrial chemical pulp, pulp	• Strategic industry formally defined: petrochemicals, shipbuilding, machinery, electronics, iron and steel, petroleum refining, power-generation-plant, chemical fertilizer, defence industry, aviation industry	• Industries receiving preferential treatment: naphtha cracking, iron and steel, machinery, electronics, shipbuilding, aviation industry
Types of preferential treatment	• Investment tax credit • Income tax deduction • Corporation or business tax exemption	• Direct forms of preference: investment tax credit, income tax deduction, corporation or business tax exemption • Indirect forms of preference: preferential depreciation, tax-free reserves for investment	• Direct forms of preference: investment tax credit • Indirect forms of preference: preferential depreciation, tax-free reserves for investment
Changing features of preferences	• Types of preferential tax treatment different for each benefiting industry • Direct forms of tax credit or tax exemption preferred	• Tax holidays rather than tax exemption • Direct as well as indirect forms in operation • Industries receiving preferential tax treatment formally defined as strategic industries	• Indirect forms of preferential treatment becoming dominant over direct forms

	Stage I (-1974)	Stage II (1975-80)	Stage III (1981-)
R & D expenditures receiving preferential treatment	• Foreign engineer's wage income • Corporation tax of research institutes • Venture business	• Foreign engineer's wage income • Corporation tax of research institutes • Reserved funds for technology development • Venture business	• Foreign engineer's wage income • Corporation tax of research institutes • Reserved funds for technology development • Research facility investments • Job training expenses • Venture business
Types of preferential tax institution	• Tax credit or exemption	• Tax credit or exemption • Tax-free reserves for expenses in technology development	• Tax credit or exemption • Tax-free reserves for expenses in technology development • Preferential depreciation
Characteristics of tax incentives	• Preferential treatment applying only to a few selected and exceptional cases	• Tax preferences generally applying to R & D activities in indirect forms such as tax-free reserves	• Pan-industry type functional approach in tax preferences rather than industry specific one • Indirect forms of tax preferences such as tax-free reserves and preferential depreciation

	Stage I (-1974)	Stage II (1975-83)	Stage III (1984-)
Preferentially treated industries	• Key industries: facility equipment, machine, raw material, parts, components	• Strategic industries: facility equipment, machine, raw material, parts, components	• Technologically leading industries: facility equipment, machine
Types of preferences	• Tariff exemption or deduction: deduction rate of 80-100%	• Tariff deduction: deduction rate of 70-90%	• Tariff deduction: deduction rate of 55-65%
Characteristics of preferences	• Individual key industries being treated independently without integrating program • Tariff exemption and high rate of tariff deduction being typical modes	• Strategic industries formally defined under integrated program of heavy-chemical industrialization • Tariff deduction being typical mode	• Technologically leading industries replacing the role of strategic industries • Tariff reduction rate gradually reduced

Source: S. Rhee, Recent Industrial Adjustments of Korean Economy and Underlying Policy Reforms, in: The Developing Economies, Bd. 26, 1988, H. 3, S. 222 - 246, S. 235 ff.

countries changed over time as the Korean example illustrates (cf. Table 2), it would be wrong to take the recent policy reforms as an indication for a fundamental change as regards the overall philosophy of economic management. On the contrary, a closer look at the ongoing policy reforms in Singapore, Taiwan and Korea (Rep.) reveals that a stronger reliance on market mechanisms is not at variance with the practice of continued government guidance and co-operative relationships of continued government and business as the most effective way of identifying needs, designing solutions and ensuring the timely implementation of necessary action. On balance, Asian NIEs will continue to bear out the contention that it is not only companies which compete in the international market. The international market is also a field of confrontation between value systems, production systems, organisational concepts and institutional structures in which business is an important agent but an agent which is integrated in a carefully designed network of relations with the education system, the technological infrastructure, the two sides of industry (management-labour relations) and the public institutions.

5. Late Industrialization - A Case for Continuous Broad Based Social Learning Rather than Planning as a Merely Technical Exercise

Since the late 1970s the developing countries have been recommended by the OECD, the World Bank, the IMF and liberal economists to press ahead with their industrialization processes within the framework of a free-market system. In particular, they are urged to strengthen market forces, to reduce government intervention, to rely on competitive markets rather than active industrial and technology policies, to lower external barriers and to integrate into the world economy.

While there is growing consensus as regards the role of export in the process of late-industrialization, recommendations on how to establish internationally efficient industries still differ. The OECD countries themselves are increasingly resorting to active industrial and technology policies and to comprehensive negotiating processes in an effort to stay ahead in the international technological race. The successful industrializing countries, too, have long since abandoned the old dichotomies of market versus plan or export diversification versus import substitution in favour of a complex overall strategy and are trying to stimulate industrial development with a skillful mix of market competition and government guidance, selective industrial and technology policies, vigorous protection of their own industries and aggressive promotion of their exports.

How much the success of industrialization depends on a broad approach to industrial transformation and restructuring and on a comprehensive social learning process becomes clear when analyzing the Southeast and East Asian models of export-oriented industrialization. It must include in particular a resolute pro-industrial grouping capable of achieving broad social consensus on the basis of a "realistic vision" of industrial and social movement. The elites in government and industry must also be able to mould the overall strategy into a package of sufficiently consistent industrial, economic and financial policy programmes and to adapt the package of measures flexibly in the light of changing exogenous and endogenous circumstances. The core sectoral policies must at least include a comprehensive education policy, so that the intellectual reserves of the people may be tapped for industrial development and social modernization, the development of national technological competence and a foreign trade policy that is pragmatic rather than geared to unrealistic textbook concepts.

Mainstream economists are, of course, not impressed whatever benefits of strategic planning, clear government guidance and selective policies are claimed. Their answer is straightforward: Performance of top-performers would even have been better without government guidance and intervention. If economists are wrong, this may not matter much. If, however, policymakers are wrong, it may have far reaching effects on the society as a whole.

EUROPE 1992 AND THE NIEs

Wolfgang Hager
Special Projects Advisor
Robinson Linton Associates s.c.
36, rue Joseph II, Box 6
B-1040 Brussels

This conference is about chances for cooperation. But to many observers from Asia and elsewhere, "1992" raises the specter of a reduction of economic exchange and the willful self-isolation of Europe. In fact, to the extent that "1992" is directed at the outside world, the program is designed to strengthen the competitive *and* adjustment capacity of the European economy, making it easier to compete in the world without resorting to protectionism. Given the brief space available, and the strength of prejudice fostered, not least in Germany, about a dirigiste Europe, this paper is largely limited to discussing the broad, liberal thrust of "1992" rather than the more marginal industrial and trade policy initiatives which are also part of the picture.

1. The Internal Market: an Internal Affair

The first thing to recognize is that 1992 is largely about matters which, at least until now, have only marginally been the subject of serious international negotiations. Increasingly, albeit politely, the EC has been forced to tell the outside world, and especially the US: this is none of your business. The United States, and others, continue to see "1992" as essentially a super "round" of regional preferential liberalization. This is largely a misunderstanding.

"1992" is in essence the integration of the regulated sectors of Member States' economies and/or of those aspects of economic

Europe-Asia-Pacific Studies in Economy and Technology
Kulessa (Ed.)
The Newly Industrializing Economies of Asia

activities (safety etc.) whose regulation has thus far been the legitimate preserve of national sovereignty.

While we speak of creating a Single Market, which is the economic goal, we should also be speaking of creating a single regulatory space - indeed, a single (mixed) economy.

Using familiar trade terminology such as non-tariff barriers (NTBs) disguises the scope and depth of the exercise. The national barriers tackled by "1992" do not exist because of their incidental protectionist effect, but because most of them involve areas where government has to intervene in some form or other (or thought it had to intervene). For "1992" to occur, two things had to happen: governments were willing to accept a modicum of "super government" at the Community level on an unprecedented scale; and there was a secular, OECD-wide trend towards de-regulation which reduced the Community's task to manageable levels - and happened to coincide with its liberal Treaty provisions.

"1992" is thus about regulation, de-regulation and re-regulation - either of whole sectors, or of certain aspects of industry or services which raise, or raised, public interest issues.

The chief comprehensively regulated sectors are:
- transport
- financial services
- telecommunications.

The main areas of partial regulation are
- public procurement
- health and safety standards
- taxation
- company law
- (liberal and technical) professions.

New or greatly strengthened areas of common policies are
- money
- regional development
- environmental policies
- industrial (R&D) policies.

Traditional areas of EC regulations which are being strengthened (or amended) because of 1992 requirements are
- competition policy: anti-trust (private);
- competition policy: anti-subsidies (public).

Making national regulations governing economic activity compatible with each other by subjecting them to a European mega-regime is a process that will take a decade - and comes at a time when the assumptions about what is good or bad in economic management are themselves undergoing constant change. Inevitably, therefore, the process of integrating national economic regulation increasingly merges with a more central politico-economic function: that of breaking new ground in economic policy making - indeed, inventing a new "model" for a European mixed economy which is continental rather than national in scope.

New or greatly strengthened elements of a "common economic government" for the Europe of the 1990s include environmental policies, common monetary and macro-economic management, regional policy, social policies, and R&D policies; but also areas forced into the common European pool by the disappearance of frontiers, such as immigration policy, drug traffic, terrorism, and organized crime in general. "Security policies" are being thrust onto the European agenda, be it through the need for a comprehensive approach to Eastern Europe, the growing need for a common arms export policy, or R&D policies which have a military-technology component. Even "culture" cannot entirely escape.

In all these cases, the need to define what is essential in present (national) practice, or which of these practices are superior to others and should be part of the common European "model", is forcing an unprecedented debate in all countries, involving industries, trade unions, and the concerned public at large: How much co-determination would there be for a European company? What is an adequate prudential ratio for a bank? Should glass bottles be banned or taxed? What license does an architect need? Is toxic waste a commercial product or a public responsibility? Which forms of regional subsidies are compatible with fair competition? How large can companies grow? The future common trade regime is only one of many such questions.

In the first instance, therefore, "1992" is an internal affair. It involves outsiders in the sense that any national economic policy change affects others; de-regulation of air transport or telecommunication in the US changed the world in these sectors; Spain's move to democracy and private capitalism added a major player to the world economy; Korea's choices regarding authoritarian vs. social consensus models will affect its export dynamism and hence help to shape the world climate of protectionism in the 1990s. But all of these were or are choices made for internal reasons, or in response to external forces which go beyond the agendas of international economic negotiation.

The over-riding, quasi-automatic effect of most of these EC-internal measures is thus one of liberalization against the outside world. Irrespective of whether the road towards a given Internal Market objective is achieved by (net) de-regulation or by mutual recognition of national regulation, third-country exporters find it easier to penetrate the market.

Two examples. The first comes from telecommunications, traditionally a sector dominated by public monopolies. It would have been very difficult to harmonize conditions of access to the various national terminals markets as long as the selling or licensing of fax machines or PBXs remained in the public domain. By decreeing that the PTTs monopoly had to stop at the plug, the Commission not only liberalized the internal market, but opened it up for outside suppliers - including those from South-East Asia.

The second example concerns mutual recognition of product standards, provided certain broad (EC-wide) performance standards are met. This means that, say, a Taiwanese exporter of a machine tool needs to have that machine certified for safety in only one Member State to have access to the other eleven - a major saving in time, effort, and uncertainty.

The same transfer of benefits to outsiders occurs in the area of public subsidies. To the extent that subsidies are controlled more tightly - as they are - to provide a "level playing field" in the Community, "financial protectionism" is also necessarily dismantled towards foreign trade competitors.

The metaphor of the "level playing field", familiar from US trade diplomacy, is in fact slightly misleading in the Community context. The real issue is to ensure that, however bumpy the field, the game is played by the same rules (and, indeed, that the same game is played). It is here that the Community becomes different from international economic regimes - GATT, OECD, IMF - not in degree but in quality. The Community has a Treaty that binds not just states but legal persons directly. It has an executive, however weak, and a Court with real clout. And it has rudimentary means of making "side payments" to groups and regions for whom formal equality of treatment means inequality of opportunity.

It is against this context that "free riders" who incur neither the constraints nor the responsibilities of a market economy are occasionally resented in Brussels. As regards EFTA, the problem is partially solved by an increasing submission - more or less unilaterally - to Community disciplines. Especially as regards essentials, such as competition, the same game is played across the whole of Western Europe. EFTA-based multinationals are more "West-European" than most EC firms, be it in pharmaceuticals, electrical engineering, white goods, automobiles or telecommunications and IT.

It is only by offering a set of interlocking rights and obligations, backed by a rudimentary but functioning government and legal system, that the bold "1992" attack on national regulatory powers becomes acceptable for the players, governments and industry alike. It is here that "reciprocity" finds its justification, not in the notion of mutually bartered access to regulated sectors as such. But an analogy of sorts, more relevant to a discussion on NIEs and "1992", is furnished by the Community's stance on the Multifibre Arrangement.

In July of this year the Community adopted a negotiating position for the future of the MFA which is rather clever. Leaving the traditional plea for limited safeguards aside, the paper calls for a substantial tightening of GATT rules - not their derogation, as in the present MFA. It says in essence: yes, let's practice free trade. But, as we do in the Community, this means strict enforcement of rules: mutual opening up of markets; no subsidies to domestic producers, e.g. in the shape of subsidized supplies of raw materials; respect for property rights: trade marks, designs, models.

In some sense, demands such as these can be compared to the threatened Super 301 action by the United States against Brazil and India. What both moves have in common is a signalling by advanced countries that the free ride in free trade, if not over, is at least being limited. The Community's approach is softer, because it puts its cards on the table ex ante.

2. General Effects of "1992" on Trading Partners

While a few of the hundreds of domestic regulations and powers to be "Europeanized" relate directly to trade, it is the general *effect* of 1992 on the partners in the world economy which is important.

2.1 Economic effects

On a purely arithmetical calculation, the forecast boost of some 7 per cent of GDP over a non-1992 status quo Europe spells markets for suppliers of goods with an above-average income elasticity of demand. But growth has a more fundamental impact: it creates objective political and economic conditions for adjustment, and hence reduces pressures for adopting protectionist measures. A prosperous, self-confident Europe is an easier trading partner.

The structural effects of 1992 will above all be seen in the modernization of productive capital - thanks to exceptionally high investment levels generated by the fear of increased internal competition. There will also be a lowering, in real terms, of those production costs which are dependent on regulated services - transport, finance, telecommunications. As regards individual sectors, the present pattern where technically marginal firms survive under national protection will be rationalized, with fewer, transnational organized units in virtually all areas of activity. These medium-to-large firms will also, on balance, be more competitive towards the outside world - and less dependent on protectionism.

Firms which are already very large will use the intra-European concentration process to simultaneously increase their international presence, able to play their part in the antagonistic-cooperative oligopoly games so typical of the emerging global capitalism. While calls for protectionism form an important part of the arsenal of these international companies, these are gambits designed to enforce a minimum of oligopolistic price and market share discipline, without which these giants cannot function.

More important to these powerful players, however, is the ability to source components and products from around the globe. This limits their protectionism to a tactical move within a strategy which is totally dependent on a high and growing level of world trade.

2.2 Negotiating power

Another general effect of 1992, however, is power. Until now, in key areas of trade and investment policies, competitors could play one Member State off against the other, effectively paralyzing the Community's ability to act. While it will still be worthwhile to lobby national governments, majority voting and the need for a truly single external regime in the area of trade and investment will force Members towards compromise.

One of the effects of treating the Twelve as a single entity is statistical: it dramatically reduces interdependence. In the 1980s, imports typically account for 9 per cent of Community GDP - the same share as that of a supposedly self-sufficient continental economy like the United States with its natural resources. (The irrelevance of the resource factor for advanced economies is of course confirmed by Japan's share of 6 per cent.) As regards exports, the EC ratio was 10 per cent in 1986 - double the US figure.

Once these figures penetrate into public consciousness, they might in time change perceptions as to the "vital importance of world trade" for our economies - perceptions which were created when *national* export dependencies - close to 25 per cent at the height of the oil crisis - were the only yardstick. The Community generates 90 per cent of its GDP internally.

The power conferred by the combination of the sheer size of the Single Market and a more cohesive decision-making procedure makes responses to trading partners' requests more of an internal matter to be decided by internal processes of politics - just as in the US or Japan. It is quickly assumed that this means greater protectionism. Yet the limits imposed on the giant Community may be greater than those on individual member states.

An example is furnished by a potential trade dispute between NIEs and the EC over a labor-intensive product, footwear. Productivity increases achieved with up-to-date machinery, combined with still relatively cheap labor, have greatly increased the competitiveness of NIEs. Since the mid-1980s, imports from South Korea and Taiwan have dealt a devastating blow to the European shoe industry, with total extra-EC imports increasing by 73 per cent - leading to a decline of 12 per cent of European production. In Italy alone, 300 footwear firms went out of business last year. However, the Commission does not act.

The NIEs' best protection against protectionism is the proven ineffectiveness of restraints imposed on them alone: As the Commission (and the trade federation pushing for control) fully know, control on Korean and Taiwanese exports would lead the firms hit by controls to relocate their expansion investments to China or Thailand. Imposing restraints on all of South-East Asia would be the only efficient remedy. But this would raise fundamental questions of regional discrimination which the Community has every political interest to avoid. As the US has found in the past, wider political responsibilities "for the system" are an effective restraint on short-term trade policy.

The common thread of this paper is precisely that the Community created by "1992" (and the Single Act) is not a trade area, but a polity. While this sets its internal economic regime qualitatively apart from the much looser international economic system, it also allows it to participate in this system as a more capable, reliable partner.

RECENT TRADE PATTERNS BETWEEN NIEs AND WESTERN EUROPE
Implications for the International Division of Labour in the 1990s

Friedrich von Kirchbach
Senior Advisor
Research Section
Division of Product and Market Development
International Trade Centre UNCTAD/GATT
54-56 rue de Montbrillant
CH-1202 Genève

Introduction

In the run-up to 1992, the general interest of Europeans in Asia is modest. Why bother with the four East Asian Newly Industrializing Economies (EANIEs) - the argument goes - if their combined GNP is of an order of magnitude of one European medium-sized economy such as Spain? Why put scarce management resources to devising complicated business strategies in relation to these four countries, which hold a combined import share in total European imports of only 3 per cent? Why undertake trade-related investment in these economies, when intra-EC trade is projected to grow faster than the EC's third-country trade, thereby pushing its overall share to close to 60 per cent of total European trade? There may be chances for increasing cooperation between Western Europe and the EANIEs, but are they worth the trouble in view of closer and possibly easier business opportunities within the EC, the perceived establishment of trading blocs, the reforms in Eastern Europe, etc?

The present paper answers with an unambiguous yes. The reason for this affirmative answer is based not only on today's importance of the EANIEs, but just as well on the lead role they have played and continue to assume in the remaking of the international division of labour. They are the forerunners in what may be perceived as the globalization of intra-industry rather than inter-industry

Europe-Asia-Pacific Studies in Economy and Technology
Kulessa (Ed.)
The Newly Industrializing Economies of Asia

trade patterns, the indigenization of production capacities in developing countries and the growing number of world market oriented production units. Cooperation with the EANIEs is therefore essential for anticipating and participating in trends which will be characteristic for the 1990s.

1. Recent Trade Patterns between the EANIEs and the EC

Since World War II, the growth of international trade has consistently outperformed that of production. All available indicators suggest that this trend will continue (see Graph 1), which implies that the internationalization of the world economy will further intensify. Few countries have benefited as much from this trend as the EANIEs with their extremely outward looking economies.

The large volume of trade between the EANIES and the EC - as compared to trade with other developing countries - is thus determined by the pronounced trade orientation of these four countries and not by the overall size of their economies. As may be seen from Graph 2, the EANIEs registered export ratios (exports divided by GNP) of between 35 and 150 per cent. In contrast, the EC showed a trade ratio of 9.7 per cent (without intra-community trade) only, and is thus less trade oriented than Japan and even the United States.

A perusal of any analysis of trade flows between Japan, USA, EC and the EANIEs shows that trade between the latter two is the weakest link (see Graph 3). European exports to the four countries under review were with US $ 21.9 billion less than half of Japanese and two thirds of US exports to this region. On the import side, the EC registered with US $ 31.1 billion only half the value of US imports from the EANIEs, but still more than Japan. This highlights once again the structural bilateral trade imbalances between the four regions: the large deficit of the USA with the EANIES, the smaller deficit of the EC (including the FRG) and Japan's substantial surplus vis-à-vis the EANIEs.

As may be gathered from Graph 3, the EANIEs were nearly as important as Japan as export market for the EC. For imports, the share of these four countries had reached in 1988 more than 60 per cent of Japanese exports to the EC. If the ASEAN countries and China are included, EC trade with these 10 countries exceeds bilateral trade with Japan both for exports and imports.

Due to the importance of intra-EC trade, the share of the EANIEs in total EC trade remains low. Imports from the EANIEs in total EC imports were just below 3 per cent in 1988, compared to 1.9 in 1980 (see Table 1). This was much lower than the corresponding shares for the USA and Japan, which not only started from a higher level in 1980, but also increased nearly two respectively threefold during the 1980s.

On the export side, the EC countries held a share of 10.5 per cent in total (cif) imports of the EANIEs. This compared with 23.8 per cent for Japan and 16.7 per cent for the USA. The share of the EC in the region's imports increased markedly during the 1980s, in contrast to that of the USA - in particular if Taiwan's gold imports from the USA in 1988 are disregarded (see Table 2).

Incidentally, the EC share in imports of the EANIEs grew faster than that in the ASEAN countries, in which the EC held a stronger position for a number of historical reasons. The gap between the EC's import market shares in these two sub-regions thereby narrowed. This follows the growing ties between the EANIEs and the ASEAN countries.

European trade with developing countries traditionally concentrated for historical and geographical reasons on the Middle

East, Africa and Latin America. The rapid rise of the EANIEs as EC trade partner documents the end of these traditional, regionalized trade patterns. Whereas the share of the EANIEs stood at 6.3 per cent in total EC exports to developing countries in 1980, it had risen to 15.6 per cent in 1988. On the import side their share had risen from 12.3 to 20.2 per cent, including primary commodities. This trend does not confirm the theory of a growing regionalization of international trade into three trade blocs. On the contrary, the developments in the EANIEs and ASEAN as well as in other parts of the world point to the disintegration of distinct, geographically defined trading areas.

It is unlikely, that the present growth differentials between the EANIEs and other regions will discontinue in the near future. Of course, structural adjustment in the EANIEs will entail periods of sector-specific stagnation and decline (see below). Recent developments in the Republic of Korea are a case in point. Present forecasts, however, point to further growth of the relative weight of the EANIEs in international trade and production. As may be seen from Graphs 4 and 5, Asian developing countries are likely to be far more important in world trade in the early 1990s than all other developing countries or than the Eastern European countries.

The designation "newly *industrializing* economies" furthermore distracts from the fact that these countries are going through the same transition to service economies as other industrialized market economies. In fact, in terms of composition of GNP, the name "new *service* economies" would certainly be equally appropriate. As may be seen in Graph 6, the share of service industries in GNP of the EANIEs was between 46 per cent for the Republic of Korea and 70 per cent for Hong Kong. Significantly, the EANIEs figure among the world's leading exporters and importers of commercial services with annual exports and imports of an order of magnitude of US $ 1 billion. In 1987, the Republic of Korea,

Singapore, Hong Kong and Taiwan occupied places 15, 17, 18 and 21 respectively in the world ranking of leading service exporters and places 19, 22, 20 and 18 among the leading service importers. These rankings were only slightly lower than those for trade in merchandise trade (see GATT, International Trade, 88-89, Vol. I).

2. Dynamics of Trade at the Product Level

Hidden behind these macro-economic data are the multitude of industry-specific developments - most of them success stories, some of them failures. Any business newspaper bears witness to the large and growing number of industries, in which the EANIEs hold a competitive or even leading position in the world market. Semiconductors are perhaps the most frequently cited example, where Malaysia, the Republic of Korea and Singapore are the world's largest producers after the USA and Japan. Hong Kong's leading role in toys and musical instruments is well known. Malaysia will shortly be the largest producer of air conditioners.

A recent study of the International Trade Centre UNCTAD/GATT (ITC) underlines this point: Export products of newly industrializing countries, for which the latter's import market share in developed market economies exceeds 75 per cent, accounted for 15.3 per cent of all manufactured exports of newly industrializing economies, and 35.5 per cent for products with an import market share of over 50 per cent (ITC, Dynamics of Exports from Developing Countries - Background Data for the Selection and Monitoring of Export Products for Trade Promotion, Geneva 1988, p. 12).

The same study sheds light on the dynamics of exports at a disaggregated product level (see Table 3). Newly industrializing countries (in the table referred to as large-size exporters of manufactures) exported 1205 different manufactured products (at the

SITC 4 and 5 digit level) to Western Europe, Japan and the USA in 1987, thereby earning US $ 164.0 billion. Among these 1205 products, there were 276, accounting for 10.6 per cent of their total exports, which had registered annual nominal growth rates of 50 per cent and above over the period from 1983 to 1987. Another 129 products accounting for additional 32.4 per cent of exports, had grown by 20 to 50 per cent per annum, starting from an already above-average market share. On the other hand, these countries lost market shares in a significant number of non-fuel primary commodity export products and simple manufactures. The decline of the Korean ceramics exports due to the competition from Thailand and China is just one example.

More generally, Table 3 emphasizes the rapid changes in the export structure at the product level not only for the NIEs but even for the least developed countries. This, in fact, characterizes the new international division of labour. The number of world market oriented production units with high locational elasticity is clearly increasing throughout the (developing) world. It is likely to become a characteristic feature of the international division of labour in the 1990s.

This trend may be illustrated by a comment from the chief of the import department of the world's largest mail order company, who noted that his company no longer selects its suppliers primarily by country, but by individual company and production units, irrespective of whether these are located in Ireland, Singapore or Bangladesh.

It goes without saying, that the world market integration of individual companies located for instance in a least developed country must not be mistaken for economic development in general.

3. Indigenization of Production in the EANIEs

Over the last three decades, the EANIEs have attracted a considerable amount of foreign investment. Inflows of foreign investment have, in fact, been so important that some observers have detected an "investment war" between Japan and the United States in the region. European investment, in contrast, has not kept pace with the inflows from the two major pacific economies, as has been pointed out by numerous studies. More importantly, the gap between the development of trade and investment flows between the EANIEs and Europe appears to be deteriorating in the late 1980s. Whereas exports and imports picked up since 1985, the outflows of European investment to the region appear to suffer from the 1992 race.

It is not the purpose of this paper to go into the details of the very different foreign investment policies and the composition of the stocks of foreign-affiliated companies in each of the EANIEs. What appears to be of interest for the international division of labour in the 1990s is the indigenization trend, which characterizes the four countries under review. In spite of the massive foreign investment inflows - of an order of magnitude of as much as US $ 1 billion a year in some countries - the share of foreign investment in total investment and the part of foreign-affiliated companies in foreign trade appears to be declining.

In Korea, for instance, the share of foreign-affiliated companies used to be below one quarter of total manufactured exports. Even in Singapore, which built its development strategy explicitly on the contributions of multinational companies, the share of local companies in direct industrial exports has increased, rising from 6.1 per cent in 1977 through 10.3 per cent in 1983 to 25.0 per cent in 1986. Similarly, the share of foreign-affiliated companies in Malaysian industrial exports fell from 82.2 per cent in 1969 to 33.2 per cent in 1982 (see ITC 1988 b).

The EANIEs are, in fact, the most advanced developing countries in what has been described as long-term indigenization cycle of production and marketing in developing countries (see Graph 7). According to this cycle, one may distinguish three stages of export development in relation to the participation of local companies in production and international marketing. In a first stage, neither locally available technical production know-how nor marketing skills in the broad sense are sufficiently advanced to render non-traditional products from local producers internationally competitive. Participation in non-traditional exports generally requires the provision of both production and marketing skills from outside sources, typically from foreign-affiliated companies.

In a second stage, the level of technical production skills in indigenous companies reaches international competitiveness, but export marketing expertise characterized by high human capital intensity is not yet locally available. In this second stage, exports are still dependent on the availability of efficient foreign export marketing channels, such as buying agents, sub-contracting, transnational corporations, etc.

During a third stage, indigenous companies participate to a larger extent in export marketing. As international marketing skills become locally available, private companies begin to undertake their own international market research for product development, and create an international distribution network over which they have some control.

In contrast to most other developing countries, many manufacturing industries in the EANIEs are in stages 2 or even 3. The internationalization of their leading companies is making rapid strides (see for instance J. R. Chaponniere 1989). This is most obvious from the growing volume of outward direct investment of the four countries under review (see Graph 8).

This indigenization trend is likely to continue into the 1990s and it appears to hold true for a growing number of other developing countries, as well. It will further contribute to differentiating the spectrum of collaborative agreements between companies in the EANIEs and in developed market economies. The differentiation of business interface and the growing importance of networking may well facilitate relations between companies in the EANIEs and in Western Europe in view of the latter's comparative openness to and significant experience with various types of technology, licensing and other contractual arrangements in East and Southeast Asia.

Incidentally, the successful completion of this indigenization cycle in the EANIEs renders their experience in export strategies and trade policy and trade promotion particularly valuable for other developing countries. More efforts will have to be put into ways and means of how to recycle such institutional and soft technology to other developing countries. In this context, an even more active participation of newly industrializing countries in institutions such as the International Trade Centre UNCTAD/GATT would be highly desirable.

4. Conclusions

Intensifying cooperation between Western Europe and the EANIEs is not only a matter of responding to a variety of opportunities, but an absolute necessity, if the two regions want to benefit fully from the international division of labour in the 1990s. The broadening of interchange will be essential - economically as well as in all other areas.

In the past, Europe has too narrowly focused on the EANIEs as markets for final products without taking full advantage of the opportunities arising from the increasing diversification and sophistication of the four economies under review. It is, however, precisely the diversity of European technology, production and demand structures as well as its way of life in general, which determines its comparative advantage over its two major Pacific rivals and makes it attractive to increasingly sophisticated consumers and producers in the EANIEs.

Determined efforts here and there will be necessary both at the political and the business level to translate these opportunities into reality.

References

1. Chaponniere J. R. (1989) L'internationalisation des nouveaux pays industriels d'Asie. Institut de recherche économique et de la planification du développement, Université des sciences sociales de Grenoble.

2. GATT (1989) International Trade 88-89, 1, Geneva.

3. International Trade Centre UNCTAD/GATT (1988 a) Dynamics of Exports from Developing Countries - Background Data for the Selection and Monitoring of Export Products for Trade Promotion, Geneva.

4. International Trade Centre UNCTAD/GATT (1988 b) Structural Change of Export Marketing Channels of Developing Countries, Geneva.

GRAPH 1

Growth of world trade and production
(annual real growth rates)

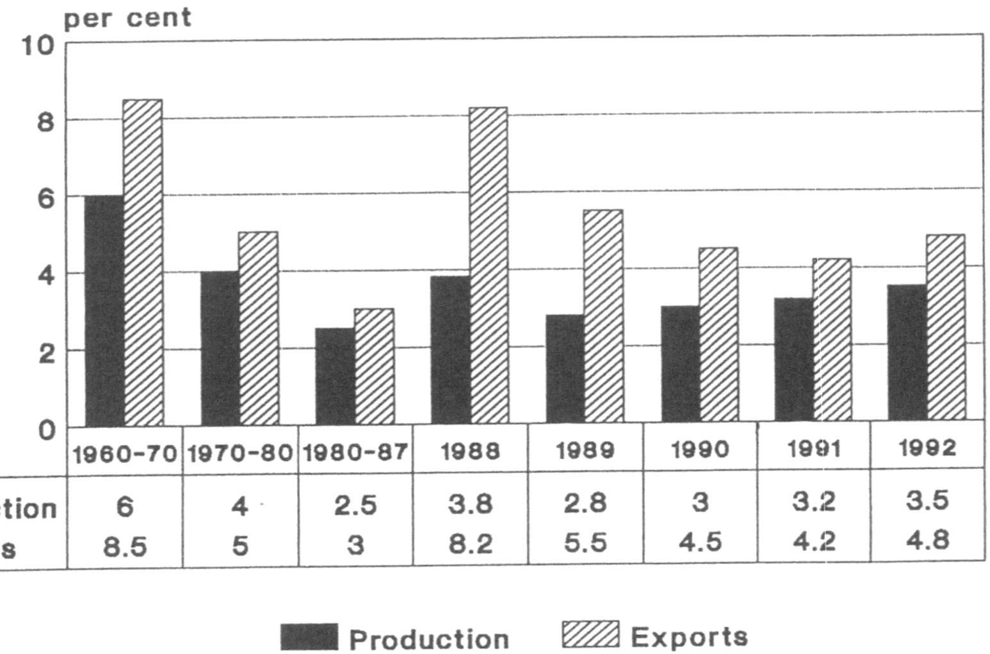

	1960-70	1970-80	1980-87	1988	1989	1990	1991	1992
Production	6	4	2.5	3.8	2.8	3	3.2	3.5
Exports	8.5	5	3	8.2	5.5	4.5	4.2	4.8

Source: GATT 1960-87, LINK 1988-92

GRAPH 2

Export ratios 1988
(exports/GNP)

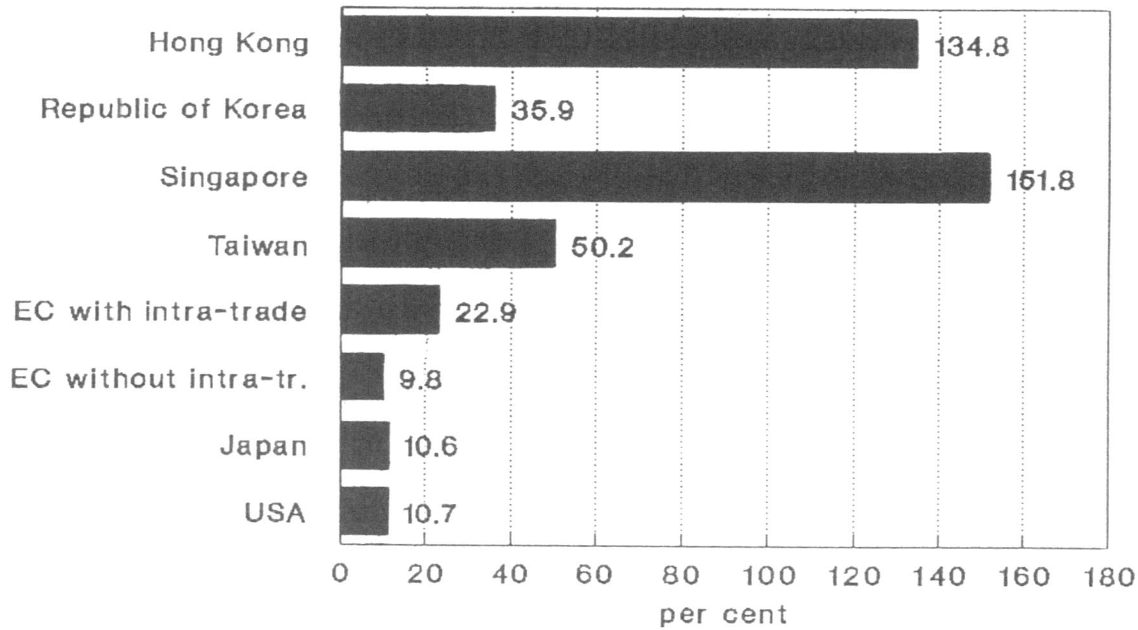

Source: LINK model and Eurostat
Note: EC data for 1986

GRAPH 3

TRADE FLOWS 1988

(US $ billion)

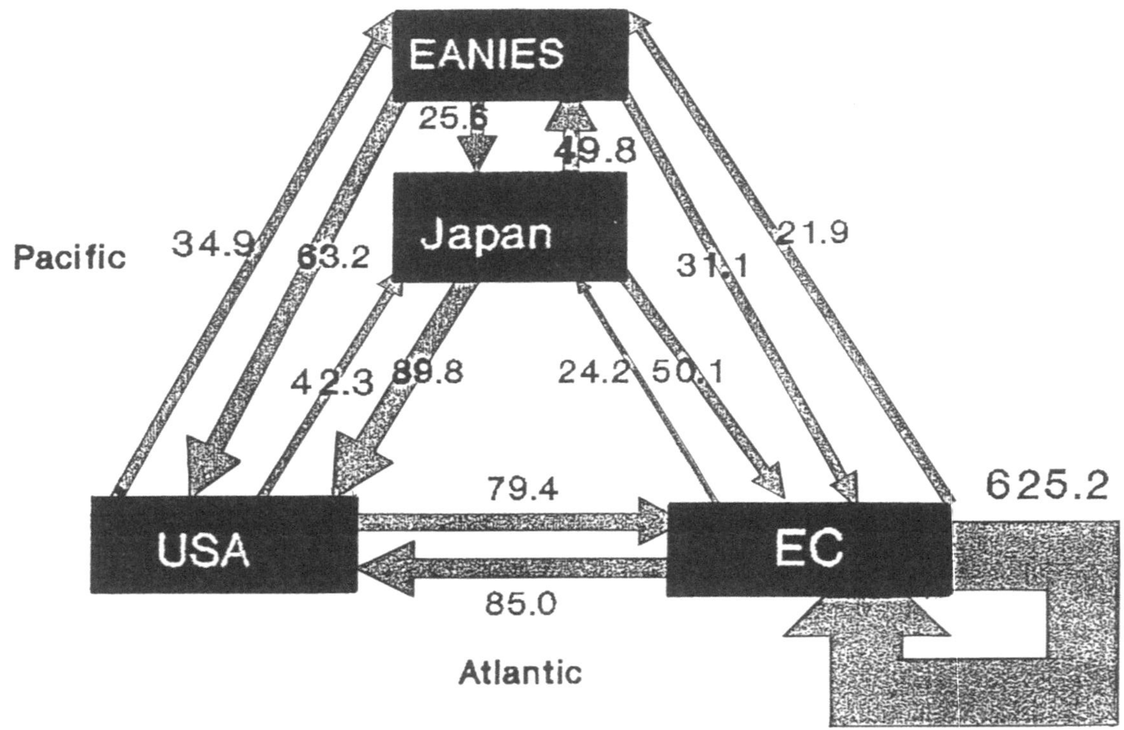

Source: OECD, cif values except for exports to EANIES

GRAPH 4

World Exports 1988 - 1992
(per cent, current $ US)

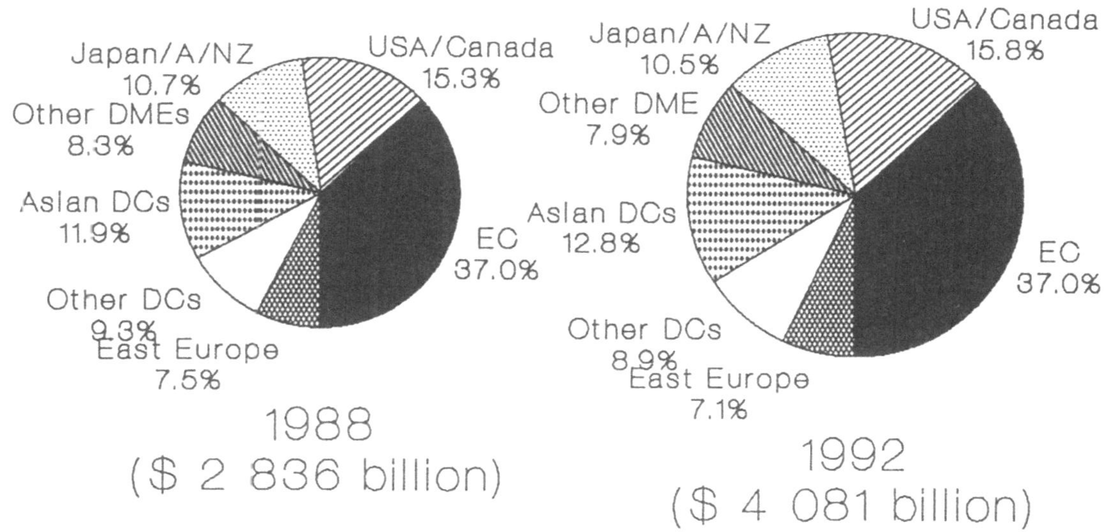

Source: LINK Model, Spring 1989
Note: including intra-reg. trade

GRAPH 5

World Imports 1988 - 1992
(per cent, current $ US)

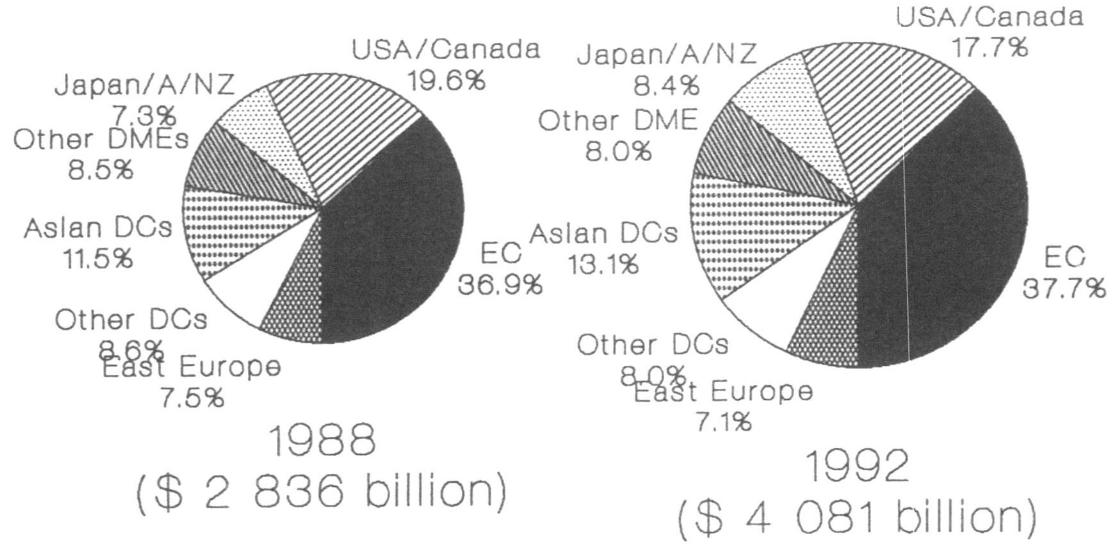

Source: LINK Model, Spring 1989
Note: including intra-reg. trade

GRAPH 6

Share of service industries in GNP
1987

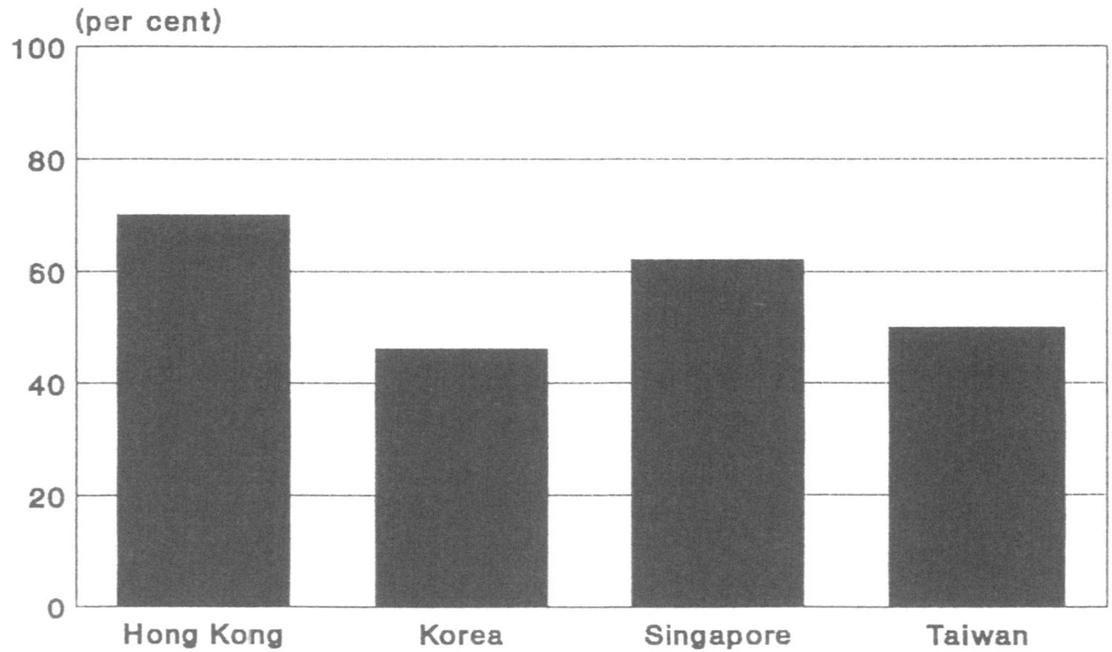

Source: World Bank

GRAPH 7

STAGES IN THE

LONG-TERM INDIGENIZATION CYCLE

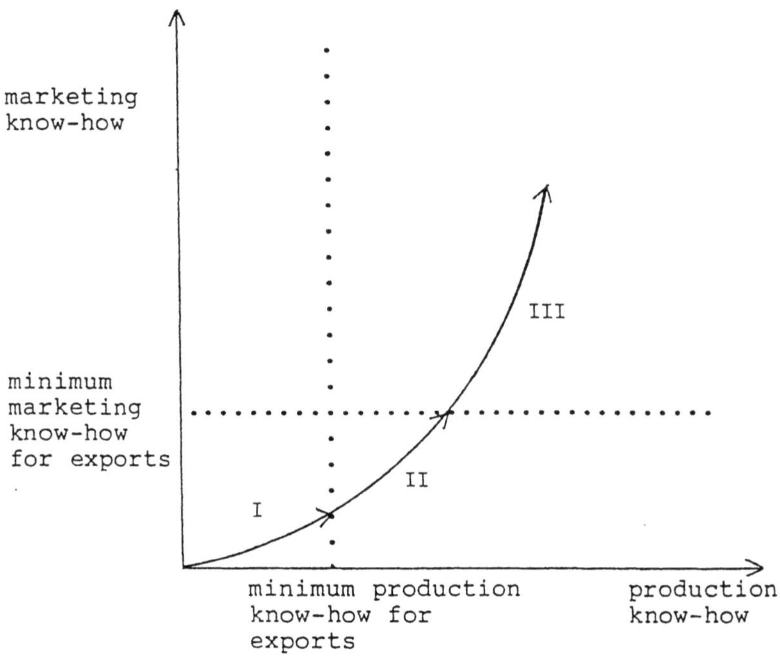

GRAPH 8

Outward investment of the Rep. of Korea and Taiwan P.o.C 1984-1988
(US $ million)

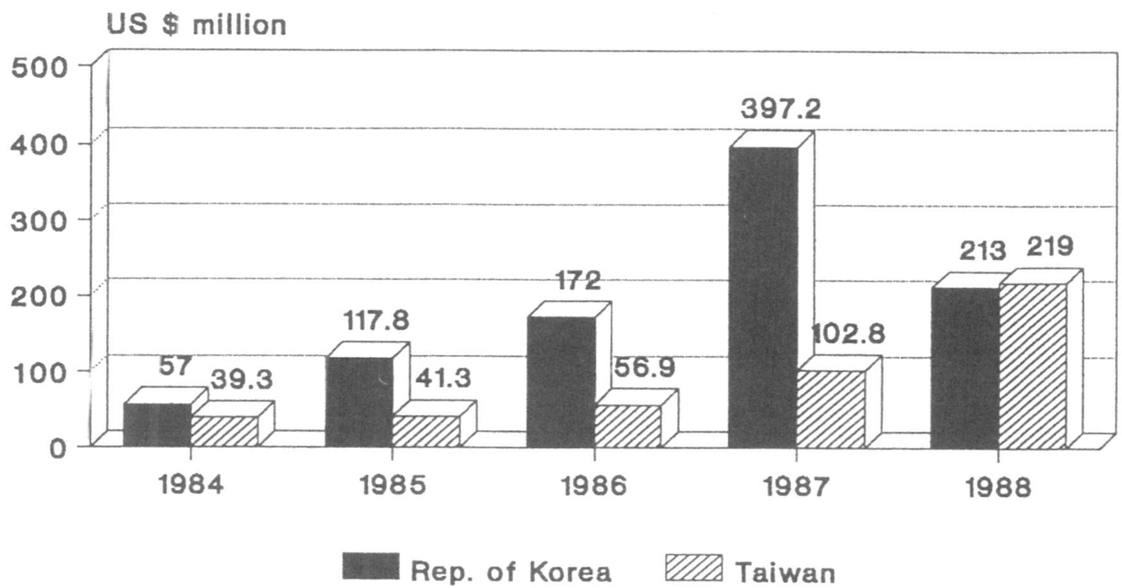

Source: TIDIC und KDI

Table 1

Exports to East and Southeast Asian countries, 1980, 1985 and 1988

(US $ billion, per cent of total imports)

to	Total imports (cif) (US$ billion)			Exports (fob) from: F.R.G.			E. E. C.			JAPAN			U.S.A		
	1980	1985	1988	1980	1985	1988	1980	1985	1988	1980	1985	1988	1980	1985	1988
Hong Kong	22.4	29.7	63.9	0.6 (2.5)	0.7 (2.5)	1.6 (2.5)	3.0 (13.4)	3.5 (11.8)	7.0 (11.0)	4.8 (21.4)	6.6 (22.2)	11.7 (18.3)	2.7 (12.1)	2.8 (9.4)	5.7 (8.9)
Korea (Rep. of)	22.3	31.1	51.8	0.5 (2.4)	0.7 (2.2)	1.8 (3.5)	1.3 (5.8)	2.1 (6.8)	5.1 (9.8)	5.4 (24.2)	7.2 (23.2)	15.4 (29.8)	4.7 (21.1)	6.0 (19.3)	11.3 (21.8)
Singapore	24.0	26.3	43.8	0.7 (2.9)	0.6 (2.4)	1.4 (3.2)	2.4 (10.0)	2.7 (10.3)	4.7 (10.7)	3.9 (16.3)	3.9 (14.8)	8.3 (19.0)	3.0 (12.5)	3.5 (13.3)	5.8 (13.2)
Taiwan, P.o.C.	19.7	20.1	49.7	0.6 (2.9)	0.7 (3.6)	1.8 (3.6)	1.2 (6.1)	1.8 (9.0)	5.1 (10.3)	5.2 (26.4)	5.1 (25.4)	14.4 (28.9)	4.3 (21.8)	4.7 (23.4)	12.1 (24.4)
EANIEs	88.4	107.2	209.2	2.4 (2.7)	2.8 (2.6)	6.6 (3.1)	7.9 (8.9)	10.1 (9.4)	21.9 (10.5)	19.3 (21.8)	22.8 (21.3)	49.8 (23.8)	14.7 (16.6)	17.0 (15.9)	34.9 (16.7)
Indonesia	10.8	10.3	13.5	0.6 (5.5)	0.6 (5.7)	0.8 (5.9)	1.7 (15.7)	1.7 (16.6)	2.3 (16.8)	3.4 (31.5)	2.2 (21.4)	3.1 (22.6)	1.5 (13.9)	0.8 (7.8)	1.1 (7.8)
Malaysia	10.8	12.3	15.0	0.5 (4.2)	0.4 (2.9)	0.5 (3.3)	1.4 (13.0)	1.2 (9.8)	1.6 (10.7)	2.1 (19.4)	2.2 (17.9)	3.1 (20.4)	1.3 (12.0)	1.5 (12.2)	2.1 (14.3)
Philippines	8.3	5.5	8.7	0.3 (3.3)	0.2 (3.0)	0.4 (4.4)	0.8 (9.6)	0.5 (9.1)	1.1 (12.3)	1.7 (20.5)	0.9 (16.4)	1.7 (20.0)	2.0 (24.1)	1.4 (25.5)	1.9 (21.6)
Thailand	9.2	9.2	20.3	0.4 (4.0)	0.4 (4.3)	0.9 (4.4)	1.0 (10.9)	1.3 (14.1)	2.4 (12.0)	1.9 (20.7)	2.1 (22.7)	5.2 (25.4)	1.3 (14.1)	0.8 (8.7)	2.0 (9.7)
ASEAN(excl. Brunei)	63.1	63.6	101.3	2.4 (3.8)	2.1 (3.4)	4.0 (3.9)	7.3 (11.6)	7.4 (11.6)	12.1 (11.9)	13.0 (20.6)	11.3 (17.8)	21.3 (21.1)	9.1 (14.4)	8.0 (12.6)	12.8 (12.6)
China	19.9	42.5	55.3	1.1 (5.8)	2.2 (5.2)	2.8 (5.0)	2.4 (12.1)	5.5 (12.9)	6.7 (12.1)	5.0 (25.1)	12.6 (29.6)	9.3 (16.8)	3.8 (19.1)	3.9 (9.2)	5.0 (9.1)
EANIEs, ASEAN and China	147.4	187.0	322.0	5.2 (3.5)	6.5 (3.5)	11.9 (3.7)	15.2 (10.3)	20.3 (10.9)	36.0 (11.2)	33.4 (22.7)	42.8 (22.9)	72.1 (22.4)	24.6 (16.7)	25.4 (13.6)	47.0 (14.6)

Source: National statistics, OECD, IMF

Table 2

Imports from East and Southeast Asian countries, 1980, 1985 and 1988
(billion U.S. dollars, per cent of total imports)

	Imports of											
	F.R.G.			E. E. C.			JAPAN			U.S.A		
from	1980	1985	1988	1980	1985	1988	1980	1985	1988	1980	1985	1988
Hong Kong	1.7 0.9	1.3 0.8	2.6 1.0	5.1 0.7	4.0 0.6	8.7 0.8	0.6 0.4	0.8 0.6	2.1 1.1	4.7 1.9	8.4 2.4	10.2 2.3
Korea (Rep. of)	1.0 0.5	0.9 0.6	2.6 1.0	2.8 0.4	2.6 0.4	8.8 0.8	3.0 2.1	4.1 3.1	11.8 6.3	4.3 1.8	10.0 2.9	20.2 4.6
Singapore	0.5 0.3	0.4 0.3	1.0 0.4	2.6 0.4	1.8 0.3	3.9 0.4	1.5 1.1	1.6 1.2	2.3 1.2	1.9 0.8	4.3 1.2	8.0 1.8
Taiwan, P.o.C.	2.0 1.1	1.0 0.6	2.8 1.1	3.1 0.4	3.2 0.5	9.7 0.9	2.3 1.6	3.4 2.6	9.4 5.0	6.9 2.9	16.4 4.7	24.8 5.6
EANIEs	5.2 2.8	3.6 2.3	9.0 3.6	13.6 1.9	11.6 1.7	31.1 2.9	7.4 5.2	9.9 7.5	25.6 13.7	17.8 7.4	39.1 11.3	63.2 14.3
Indonesia *	0.4 0.2	0.4 0.3	0.5 0.2	1.7 0.2	1.4 0.2	2.5 0.2	13.2 9.4	10.3 7.8	9.6 5.1	5.2 2.2	4.6 1.3	3.2 0.7
Malaysia	0.8 0.4	0.7 0.4	0.9 0.4	2.5 0.3	2.3 0.3	3.6 0.3	3.5 2.5	4.4 3.4	4.7 2.5	2.6 1.1	2.3 0.7	3.7 0.8
Philippines	0.4 0.2	0.3 0.2	0.5 0.2	1.2 0.2	1.0 0.2	1.5 0.1	2.0 1.4	1.3 1.0	2.0 1.1	1.7 0.7	2.1 0.6	2.7 0.6
Thailand	0.6 0.3	0.5 0.3	0.9 0.4	1.8 0.2	1.7 0.3	3.5 0.3	1.1 0.8	1.0 0.8	2.8 1.5	0.8 0.3	1.4 0.4	3.2 0.7
ASEAN (excl. Brunei)	2.7 1.5	2.3 1.5	4.0 1.6	9.6 1.3	8.1 1.2	15.0 1.4	21.4 15.2	18.6 14.2	21.4 11.4	12.3 5.1	14.7 4.3	20.8 4.7
China	0.8 0.4	0.9 0.6	2.5 1.0	2.6 0.4	3.0 0.5	7.7 0.7	4.3 3.0	6.6 5.0	9.9 5.3	1.1 0.5	3.9 1.1	8.5 1.9
EANIEs, ASEAN and China	8.2 4.4	6.3 4.0	14.5 5.8	23.2 3.2	20.9 3.2	49.9 4.6	31.6 22.4	33.5 25.5	54.6 29.1	29.3 12.1	53.4 15.5	84.5 19.1
World	185.9 100.0	157.6 100.0	250.5 100.0	730.2 100.0	663.1 100.0	1080.5 100.0	141.1 100.0	131.3 100.0	187.5 100.0	241.2 100.0	345.3 100.0	441.3 100.0

Source: OECD data

Table 3

Export performance at the product level by country group, 1987

(Distribution by export performance)

Criteria		Sustained Success	New-comers	Losers	Other	All
trend 1983-87, p.c. pa		20 to 50	> 50	< 0	}	
import market share 87		> than average share[a]			} all } others	
acceleration ratio		> 1.00		< 1.00	}	
Least developed countries (av.share: nfpp[b] 0.95; manufactures 0.17)						
non-fuel prim.products	nr. of prod.	30	92	60	60	242
	value	21.0	3.0	6.7	69.3	100.0
manufactures	nr.of prod.	30	255	90	121	496
	value	16.2	24.6	8.5	50.7	100.0
Large-size exporters of manuf. (av.share: nfpp[b] 8.46; manuf.11.17)						
non-fuel prim. products	nr. of prod.	100	107	87	208	502
	value	22.4	5.9	14.9	56.8	100.0
manufactures	nr. of prod.	129	276	77	723	1205
	value	32.4	10.6	1.5	55.4	100.0
Medium-size exporters of manuf. (av.share: nfpp[b] 8.68; manuf. 3.86)						
non-fuel prim. products	nr. of prod.	84	108	106	193	491
	value	11.5	4.2	14.6	69.6	100.0
manufactures	nr. of prod.	128	369	124	526	1147
	value	39.5	11.2	4.1	45.2	100.0
Other developing countries (av.share: nfpp[b] 8.56; manuf. 1.09)						
non-fuel prim. products	nr. of prod.	84	142	105	136	467
	value	5.7	2.0	15.5	76.8	100.0
manufactures	nr. of prod.	79	423	130	336	998
	value	43.4	20.7	6.7	29.2	100.0
All developing countries (av.share: nfpp[b] 24.4; manuf. 16.3)						
non-fuel prim. products	nr. of prod.	87	76	92	281	536
	value	7.6	2.1	9.3	81.0	100.0
manufactures	nr. of prod.	149	214	77	778	1218
	value	34.2	8.0	1.3	56.5	100.0

Source: UNSO/COMTRADE, own calculations.

Notes: a) Average percentages shares in imports of the major developed market economies

b) Non-fuel primary products

THE NIEs VIEWED FROM THE GERMAN AND EUROPEAN PERSPECTIVES

Lorenz Schomerus
Director-General
Federal Ministry of Economics
Villemombler Strasse 76
D-5300 Bonn 1

The terms "newly industrializing countries" and "newly industrializing economies" - and even more so their derivative acronyms "NICs" and "NIEs" - have become just as much a part of our economic and political vocabulary as the terms "global interdependence", "globalization", and "multipolarity". They stand for penetrating changes in the network of world economic and political structures, both at the national and supranational level, to which economic policy must appropriately respond. This, in my opinion, is one of the major challenges to economic policy in the nineties. In history books yet to be written, the period in which we now live will perhaps be interpreted as the phase which, more than any other, has shaped the global economic and political landscape of our planet for the coming century. Traditional seats of economic power are losing their influence to rising centers of regional growth; time-worn patterns of the international division of labor are assuming new profiles both in regional and sectoral terms; and boundaries once defining the spheres of geopolitical power are becoming blurred. Fixed patterns of thinking, valid for decades, are now losing relevance as the traditional North-South and East-West patterns reflect realities less and less. A new way of thinking is needed - not only in the Eastern countries where unbearable and continued economic shortcomings are forcing the implementation of reforms - but in the West as well. The struggle against thinking in terms of the status quo, against a refusal to adapt, and against a defensive posture of merely preserving previous gains is far from being won. The battle will have to be waged with undiminished determination. Events such as this forum are an important contribution to such efforts.

Europe-Asia-Pacific Studies in Economy and Technology
Kulessa (Ed.)
The Newly Industrializing Economies of Asia

And now, using the terms cited, I want to outline the new elements in global political and economic relations that have made the latter part of the eighties so different from the rest of the post-war era.

First:

Global interdependence: aided by rapid progress in transport and transportation and in the information and communication technologies, our globe is becoming smaller and smaller. The internationalization of the world economy has advanced to an extent hardly imaginable at an earlier stage. An important indicator of this is world trade, which for a number of years has been expanding at a significantly more rapid pace than the aggregate volume of goods produced. National economies are thus becoming the individual components of an entity we might well call the "mondial-economy". The functional loss incurred by the nation-state, initial signs of which can only just be discerned in the political field (perhaps most clearly in the field of security policy), has to a large extent already become reality in the economic sector. No national economy can seriously consider leaving the close network of mutual dependencies without endangering the prosperity of its citizen.

These dependencies have deep roots and are to be found in nearly every sector. The image of "Starship Earth" implies this in the ecological field. Another particularly obvious example is the industrialized states' farm policy and its influence on the developing countries' debt servicing capabilities. The same is true of the industrialized countries' textile and steel policy. These interdependencies must be taken into greater account if conflicts are to be prevented and backlash ruled out. The protectionist measures applied by the industrialized states, for example, directly affect developing nations' export opportunities, and they indirectly weaken the latter's ability to absorb imports, thus shrinking their own export opportunities.

Second:

Another important feature that characterized the end of the post-war era is the evolution of a multipolar power system. The bipolar system built and dominated by the United States and the Soviet Union in the wake of the Second World War has largely entered the realm of history. Viewed at least in economic terms, our world has long been multipolar. The "Pax Americana", based on the United States' undisputed leadership role in the economic-technological fields no longer applies. Statistics prove my contention. America's share of the overall economic output in the non-communist world has fallen from some one-half in 1950 to less than a third. During the same period, Japan's contribution has risen more than fivefold, while Europe's share has remained more or less constant. But this is true only in a purely economical context. Another picture results when the situation is viewed from a political perspective. The European Community will gain in geopolitical importance when it becomes a political entity. Its responsibility for the global economy and global political affairs will then grow accordingly.

The trend toward multipolarity serves the interests of all concerned. On the one hand, it increases development opportunities in economically slower areas of our planet. On the other hand, a more balanced distribution of strength can increase the pressure toward economic and political cooperation which, in turn, benefits international relations.

But the replacement of American hegemony over the world economy by the trilateral configuration comprising the United States, Europe, and Japan certainly does not mean that the multipolarization tendencies have drawn to an end. The appearance of the "newly industrializing countries", above all in the Asian-Pacific region, has further developed the geometry of forces rather visibly in the direction of a square. I shall refrain from projecting the geometry of global economic forces in the medium or long term.

I view the evolution of a new dynamic growth center on the Western rim of the Pacific as an additional and major structural element of the global economy at the end of this decade and century. The numbers are impressive. Taken together, the countries on the Pacific basin's western rim[1] have doubled their share of global GNP since the mid-sixties. No less than one-fifth of the absolute rise in prosperity during this period was accounted for by the region. Even without Japan, the growth lead remains considerable when comparison is made with Western Europe and the United States.

The growth dynamic of the Pacific basin is reflected by world trade figures viewed by regions. In 1988, just as has been the case since the beginning of this decade, the highest growth rate was registered for commerce within the Western Pacific region. Trailing behind were transpacific trade (North America - Western Pacific) and Euro-Pacific commerce. Only then do we find merchandise trade within North America, followed by transatlantic (North America - Western Europe) and finally intra-Western European trade. But the level of intra-European trade is still far in the lead.

Generally viewed as the prime mover behind this trend is a small group of economies that, relatively speaking, have progressed rather far toward industrialization, and that, owing to their un-

---

1 Australia, Japan, New Zealand, Hong Kong, Singapore, South Korea, Taiwan, Indonesia, Malaysia, Philippines.

usually dynamic economic expansion and astonishing success on world markets, are called the "four little tigers", a name reflecting both admiration and fear.[2] As they have matured, these four appear to have succeeded in ending the "Pax Japonica" in the Pacific-Asian region just as the "Pax Americana" has been eclipsed in the Atlantic region. These countries' surge to the fore on many markets only recently dominated by the Japanese, such as computer chips, televisions, videos, and automobiles, emits a clear message.

No other example could illustrate as convincingly the historically proven thesis that global economic growth is a constant process of catching up and overtaking, not only on the part of individual countries but also in terms of regions and groups of countries. The development of the Asian NICs is representative of the most impressive success story in modern economic history. The following are only some of its highlights:

- In past years, the four NICs have consistently advanced on the list of the world's leading exporters. In 1988, their total share of nearly 8 % of world exports put them in fourth place, behind Germany, the United States, and Japan.

- Their share of world trade has thus risen fivefold since the mid-sixties.

  This trend is likely to continue. The IMF forecasts that the foreign trade of these countries will continue to expand in 1989 and 1990 considerably faster than world trade.

But their export success lets us forget all too easily that the NIEs are also increasingly important as import markets. On the

----

2 Hong Kong, Singapore, Taiwan, South Korea.

list of the most important importers, the "four tigers" now take third place behind the United States and Germany, thus even ahead of the United Kingdom, Japan, and France. This also reflects the measures that have been applied in recent years to make domestic markets more accessible to foreign vendors.

For German and European producers, this opens up opportunities that so far unfortunately have been ignored all too often.

There is no simple recipe for these countries' success, if only because of the structural heterogeneousness within the group. But among the array of decisive factors, the following are the most important:

- An export-oriented development strategy that contrasts with the domestic market strategy of import substitution associated with many other developing countries, particularly in Latin America.

- A high degree of political stability.

- The availability of a critical mass of human capital.

- Finally, factors yielding a work ethic such as the Confucian outlook emphasizing thrift, industry, discipline, and respect for authority.

It should, however, not be overlooked that questionable practices such as subsidization and import restraints played a role at the beginning of the trend, even though they have lost significance.

Rapid industrialization in the advanced developing countries has been a powerful motor for redistributing influence in the global power network. This process is irreversible. It offers substantial opportunities for the global economy, but also creates problems. The opportunities are evident. Growth dynamism in the NIEs exerts strong impulses on world trade and on the direction of global economic activity. We all ultimately profit, even those of us in the traditional industrial states.

On the other side, the resolute advance of new and capable competitors on world markets confronts traditional vendors with new challenges. Competition becomes rougher, in turn compelling adjustment. The process of adjustment is not without friction, particularly when it encounters rigid structures. Above all in areas with employment problems, it can easily provoke opposition and defensive reactions. This particularly applies when competition by the newcomer is perceived as unfair.

A defensive attitude toward global economic structural change is the most serious danger. The need for structural adjustment cannot be avoided by attempting unilaterally to withdraw from the network of mutual dependencies; for the resulting relief would be short term at best. In the long run, such a course leads the global economy into a blind alley, making growth and employment losses even worse.

The best guarantee for the maintenance of multipolarity is an economic system based on the division of labor and functioning in as open a manner as possible, a system that adjusts flexibly to rapid and far-reaching structural changes. Openness is to be equated with multipolarity. The development of the multilateral GATT system has been one of our major achievements of post-war reconstruction. For it laid the basis for prosperity without precedent in world history. This concept of a multilateral economy is superior to every other type of economic system. Not only open to all countries, it also actively promotes their global economic integration by making physical, economic, and political boundaries more permeable by means of trade, investment, and capital transactions. Since this approach questions the primacy of thinking in categories of power and military policy, it is at the same time inherently peaceful. And this is the basis for the opportunity for peace offered by the current reforms and openness in the centrally planned economies.

Openness and the willingness to cooperate on the basis of multilateral rules of play would also determine the relationship of the "old" to the "new" industrial countries. The NIEs must be treated as participants with equal rights in the peaceful global economic test of strength. Generally accepted rules of fair play must set the framework for competition for market shares and determine the leaders in the technological contest. To the same extent, however, there must be the assurance that infractions against the rules will be punished.

Such infractions have increased at a frightening rate in the past years with the result that there has been a dangerous erosion of the system governing the worldwide exchange of merchandise and services, that is based on the most-favored-nation and non-discrimination principles. Unilateralism and bilateral arrangements that ignore the GATT rules are particularly serious violations; above all they threaten capable producers from the so-called threshold countries. The United States' new trading bill and the possibilities it gives for unilateral protective and retaliatory measures are only one rather striking example of a global tendency. Violations of the rules are hardly to be kept in check, particularly in the gray-zone trading areas. They range from increased requests for anti-dumping proceedings and for the imposition of countervailing duties, to more restrictive application of rules of origin, local-content requirements, and voluntary restraint arrangements.

More fundamental in nature is the fear that our multilateral trading system could disintegrate into trading blocs more or less insulated from one another owing to the establishment of regions featuring a particularly high degree of economic integration. The free trade agreement between the United States and Canada, the completion of the Single European Market, and thoughts on the creation of a Pacific free trading zone trigger such concerns as are being discussed under the term "regionalization of the global economy". These should be regarded with all due seriousness, although I warn against dramatization. Regional shifts in growth centers and trading hubs merely reflect the structural change in the world economy and are thus not negative in themselves. Nor is regional integration a reason for concern as long as it is not aimed against binding rules under the GATT, that is, as long as openness and multilateralism remain guaranteed. On the contrary, the linking up of national economies into an integrated trading area can catalyze liberalization efforts of even larger dimensions simply by provoking imitation. But a condition for this, and I want to reiterate this point, is that trade policy liberality at home not be sacrificed by reducing access for third parties. At a time of growing multipolarity and interdependence, there is no longer any justification for a "fortress" mentality.

This naturally also fully applied to economic integration in Europe. The NIEs particularly tend to view the trend toward the international market with suspicion. I admit that some elements of the discussion as to the shape of the Community's trade relations with third countries after completion of the internal market might provide occasion for mistrust. But those whose eyes are fixed on the "fortress Europe" as a rabbit's eyes on an approaching snake, can easily overlook the solid benefits for trading partners outside the Community that will result from the internal market. The elimination of intra-Community borders will also make it easier and less expensive for third-country producers to sell on the European market. The resultant lowering of transaction costs within the Community will doubtlessly have a certain trade-redirecting effect which for non-EC members will be greatly overcompensated for by the trade-creating impact.

The growth effects of the single European market are already visible in Europe. The EC's trading partners will, of necessity, profit from the prospering and dynamically growing markets within Europe. This also applies to the NIEs. They have already been able to considerably expand their market share within the EC. This share rose from some 2.5 % of total EC imports in the 1960s to 4.6 % in 1987[3]. In the field of finished manufactures, sales have been even more impressive.

The deadline for completion of the internal market by the end of 1992 is, therefore, not a threat which the trading partners outside the EC must fear. Rather, it is an excellent opportunity for more market economy, more competition, and thus also for more growth and employment both within and outside Europe. This opportunity must be seized by the NIEs.

With the growing economic integration, there is also an increase in the potential for conflicts with unforeseen consequences to the detriment of all concerned. For this reason it is all the more important that existing rules and mechanisms be adjusted to the new realities and that new institutional safeguards be developed to reduce the risk of self-destructive conflicts. Since 1985 there have been more than twenty "trade wars" alone between the United States and Europe; these conflicts forced the principal crisis managers to hold their breath for weeks at a time. This shows the urgent need for more dependable rules, additional transparency, and greater competency for dispute settlement.

The current round of negotiations under the GATT provides us with a unique opportunity for this. Besides the continuous trade liberalization, the goal is also an institutional strengthening of the GATT system so as to defend it from the dangers arising from

---

3 In the OECD statistics, the NIEs comprise: Yugoslavia, Mexico, Brazil, Singapore, South Korea, Taiwan, and Hong Kong.

protectionism and bilateralism. Hopes attached to the GATT round, particularly by the small and weaker trading partners, above all the highly indebted countries of the Third World, should not be disappointed. For growth and development reasons, these countries are particularly dependent on free market access and on the protective function of an internationally safeguarded rule-setting system. Failure of the negotiations would place into serious question the basic consensus on the advantages of the existing multilateral system and would make unilateral and bilateral options more attractive. The consequences for the global economy cannot be calculated. For failure would be tantamount to striking a main artery in the blood stream not only of the industrial countries but also of the NIEs whose rapid prosperity has been based on the transfer of merchandise, capital, and know-how in as free a form as possible.

The shared interest in maintaining the free system of world trade must therefore be accompanied by the willingness of the "old" and "new" industrial countries to assume trade policy obligations and global economic responsibility. This means that all must have the will to compromise, even in areas as sensitive as trade in textiles and services or the protection of intellectual property.

In an interdependent world, we are all in the same boat. Cooperation and mutual coordination are vital; for many conflicts have their roots in misunderstandings and communication problems. Common interests can only be identified on the basis of better mutual understanding. This can best be done within the framework of an open and prejudice-free dialogue. The OECD has inaugurated a new and promising route by inviting a number of advanced developing nations from the Eastern Asian area to a discussion of issues of interest to both sides. The framework for dialogue is informal and divorced from the political framework. This guarantees an exchange of opinions free from the compulsions of politics or protocol.

The dialogue started out with a seminar uniting representatives from the OECD countries and those of South Korea, Taiwan, Hong Kong, and Singapore at the beginning of the year in Paris. In the winter of 1989/90 it will continue in a number of workshops on specific topics (trade and financial markets, for example). The dialogue is based on the principle of regional openness, making possible the later inclusion of additional NIEs. The OECD Council of Ministers expressly reiterated this principle at its meeting on May 31 and June 1 of this year.

A new structure for cooperation is thus developing, one for which the existing institutional mechanisms offer no room since they are defined either too narrowly on a regional basis (such as the G-7) or because their politicized climate automatically makes a prejudice-free dialogue difficult (United Nations bodies, for example). By contrast, the multilateral framework of the OECD and its clean working style provide optimal conditions for creating mutual understanding and trust by the exchange of facts and opinions.

The more rapidly and comprehensively this occurs, the greater will be the opportunity for finally removing whatever antagonisms might still exist from obsolete North-South perspectives and for replacing them with a partnership based on equality and fairness. The forum which begins today will doubtlessly also make an important contribution.

THE ABILITY OF THE GERMAN ECONOMY TO FACE OPPORTUNITIES AND CHALLENGES OF EMERGING NIEs (NEWLY INDUSTRIALIZING ECONOMIES)

Helmut Giesecke
Director
Foreign Trade Department
Association of German Chambers of Industry and Trade
Adenauerallee 148
D-5300 Bonn 1

OECD claims that the continuing large trade surpluses of Japan and Germany, recorded since 1987, have been held to reflect in part these countries' positions as major exporters of investment goods. The current upswing in activity in the OECD area - and subsequently in the closely related NIEs - has been marked by a strong recovery in machinery and equipment investment, which on average has grown more than twice as fast as GNP and by more than 50 % since 1982. Additionally, in recent years there has been a distinct tendency for investment to grow more dynamically, with growth more evenly spread geographically. As Japan's and Germany's exports show a higher degree of specialization in capital goods compared to other industrial countries, both economies have the potential to further improve their international trading position.

Whereas the Japanese foreign trade in post-war times heavily concentrated on the United States' markets and the neighbouring East and South-East Asian countries, German industries after the war resumed their role as suppliers of machinery and equipment to European countries, including - as far as possible - the Eastern European state trading countries. German multinationals and an ever growing number of medium scale and even smaller German industries embarked on this international business. The international competitiveness of German industries was strengthened by the traditional open-market policy of the German post-war governments. The opening-up of the European markets under the EEC in

Europe-Asia-Pacific Studies in Economy and Technology
Kulessa (Ed.)
The Newly Industrializing Economies of Asia

the sixties was an additional challenge for German industries. The industrial adjustment process accelerated to a rapid pace of structural change due to new developments in the 1970s. The two oil-price shocks had severe effects on the world economy. The strong revaluation of the DM against the US dollar led to a loss of international price competitiveness of German goods and - at the same time - gave Asian products, under the lead of those of Japanese origin, the opportunity to penetrate into some of Germany's domestic and foreign markets.

An OECD study of industrial adjustment reveals different developments from country to country. It states that in Germany, which combines long-run real-wage flexibility with pronounced price rigidity, the corporate sector as a whole has demonstrated a remarkable ability to maintain overall profit ratios in the face of the short-term shocks and movements in foreign competitors' prices. Germany's strong foreign trade performance stems primarily from the fact that its exports are concentrated in relatively "traditional" products where economies of scale play an important role. Thus, although Germany's performance in high technology markets has not improved significantly over the years, its industry has managed to maintain pools of competitiveness in areas such as automobiles, engineering and chemicals. The robustness of these "strong-points" lies primarily in the speed with which technological innovations are implemented, thereby allowing German industry to outpace competitors in moving to up-market product niches. (Economies in Transition, Structural Adjustment in OECD countries, OECD, Paris (1989), pp. 134,148,149).

One main feature of the 1980s is the new trend in industrial specialization, and the new types of economic and industrial relationships between developed and developing countries. They constituted the most visible result of the industrial take-off of a limited number of countries in Latin America, Asia and Southern Europe, which had begun in the 1960s. Exports of these countries, while rapidly increasing, were essentially limited to such sectors as textiles and clothing, leather goods and foot-wear, and electronic assembly operations. Accordingly, German companies' direct investment had actively participated by transferring of production facilities into the NIEs, chiefly motivated by the desire to reduce production costs. The decisive comparative advantage of these countries was found in their low wage levels. Concern about the rising competition from the NIEs on domestic and foreign markets was only voiced as a reaction to the worsening economic situation of the 1970s. Increased imports from the NIEs were seen as aggravating the economic problems such as the slowdown of growth and the rise of unemployment in European countries. The affected German industrial sectors responded in various ways, from pulling-out of mass market production to more product and process sophistication. The philosophy of open-market policy of the German governments was never in jeopardy.

By the mid-1980s the NIEs had considerably changed their role in the world economy. The comparative advantages enjoyed by the first NIEs, especially in Asia, began to decrease under the pressure of a new wave of developing countries such as India, Indonesia, Malaysia, Thailand and, increasingly, China. The first-wave NIEs tried to develop more technology-intensive products which require more skilled manpower and for which quality and innovation content are as important as price in determining competitiveness. Higher levels of skill and improved technological capabilities are engaged in these countries which attach a great importance to the acquisition of new technologies.

German industries responded to these new developments in the Asian NIEs in various ways. In the export field traditionally they are strong partners by purchasing sophisticated chemical and machinery products for specialized industry and transport equipment from international suppliers. But the "Four Dragons", in their total imports, increased their share of German goods from

1980 to 1988 only from 1.2 % to 2.0 %. A recent survey of the bilateral German Chambers of Industry and Commerce located in the Asian NIEs indicates a steady and remarkable increase of purchases from German sources in the current year. In fact, German industry ranks as number three supplier to Korea and Taiwan, but far behind Japan and USA.

Finally, the small share of 1.3 % in German foreign direct investment (1986) has stirred up public discussion of whether German industries are taking full advantage of the market potential and the cost differentials for export productions available in this dynamic growth region. In 1986 the federal parliament took up this topic with the German government and discussed the efficiency of German foreign trade promotion measures in specific Asian countries. Taking into consideration the differences amongst the industries' strategies, the "traditional" German lagging behind of investment performance compared to export turnover, and the specific locational factors of the Asian NIEs, there was full agreement to further develop the promotional infrastructure for German business. It was agreed to strengthen the activities of the bilateral Chambers of Industry and Commerce, of the commercial sections of the German embassies and to intensify the flow of information from the Federal Agency for Foreign Trade Information in the region. The Federation of German Industries and the German Chambers of Industry and Commerce stepped up their trade information of the relevant markets, and more frequently set out for business delegations and participation in local fairs in the region. Several exhibitions and technological symposia took place which were tailored to the specific demands of the Asian NIEs. Thus, environmental technologies were presented in Taipei. A highly specialized German industries' presentation will be the "Technogerma 1991" in Seoul. Another example is Germany's participation with a national pavilion in the First International Design Forum Singapore, 1988. In addition, German government and industries are trying to overcome problems in the fields of expatriate legislation and of intellectual property rights which still are an impediment to stepping up German activities. German textile and shoe industries claim that the access to the growing NIEs markets should be facilitated. The investment climate of some countries of the region still causes problems particularly to medium-sized German industries. There sometimes seems to be evidence that US-suppliers for various reasons are favoured. The German bilateral chambers report an increasing trend in the NIEs to diversify their imports.

The "Four Dragons" in 1988 accounted for a share of 3.6 % (after 2.5 in 1980) of total German imports. In total NIEs' exports, the share of textiles and clothing deliveries to Germany has fallen, much as is the case with "other" products, which often come from the consumption-based light industry, too. Compensating for this, the German bilateral chambers report large increases in computers and components, consumer electronics, TV, cameras and toys from Hong Kong. The Korean-German Chamber notices considerable advances in quality and sophistication of technical products, particularly in the fields of consumer electronics. Taiwan at present seems to be suffering from recent revaluations of the local currency (as Korea does), although electronics appear to have made inroads in markets in Germany. Opportunities for the sale of technical products from Thailand also seem to be improving quickly.

There is clear evidence that all Asian NIEs are trying hard to shake off their dependence on exports to the US and Japan. They are diversifying for the envisaged EEC Internal Market. The Asian Development Outlook (Asian Development Bank, 1989) points out that the EEC is the largest trading region in the world, accounting for about 40 % of world trade. During the 1980s, the EEC became more Europe-oriented in its trade, particularly with respect to imports. Between 1980 and 1987 the proportion of intra-Community imports increased from 52 % to 61 %. It seems likely that as

Europe moves towards full integration by 1992, this tendency will be accentuated and may pose serious adjustment problems for its non-European trading partners (page 20). According to the Bank, Asian exports to the EEC and Japan increased by over 30 % in 1987 and to the US by 19 %. Deceleration in 1989 and 1990 is expected, as economic activity in industrial countries and the expansion in world trade may slow down. This tendency may be intensified by currency appreciations in the NIEs, capacity constraints in Thailand, and softening of primary commodity prices over the next two years.

German industries are well aware that the envisaged completion of the Internal Market by 1992 requires the shaping of a common external economic policy for the EEC. It needs to be examined to what extent openness within the Internal Market will affect economic relations with third countries. At present, the individual EEC member states still have protective mechanisms of their own, Germany operating the fewest. In accordance with their free trade convictions and experiences German industries welcomed the declaration by the European Council in Rhodes of December 2nd, 1988, to the effect that "the Internal Market will not close in on itself". In the previous discussions German industries had strongly underlined the gist of the free trade commitment of the EEC Treaty. Nonetheless, in various sectors of German industries, too, growing competition from within and from abroad is already strongly felt. The main players in this field are industries from other EEC member states, from EFTA countries from the United States and particularly also from the NIEs. The Internal EEC Market and the resultant opportunities for intra-Community trade create an additional growth potential which will probably attract more imports from third countries. Secondly, the homogeneity of the EC market may considerably facilitate sales by suppliers from third countries because they will no longer have to deal with fragmented markets.

In fact, a lot of new movement has already started in European markets, not the least in Germany. Ossified structures have been broken open and entrepreneurial energy has been released. Company acquisitions within EEC are increasing in number. There is a resolute determination to secure a strong position in what the companies consider to be their most important market. Investment in R & D is on the increase. The suppliers' structure is being reviewed everywhere. Components sourcing is changing from traditional domestic suppliers to other member countries and overseas. Better use is being made of high human skills in more flexible production lines.

Japan's highly competitive exports into open German markets have, in the past, eliminated complete industrial sectors. The attitude of German industries in this context is best explained by one Siemens executive stating that consumer electronics is that part of business which uses a high volume of semiconductor products. So the Japanese achieve two things if you surrender your market to them - first they get control of the consumer products, then they move into manufacturing the micro-electronics that go with them. Consequently, Siemens determinedly hangs on to these markets.

In the opinion of German industry the advantages of the "open-market concept" are obvious. Not only in the EEC, sectoral problems require solutions involving adjustment based on free-market principles. As the world's largest trading partner the EEC must contribute through a dedicated and constructive effort to improve the world trade system. Accordingly, German industries look with some skepticism upon the EEC proposals which should replace the existing quantitative restrictions applied by individual EEC countries. At present it would seem that the EEC Commission is considering converting at least some of them into EEC-wide voluntary restraint agreements.

On the other hand liberal trade policy is based on the concept of world wide reciprocity. Restricting access to overseas markets, be it openly or covertly, is no valuable starting point. Also, third-country suppliers should not abuse the freedoms granted by employing unfair practices, thus becoming a threat to free competition. Distortions of competition must be firmly countered under the GATT rules.

German industries have mastered all the economic challenges of the past by a continuous process of structural adjustment. They have with some minor exceptions refrained from demanding a protectionist response and have put instead favoured open-market strategies, also vis-á-vis the Asian NIEs.

German industry's presence on the NIEs' markets in all the forms appropriate to the opportunities of the region shows only slow growth because many German industries put their priorities on the opening EEC-markets, the other European and the large US/Canada markets. The great many middle-sized companies can only afford to expand within the limits of their human and financial resources.

RECOMMENDATIONS FOR A EUROPEAN POLICY TOWARD THE ASIAN NEWLY INDUSTRIALIZING ECONOMIES

Achim von Heynitz
Senior Economic Researcher
Stiftung Wissenschaft und Politik (SWP)
Haus Eggenberg
D-8026 Ebenhausen

The Asian NIEs have become major economic players with a lasting impact on the world economy. This transformation is not without its difficulties and conflicts on the social, economic, as well as political level, as the NIEs are NDEs as well - newly democratizing economies. In the near future, the most acute international conflicts will probably occur in the Pacific arena, as this is the region where the decline of the American hegemonic power and the ascendence of fast-growing peripheral economies will confront each other most directly.

Assuming normal external conditions, the NIEs' growing weight and influence have to be viewed as an integral part in a growing multilateral economy and as irreversible. They will mark a continuing shift in the world's center of economic gravity.

Any policy set to defend home markets for job security reasons will prove a risky strategy. Short-term advantages turn into losses in international competitiveness and well-being in the longer run. Much more serious would prove the view in the US that a plausible policy initiative to relieve pressure from the US market would have to be bilateral, with the Asian NIEs agreeing. Such a move would leave the Europeans isolated.

Thus, it is clearly not sufficient for a European policy to react defensively with endless proliferations of non-tariff barriers. This is the time for the Europeans to adopt a policy aiming at integration of the NIEs into the world economy and its multi-

Europe-Asia-Pacific Studies in Economy and Technology
Kulessa (Ed.)
The Newly Industrializing Economies of Asia

lateral institutions.

This general guideline may be translated into a number of more detailed recommendations.

(1) *The NIEs' trade surplus does not need corrective action.*

Young and shaky, as the group's trade surplus is, it does not need any corrective action. In the past, import restrictions were legitimate on grounds of infant-industry protection. Since 1980, the NIEs have started a thorough liberalization process, going definitely further than Japan's in the early 1960s, when her stage of development was similar to the NIEs' position today. This liberalization process needs to be advanced further.

Part of the NIEs' external surplus is caused by their savings-investment gap and may prove transitory[1], another part is caused by unusually favorable worldwide economic developments[2]. It reflects internal saving surpluses, as domestic saving rates have developed beyond actual investment opportunities.

(2) *Reverse the past European trend toward protectionist trade policy measures. Favor instead structural adjustment and more flexible adaptation at home.*

For several reasons the industrial countries in particular should refrain from a restrictive trade policy: First, trade restrictions are not solving the surplus problem but rather diverting it to others. Second, trade restrictions are tending to push the Asian producers into more advanced technological areas and there-

----

[1] Shifts in investment patterns and growth-caused gaps in consumption behavior.
[2] Low commodity and oil prices, decline of the dollar and interest rates.

by heating up the "technology race". Third, trade restrictions are poorly balancing short-term advantages against longer-term losses and do not help European industry to adapt rapidly and flexibly to the various challenges of the new international economic environment. Fourth, abstention from trade restrictions is the best way to promote further integration of the NIEs into the world economy and its multilateral institutions, and to pursue further gradual market liberalization within the NIEs.

(3) *The question of adjustment in NIEs cannot be addressed independently from the American trade deficits*[3] *or the relatively closed Japanese and European domestic manufacturing markets.*

Prospective cuts in the *American budget* and, simultaneously, a broader exposure of the European and Japanese domestic markets to imports from NIEs seem suitable for reducing some of the political friction linked to growing economic imbalances. As expansionary (European and Japanese) measures are easier to implement than restrictive (American) budget cuts, the expansive steps should be taken first and independently of American action.

In *Japan*, this process has set in vigorously since the appreciation of the yen in 1985. After years of a nearly closed domestic market for manufacturing imports from the NIEs, several expansionary policy packages directed toward a stimulation of the Japanese domestic market have allowed a steep surge of imports from the NIEs.

----

[3] Dornbusch and Park suggest that this policy conclusion seems uncomfortable because US policymakers somehow believe that the trade problem can be solved without budget action, see Dornbusch and Park, Korean Growth Policy, p. 438. The Europeans are not confronted with the same problem but have preferred the easier protectionist route to structural adjustment which is more rewarding in the longer run.

Europe, however, is still lagging behind. A commitment of the European Community to open its market far beyond the narrow limits of the past 15 years would provide the NIEs with an additional outlet for their manufactures and take some of the pressures off the US.

(4) *Restructure adjustment from defensive trade-policy-related measures toward an active policy of encouragement of technological upgrading, given the future technological challenges posed by the Asian economies Japan and the NIEs. Improve technology transfer within and from outside Europe.*

While technological cooperation within Europe has started in a wide range of areas, there is still some room for improvement toward an extended extra-European technological cooperation with the US and Asia. This is part of a broad improvement in adjustment policies. Its costs are smaller and its prospective rewards higher than those of the defensive trade policy pursued so far. Lower barriers for the NIEs' access to European markets provide European entrepreneurs with more reliable incentives for adjustment than those stemming from policy efforts.

(5) *Strengthen the multilateral world economic order and push for a further integration of the NIEs into multilateral institutions.*

Due to a lack of a political framework of the ASEAN type among the NIEs, there is no cooperation agreement between the EEC and the NIEs. Given the precarious political situation of Hong Kong and Taiwan, this is not going to change in the future. Therefore, political efforts should pursue other avenues of cooperation, in particular multilateral institutions.

GATT: Push for general progress in the Uruguay Round.

The Asian NIEs have recently shown some readiness to accept wider GATT responsibilities. Areas of main interest for them are limitations on NTBs, improved transparency of the escape clause (Art. XIX), the race for subsidies in steel and textiles, market access and the new areas of TRIMs and TRIPs. In political terms, their main concern is to avoid a special NIC classification within GATT which would separate them from the wider group of developing countries.

EEC: Propose NIE graduation out of the EEC-GSP scheme on the basis of "self-selection" parallel to a general lowering of market access barriers.

The principle of graduation is already practised and recognized in the monetary sector (credit criteria of IMF, ADB) and in development policy (per capita income benchmark, used by the World Bank[4]). As far as trade policy is concerned, the economic impact of a graduation from EEC-GSP privileges for the NIEs would be minor[5]. Yet, it offers a chance to restructure the GSP in favor of low-income developing countries. So far, the GSP privileges have been heavily biased in favor of the NICs (primarily Asian NIEs and some other middle-income developing countries)[6]. On the other hand, such a signal would make it clear that the developed countries also need to "graduate" (or to underdevelop).

In political terms, however, graduation is a sensitive issue. As the granting of preferences was offered on the basis of self-se-

---

[4] The World Bank normally graduates a country five years after it reaches a per capita GNP benchmark, see O'Neill H. (1984) HICs, MICs, and LICs: Some Elements in the Political Economy of Graduation and Differentiation. World Development, Vol. 12, No.7, p. 706

[5] Taiwan does not receive EEC preferences within the GSP.

[6] Langhammer R. J. and Sapir A. (1987) Economic Impact of Generalized Tariff Preferences. London, pp. 48-59

lection, graduation should be based on the same principle. Thus, the industrial countries' approach should change from one of demand or unilateral coercion (US[7]) to one of negotiation[8].

OECD: Support the opening of an informal dialogue with interested Asian NIEs and their broadened participation in OECD working groups.

In May 1988, the OECD Ministerial Council decided to form a working group to review the possibilities of broader cooperation with the NIEs within OECD. Possible candidates for later OECD membership are South Korea and Singapore[9]. This initiative would be in line with the general idea of graduation. Its symbolic value lies primarily in the international recognition of the NIEs as equal members in the group of industrial countries. Its major goal is the transfer of bilateral trade conflicts into the multilateral framework of OECD working groups. This is important, as the EEC does not have an ASEAN-type cooperation agreement with the NIEs[10], and to avoid increasing support for the building of economic blocs in the style of "Pacific Free Trade Area Agreements" which would exclude Europe.

---

7 The US has withdrawn GSP preferences for the four Asian NIEs beginning January 2, 1989. Economically, the impact of this decision remains rather limited. The trade volume affected is about $ 8-10 billion, nearly 60 % of all US GSP-favored imports. The average tariff on those items will be about 5 %. These unilateral US measures, however, stirred some political protests, as the US have used the GSP preferences as an incentive for improvements of the patent and copyright laws in the NIEs. After improving these laws, the NIEs now feel disappointed about the withdrawal of the incentive, see New York Times, January 30, 1987, p. 1,34 and IHT, February 1, 1988, p. 3.

8 O'Neill, op. cit., p. 709. Martin Wolf has accurately observed: "Developing and industrial country attitudes present a mirror image: both fear the general application of universal and liberal rules vis-à-vis one another and both are prepared to accept derogations from such universality, hoping thereby either to obtain special favors, as in the case of developing countries, or to avoid liberalism toward the more dynamic developing countries, as in the case of industrial countries." Ibid., p. 703.

9 At this time, an OECD membership of Hong Kong and Taiwan is hardly conceivable.

10 With the exception of the ASEAN member Singapore.

Regional Pacific Cooperation: Support regional integration and cooperation, but oppose the inclusion of the US in a Pacific free trade zone. In exchange make a commitment to open access to the European internal market for the Asian economies after 1992.

The Pacific Basin is the region which is least integrated compared with the other world economic centers of the triad. This is mainly due to the catching-up process of the region and the closed Japanese market for manufactures. Regional integration efforts deserve special support, as the European integration process has inspired Asian thinking about regional integration to some degree.

In Asia, however, there are considerable reservations about a renewed Japanese leadership in the area, going back to the old imperial Japanese concept of "Greater Asian Coprosperity Sphere" and to present Japanese preponderance in the region. On the other hand, the Basin's link with the US market is overwhelming, as it is its most important asset for further growth and development. Given a persisting huge American trade imbalance with the region (see Chart 10) and the lack of efforts to adjust on the American side, US pressures for the establishment of a "Pacific-Asia Free Trade Area Agreement" (PAFTA) have been recently mounting again. To date, the discussion is mainly focussing on the US-Japanese relationship, but is hardly conceivable to leave the neighboring NIEs out of a trade agreement in the longer run. With the inclusion of the US in a regional free trade area agreement, however, the Europeans would find themselves excluded from the largest trading bloc in the world. That, certainly, would modify the international economic order profoundly.

The most effective steps the Europeans can take, in order to prevent such developments, consist in their commitment to keep the European market open, more so after 1992 than before. The threat, of Japan and the NIEs facing closed European doors in the near future, would certainly propel their thinking toward a free trade area agreement with the US.

Chart 10: USA: Regional Trade Balance in 1986 and 1987, Bn. Dollar

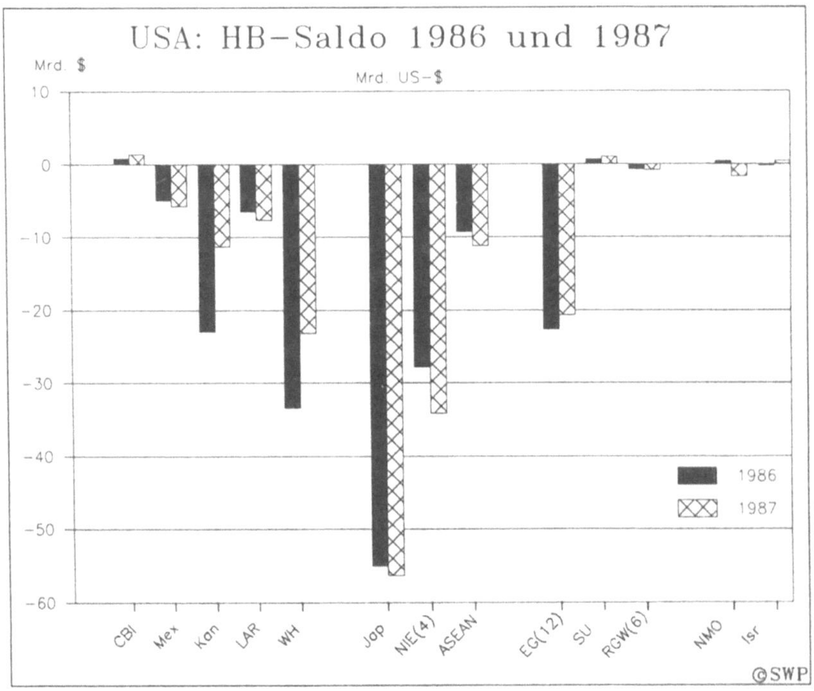

Legend:
CBI = Caribbean Basin Initiative Members
Mex = Mecico
Kan = Canada
LAR = Other Latin America
WH = Western Hemisphere Total
Jap = Japan
NIE(4) = Asian NIEs (Korea, Taiwan, Hong Kong, Singapore)
ASEAN = Asean
EG(12) = EG(12)
SU = Soviet Union
RGW(6) = Six Eastern European CMEA-members
NMO = Middle East
ISR = Israel

Source: Based on Data of D.o.C., Bureau of the Census, Statistical Abstract of the United States

A N N E X E S

Statistical Country Profiles

by

Harald Mücke

Hong Kong

E C O N O M I C   S T A T I S T I C A L   P R O F I L E

/ SEPTEMBER 1989 /

- latest available figures -

Economic Performance	1986	1987	1988 (e)	1989 (p)
GDP (US$ bn)	38.4	46.2	53.4	61.0
Real GDP (changes in %) 1)	11.2	13.6	6.7	5.8
GDP per capita (US$)	6,948	8,279	9,449	10,627
Real GDP per capita (changes in %) 1)	9.0	12.6	5.3	4.4
Real industrial production (changes in %) 1)	14.8	14.2	10.5	10.0

Foreign trade (US$ bn)	1986	1987	1988 (e)	1989 (p)
Exports (fob)	35.4	48.5	63.0	74.4
Imports (cif)	35.4	48.5	63.7	75.2
Current account	1.97	2.71	2.30	2.18

Main destinations of exports

% of total	1988
China	27.0
U.S.A.	24.8
Japan	5.9
West Germany	5.0
UK	4.5

Main origins of imports

% of total	1988
China	31.0
Japan	18.6
Taiwan	8.9
U.S.A.	8.3
South Korea	5.3

Foreign debt	1986	1987	1988 (e)	1989 (p)
Total (US$ bn)	10.4	10.5	10.7	10.2
in % of GDP	27.2	22.7	20.0	16.8

Social indicators	1986	1987	1988 (e)
Labour force (mn)	n.a.	n.a.	2.79
Unemployment rate	2.8	1.6	1.3
Inflation rate	1.5	4.7	7.1

Origins of GDP

% of total	1987
Wholesale & retail import & export trade, hotels and restaurants	23.2
Manufacturing	22.1
Finance insurance, real estate & business services	18.4
Construction	4.6

Employment by industry

% of total	1988(e)
Manufacturing	38.5
Wholesale, retail import & export trade, hotels and restaurants	31.8
Financing, insurance, real estate & business services	10.5

Main commodities exported

	(1988 US$ bn)
Clothing	8.62
Watches & clocks	2.13
Textiles	1.69
Electronic components	.91
Metal manufactures	.73
Radios	.34

Main commodities imported

	(1988 US$ bn)
Raw materials and semi-manufactures	27.72
Consumer goods	21.96
Capital goods	9.89
Foodstuffs	4.11
Fuels	1.13

---

e: estimated; p : projected; n.a.: not available

1) Base: standard currency
2) including re-exports

Source: Asian Business, Asian Finance,
The Hongkong and Shanghai Banking Corporation: Business Series,
F.A.Z. GmbH: Informationsdienste, The Economist Intelligence
Unit: Country Profiles

Indonesia

ECONOMIC STATISTICAL PROFILE

/ SEPTEMBER 1989 /

- latest available figures -

Economic Performance		1986	1987	1988 (e)	1989 (p)
GDP	(US$ bn)	74.7	69.7	74.8	76.7
Real GDP (changes in %)	1)	3.2	3.4	3.9	4.1
GDP per capita	(US$)	447.5	408.8	430.0	431.4
Real GDP per capita (changes in %)	1)	1.0	1.3	1.7	1.9
Real industrial production (changes in %)	1)	4.1	1.9	4.8	5.3

Foreign trade (US$ bn)	1986	1987	1988 (e)	1989 (p)
Exports (fob)	14.8	16.5	19.1	20.6
Imports (cif)	10.7	10.2	11.7	13.0
Current account	- 3.9	- 2.2	- 2.5	- 2.2

Main destinations of exports

% of total	1987
Japan	54.2
U.S.A.	20.0
Singapore	8.4
South Korea	3.9
Netherlands	2.8
Taiwan	2.8

Main origins of imports

% of total	1987
Japan	29.5
U.S.A.	10.9
Singapore	8.9
West Germany	6.5
Saudi Arabia	5.1
Australia	3.7

Foreign debt		1986	1987	1988 (e)	1989 (p)
Total	(US$ bn)	5.54	6.82	8.33	8.39
in % of GDP		7.4	9.8	11.1	10.9

Social indicators	1987	1988 (e)	1989 (p)
Labour force (mn)	n.a.	69.1	n.a.
Unemployment rate	7.0	7.5	7.0
Inflation rate	8.9	7.0	n.a.

Origins of GDP

% of total	1987
Agriculture	25.5
Wholesale & retail trade	16.8
Manufacturing	13.9
Mining & quarrying	13.1

Foreign Investment

	1985	1986
Number of Projects	50	50
Value in US $ (bn)	.9	.8

Main commodities exported

	(1987 US$ bn)
Crude oil products	6.2
Wood & products	2.4
Natural gas	2.4
Textiles & garments	1.0
Rubber & products	1.0

Main commodities imported

	(1987 US$ bn)
Machinery & equipment	3.7
Chemicals	1.8
Base metals	1.3
Mineral products	1.3
Transport and equipment	1.1

e: estimated; p : projected; n.a.: not available

1) Base: standard currency
2) including re-exports

Source: Asian Business, Asian Finance, The Hongkong and Shanghai Banking Corporation: Business Series, F.A.Z. GmbH: Informationsdienste, The Economist Intelligence Unit: Country Profiles

Korea

ECONOMIC STATISTICAL PROFILE

/ SEPTEMBER 1989 /

- latest available figures -

Economic Performance	1986	1987	1988 (e)	1989 (p)
GDP (US$ bn)	98.3	121.3	162.8	203.7
Real GDP (changes in %) 1)	11.7	11.1	10.8	7.5
GDP per capita (US$)	2,364	2,883	3,823	4,726
Real GDP per capita (changes in %) 1)	10.4	9.8	9.5	6.2
Real industrial production) (changes in %) 1)	17.1	16.0	13.0	10.0

Foreign trade (US$ bn)	1986	1987	1988 (e)	1989 (p)
Exports (fob)	34.7	47.3	60.7	72.8
Imports (cif)	31.6	41.0	51.8	66.7
Current account	4.6	9.9	14.0	10.3

Main destinations of exports

% of total	1988
U.S.A.	35.3
Japan	19.8
Hong Kong	5.9
W. Germany	3.9
U.K.	3.2
Canada	2.8

Main origins of imports

% of total	1988
Japan	30.7
U.S.A.	24.6
W. Germany	4.0
Australia	3.5
Malaysia	2.6
Saudi Arabien	1.6

Foreign debt	1986	1987	1988 (e)	1989 (p)
Total (US$ bn)	44.5	35.6	29.9	23.4
in % of GDP	45.3	29.3	18.4	11.5

Social indicators	1987	1988 (e)
Labour force (mn)	n.a.	16.87
Unemployment rate	n.a.	2.5
Inflation rate	3.9	7.2

Origins of GDP

% of total	1986
Manufacturing	31.0
Trade	13.5
Agriculture	12.7
Transport and communication	8.3
Construction	8.0

Main origins of foreign investment

accumulated 1982 - Nov. 1988 (total: US$ bn	3.98)
Japan	47.8%
U.S.A.	26.4%
W. Europe	17.7%
Hongkong	3.8%

Main commodities exported

	(1988 US$ bn)
Textile products	13.35
Electronic products	18.33
Iron & steel products	5.38
Machinery	5.17
Automobiles	3.59
Footwear	3.41

Main commodities imported

	(1988 US$ bn)
Machinery	7.90
Electric & electronics	7.18
Chemicals	4.25
Crude Oil	3.69
Food & direct consumer goods	2.64
Iron & steel products	2.43

e: estimated; p : projected; n.a.: not available

1) Base: standard currency
2) including re-exports

Source: Asian Business, Asian Finance, The Hongkong and Shanghai Banking Corporation: Business Series, F.A.Z. GmbH: Informationsdienste, The Economist Intelligence Unit: Country Profiles

Malaysia

ECONOMIC STATISTICAL PROFILE

/ SEPTEMBER 1989 /

- latest available figures -

Economic Performance		1986	1987	1988 (e)	1989 (p)
GDP	(US$ bn)	27.6	32.0	33.7	34.7
Real GDP (changes in %) 1)		1.2	5.2	6.8	4.7
GDP per capita	(US$)	1,711	1,935	1,979	1,977
Real GDP per capita (changes in %) 1)		-1.5	2.3	3.8	1.8
Real industrial production (changes in %) 1)		9.5	8.3	15.5	9.6

Foreign trade (US$ bn)	1986	1987	1988 (e)	1989 (p)
Exports (fob)	14.0	17.9	21.1	22.0
Imports (cif)	10.8	12.7	14.9	16.3
Current account	-0.1	2.4	2.6	1.4

Main destinations of exports

% of total	1988
Singapore	19.3
U.S.A.	17.3
Japan	17.2
South Korea	5.0
UK	3.5
Hongkong	3.5

Main origins of imports

% of total	1988
Japan	23.4
U.S.A.	17.7
Singapore	13.2
UK	4.9
Taiwan	4.6
Australia	4.1

Foreign debt		1986	1987	1988 (e)	1989 (p)
Total	(US$ bn)	22.0	22.4	21.2	20.7
in % of GDP		79.8	69.8	62.9	60.0

Social indicators	1987	1988 (e)	1989 (p)
Labour force (mn)	6,3	n.a.	n.a.
Unemployment rate	9.5	8.1	7.8
Inflation rate	0.9	2.5	2.8

Origins of GDP

% of total	1988
Manufacturing	24.0
Agriculture	21.2
Wholesale, retail trade & hotels	10.6
Mining	10.4

Crude oil exports by destination

% of total	1988
Singapore	29.3
Japan	23.2
South Korea	14.7
Thailand	12.6

Main commodities exported

	(1987 US$ bn)
Electronic components	3.3
Petroleum	2.3
Logs & timber	2.2
Rubber	2.0
Palm oil	1.7

Main commodities imported

	(1987 US$ bn)
Manufacturing inputs	5.8
Machinery & transport equipment	2.0
Metal products	1.1
Food, beverages & tobacco	1.0

e: estimated; p : projected; n.a.: not available

1) Base: standard currency
2) including re-exports

Source: Asian Business, Asian Finance, The Hongkong and Shanghai Banking Corporation: Business Series, F.A.Z. GmbH: Informationsdienste, The Economist Intelligence Unit: Country Profiles

Philippines

ECONOMIC STATISTICAL PROFILE

/ SEPTEMBER 1989 /

- latest available figures -

Economic Performance	1986	1987	1988 (e)	1989 (p)
GDP (US$ bn)	31.0	34.6	39.2	41.0
Real GDP (changes in %) 1)	2.0	5.7	6.1	3.5
GDP per capita (US$)	564	614	683	701
Real GDP per capita (changes in %) 1)	1.4	3.1	4.2	1.8
Real industrial production (changes in %) 1)	2.1	8.0	8.1	3.8

Foreign trade (US$ bn)	1986	1987	1988 (e)	1989 (p)
Exports (fob)	4.8	5.7	6.7	7.7
Imports (cif)	5.2	6.9	8.2	9.6
Current account	1.0	- .5	- .4	- .9

Main destinations of exports

% of total	1987
U.S.A.	36.1
EEC countries	19.0
Japan	17.2
ASEAN countries	8.9
Hong Kong	4.9

Main origins of imports

% of total	1987
U.S.A.	22.1
Japan	16.6
Middle East countries	12.4
EEC countries	11.6
ASEAN countries	10.2

Foreign debt	1986	1987	1988 (e)	1989 (p)
Total (US$ bn)	28.3	28.7	30.6	32.2
in % of GDP	91.1	82.7	78.0	78.7

Social indicators	1986	1987	1988 (e)
Labour force (mn)	22.4	n.a.	24.4
Unemployment rate	11.1	n.a.	13.4
Inflation rate	- 1.4	6.9	9.4

Origins of GDP

% of total	1987
Agricultur, forestry and fishing	25.1
Manufacturing	24.6
Trade	19.4
Finance and housing	6.8

Main origins of foreign investment

% of total	1988
Japan	27
United Kingdom	21
U.S.A.	18

Main commodities exported

	(1987 US$ bn)
Electronics and electrical equipment	1.12
Garments	1.10
Coconut products	.56
Chemicals	.25
Forest products	.24

Main commodities imported

	(1987 US$ bn)
Mineral fuels and lubricants	1.25
Manufactured goods	.96
Chemicals	.92
Materials for the manufacture of electrical equipment	.77
Non-electrical machinery	.54

e: estimated; p : projected; n.a.: not available

1) Base: standard currency
2) including re-exports

Source: Asian Business, Asian Finance, The Hongkong and Shanghai Banking Corporation: Business Series, F.A.Z. GmbH: Informationsdienste, The Economist Intelligence Unit: Country Profiles

Singapore

ECONOMIC STATISTICAL PROFILE

/ SEPTEMBER 1989 /

- latest available figures -

Economic Performance	1986	1987	1988 (e)	1989 (p)
GDP (US$ bn)	17.5	19.9	20.9	23.3
Real GDP (changes in %) 1)	1.8	8.8	9.2	6.4
GDP per capita (US$)	6,766	7,594	7,965	8,834
Real GDP per capita (changes in %) 1)	.6	7.6	9.2	5.6
Real industrial production (changes in %) 1)	8.6	17.5	20.2	11.4

Foreign trade (US$ bn)	1986	1987	1988 (e)	1989 (p)
Exports (fob)	22.50	28.60	34.87	39.45
Imports (cif)	25.51	32.50	39.73	44.92
Current account	.54	.54	.69	.71

Main destinations of exports

% of total	1987
U.S.A.	23.8
Malaysia	13.6
Japan	8.6
Hong Kong	6.3
Thailand	5.5

Main origins of imports

% of total	1987
Japan	21.9
U.S.A.	15.5
Malaysia	14.6
Taiwan	4.5
Saudi Arabia	4.4

Foreign debt	1986	1987	1988 (e)	1989 (p)
Total (US$ bn)	16.3	19.0	21.7	24.1
in % of GDP	92.9	95.4	103.8	103.4

Social indicators	1987	1988 (e)	1989 (p)
Labour force (mn)	1.25	n.a.	n.a.
Unemployment rate	4.7	n.a.	n.a.
Inflation rate	.5	1.9	2.3

Origins of GDP

% of total	1988 (e)
Manufacturing	28.8
Financial business services	27.5
Commerce	17.9
Transport and communications	14.2
Construction	5.7

Foreign investment commitments by origin

S$ mn	1988 1 Qtr	1989 1 Qtr	%change
U.S.A.	164.1	138.9	- 15.4
Japan	182.0	133.3	- 26.4
EC	64.2	123.3	92.1
Total incl. others	431.0	409.5	- 5.0

Main commodities exported

	(1988 US$ bn)
Machinery & equipment	18.9
Mineral fuels	5.0
Manufactured goods	3.2
Chemicals	2.6
Crude materials	2.0
Food	1.6
Clothing	1.2

Main commodities imported

	(1988 US$ bn)
Machinery & equipment	19.1
Manufactures goods	6.5
Mineral fuels	6.2
Chemicals	2.9
Food	2.3
Crude materials	1.5
Beverages & tobacco	.4

---

e: estimated; p : projected; n.a.: not available

1) Base: standard currency
2) including re-exports

Source: Asian Business, Asian Finance,
The Hongkong and Shanghai Banking Corporation: Business Series,
F.A.Z. GmbH: Informationsdienste, The Economist Intelligence Unit: Country Profiles

Taiwan

ECONOMIC STATISTICAL PROFILE

/ SEPTEMBER 1989 /

- latest available figures -

Economic Performance	1986	1987	1988 (e)	1989 (p)
GDP (US$ bn)	71.4	94.6	114.8	133.7
Real GDP (changes in %) 1)	10.6	11.1	7.2	5.5
GDP per capita (US$)	3,690	4,844	5,829	6717,8
Real GDP per capita (changes in %) 1)	9.5	9.9	6.3	4.6
Real industrial production (changes in %) 1)	14.1	11.8	8.0	6.1

Foreign trade (US$ bn)	1986	1987	1988 (e)	1989 (p)
Exports (fob)	39.8	53.5	60.5	69.0
Imports (cif)	24.2	34.5	50.0	62.5
Current account	16.2	18.1	11.7	9.0

Main destinations of exports

% of total	1988 (e)
U.S.A.	38.7
Japan	14.5
Hongkong	9.2
West Germany	3.9
UK	3.1
Canada	2.6

Main origins of imports

% of total	1988 (e)
Japan	29.9
U.S.A.	26.2
West Germany	4.3
Hongkong	3.9
Australia	2.7

Foreign debt	1986	1987	1988 (e)	1989 (p)
Total (US$ bn)	13.7	22.8	19.6	16.8
in % of GDP	19.2	24.1	17.1	12.6

Social indicators	1986	1987	1988 (e)	1989 (p)
Labour force (mn)	7.9	8.2	8.5	n.a.
Unemployment rate	2.7	2.0	1.7	1.8
Inflation rate	0.7	0.5	1.3	5.0

Origins of GDP

% of total	1988 (e)
Manufacturing	38.1
Wholesale & retail trade	15.7
Banking, insurance, real estate	11.2
Agriculture forestry & fishing	6.1
Transport, storage & communications	5.5

Foreign Investment

US$ mn	1986
Japan	254
Europe	187
U.S.A.	138
Total	770

Main commodities exported

	(1988 (e) US$ bn)
Electronic products	16.6
Textile garments	5.1
Metal products	3.5
Plastic products	3.1
Machinery	3.0

Main commodities imported

	(1988 (e) US$ bn)
Basic metals	10.4
Electronic products	8.7
Machinery	5.0
Chemicals	4.9
Transport equipment	2.8
Crude petroleum	2.2

e: estimated; p : projected; n.a.: not available

1) Base: standard currency
2) including re-exports

Source: Asian Business, Asian Finance,
The Hongkong and Shanghai Banking Corporation: Business Series,
F.A.Z. GmbH: Informationsdienste, The Economist Intelligence
Unit: Country Profiles

Thailand

ECONOMIC STATISTICAL PROFILE

/ SEPTEMBER 1989 /

- latest available figures -

Economic Performance	1986	1987	1988 (e)	1989 (p)
GDP (US$ bn)	41.8	47.1	54.1	63.8
Real GDP (changes in %) 1)	3.5	6.3	9.8	6.1
GDP per capita (US$)	809	888	1,018	1,162
Real GDP per capita (changes in %) 1)	1.9	4.3	7.9	4.3
Real industrial production) (changes in %) 1)	5.5	8.5	11.1	5.9

Foreign trade (US$ bn)	1986	1987	1988 (e)	1989 (p)
Exports (fob)	8.8	11.7	15.0	17.0
Imports (cif)	9.2	13.0	18.5	21.0
Current account	.3	- .7	- 2.5	- 3.1

Main destinations of exports

% of total	1987
U.S.A.	19
Japan	15
Singapore	9
Netherlands	7
W. Germany	5

Main origins of imports

% of total	1987
Japan	26
U.S.A.	22
Singapore	8
W. Germany	6
Malaysia	4

Foreign debt	1986	1987	1988 (e)	1989 (p)
Total (US$ bn)	18.3	18.9	19.7	20.7
in % of GDP	43.9	40.1	35.9	32.4

Social indicators	1987	1988 (e)	1989 (p)
Labour force (mn)	28.0	28.9	n.a.
Unemployment rate	4.1%	6.8%	n.a.
Inflation rate	2.5%	6.2%	5.8%

Origins of GDP

% of total	1987
Manufacturing	24.1
Agriculture, forestry, fishing and mining	19.0

Main origins of foreign investment

(accumulated 1980 - 1988)	
Japan	23 %
Singapore	23 %
U.S.A.	22 %
Hongkong	16 %
Netherlands	4 %

Main commodities exported

	(1987 Bt bn)
Textiles	48.6
Rice	22.7
Tapioca products	20.7
Rubber	20.5
Integrated circuits	15.2
Precious stones	11.6
Canned fish	9.5

Main commodities imported

	(1987 Bt bn)
Non-electric machinery	49.4
Fuel & lubricants	44.5
Chemicals	36.1
Base metals	33.8
Electric machinery & parts	31.8
Vehicles & parts	15.2

e: estimated; p : projected; n.a.: not available

1) Base: standard currency
2) including re-exports

Source: Asian Business, Asian Finance, The Hongkong and Shanghai Banking Corporation: Business Series, F.A.Z. GmbH: Informationsdienste, The Economist Intelligence Unit: Country Profiles

THE NEWLY INDUSTRIALIZING ECONOMIES OF ASIA

Chances for Increasing Cooperation

Berlin (West), 25 to 29 September 1989

I n t e r n a t i o n a l   R o u n d   T a b l e

organized by the
Development Policy Forum
of the
German Foundation for International Development (DSE)

in cooperation with the
Asia Pacific Society, Cologne

Venue and Accommodation:

Deutsche Stiftung für internationale Entwicklung (DSE)
Villa Borsig, Reiherwerder
D 1000 Berlin 27

Programme

<u>Monday, 25 September 1989</u>

19.30 hrs. Villa Borsig	Welcome Dinner hosted by the German Foundation (DSE)

<u>Tuesday, 26 September 1989</u>

9.30 to 12.10 hrs.	**Opening and First Working Session**
	The Chairman, DSE Development Policy Forum
	Addresses
	Mr. Fritz Hermanns for the Asia Pacific Society
	State Secretary Jörg Rommerskirchen for the Senat of Berlin
	Professor S. C. Tsiang for the participants from Asia
	Keynote address
	Dr. Lorenz Schomerus Director-General Federal Ministry of Economics
	Address
	Professor Dr. Theodor Leuenberger
	ASEAN panel
	"The role of Europe as partner in cooperation - viewed from the East" Moderator: Mr. Augustine H. H. Tan, M.P.
	General discussion

Tuesday, 26 September 1989

14.00 to 17.00 hrs.	**Second Working Session** Address Mr. Hans-Peter Repnik Parliamentary State Secretary to the Federal Minister for Economic Cooperation Presentations and discussions - ASEAN 2000 (Siddique) - Japanese-NIE strategic interdependence (de Bettignies) - Capacity of German economy (Giesecke) - Cooperation between small and medium-sized enterprises (Régnier)
18.00 hrs.	Opening ceremony of Overseas Import Fair "Partners for Progress" followed by reception
20.00 hrs	Dinner at Pullman Restaurant, International Conference Centre (ICC)

Wednesday, 27 September 1989

9.30 to 12.00 hrs. Fair Ground	Tour of the Overseas Import Fair conducted by The Governing Mayor of Berlin
	Luncheon at the invitation of The Senator for Economics, at the "Esplanade", Berlin
14.30 to 16.15 hrs.	**Third Working Session**
	Taiwan - claims and strategies towards Europe Presentation: S. C. Tsiang, CHUNG-HUA Institution for Economic Research, Taipei
	The Hong Kong economy in a changing international economic environment - some implications for Europe Presentation: Edward K. Y. Chen, Centre of Contemporary Asian Studies, University of Hong Kong
	The concept of international division of labour and principles of cooperation Presentation: Rolf Langhammer The Kiel Institute for World Economics
	Address
	Göran M. Engblom Executive Director International Trade Centre UNCTAD/GATT, Geneva

Wednesday, 27 September 1989

16.30 to 19.00 hrs.	**Fourth Working Session**
	Korea 2000: economic and social targets and development strategies Presentation: Rhee Hak-Yong, Korea University, Seoul
	Recent trade patterns between NIEs and Western Europe and implications for the international division of labour in the 1990s Presentation: Friedrich von Kirchbach International Trade Centre, Geneva
	New technologies, global competition and latecomer industrialization - the challenge ahead for NIEs Presentation: Dieter Ernst, OECD, Paris
	State intervention, state involvement and market forces: Singapore and South Korea Presentation: Hans Christopher Rieger and Wolfgang Veit, South Asia Institute, Heidelberg

Thursday, 28 September 1989

9.00 to 13.00 hrs.	**Fifth Working Session**
	NIEs as models: what lessons to draw? Presentation: Wolfgang Hillebrand German Development Institute, Berlin
	The role of technical capability in industrialization: Lessons for Sri Lanka Presentation: Ponna Wignaraja United Nations University, Colombo
	Europe 1992 and the NIEs Presentation: Wolfgang Hager Robinson Linton Associates S.C., Brussels
	Some reflection on prospects for regional co-operation in the Asian-Pacific region Presentation: S. M. Naseem ESCAP, Bangkok
15.00 hrs.	Sightseeing tour
18.00 hrs.	Supper at the "Mövenpick" restaurant
20.00 hrs.	Concert at the Berlin Philharmonic Hall

Friday, 29 September 1989

9.30 to 12.00 hrs.	**Closing Session**
	General discussion Summary presentation Conclusions and recommendations Closing remarks

LIST OF PARTICIPANTS AND AUTHORS

Günther Becher
Member of the Board
Asia Pacific Society
Chairman
Supervisory Board
Lufthansa German Center GmbH & Co. KG
Von-Gablenz-Strasse 2-6
D 5000 Köln 21

Henri-Claude de Bettignies
Professor
Institut Européen d'Administration des Affaires (INSEAD)
Boulevard de Constance
F 77305 Fontainebleau
France

Markus Biermann
Research Assistant
Institute for Technology Management
University of St. Gall
Unterstrasse 22
CH 9000 St. Gallen
Switzerland

Raymond J. M. Chang
President
Institute for National Policy Research
114, Chienkuo N. Road Sec. 2
10433 Taipei
Taiwan

Edward K. Y. Chen
Director
Centre of Asian Studies
University of Hong Kong
Member of the Central Policy Unit of the Hong Kong Government
Pokfulam Road
Hong Kong

Vincent H. C. Cheng
Central Policy Unit
Hong Kong Government
33 Garden Road
St. John's Building, 1st floor
Hong Kong

Chia Siow Yue
Associate Professor
Department of Economics and Statistics
National University of Singapore
Kent Ridge Crescent
Singapore 0511

Bhagirath Lal Das
Director
Coordinator
International Trade Programmes
United Nations Conference on Trade and
Development (UNCTAD)
Palais des Nations
CH 1211 Genève 10
Switzerland

Linin Day
Consultant to the Minister of Finance
Ministry of Finance
2, Aikou W. Road
Taipei
Taiwan

Rolf Dittmar
Counsellor
East and Southeast Asian Section
Federal Ministry of Economics (BMWi)
Villemombler Strasse 76
D 5300 Bonn 1

Göran M. Engblom
Executive Director
International Trade Centre UNCTAD/GATT
Palais des Nations
CH 1211 Genève 10
Switzerland

Dieter Ernst
Senior Advisor
Research Programme "New Technologies, Industry and Trade"
Organisation for Economic Cooperation and Development (OECD) Development Centre
94, rue Chardon-Lagache
F 75016 Paris
France

Gundi Feilner (Mrs.)
Ambassador (rtd.)
Dall'Armistr. 3 a
D 8000 München 19

Alexander G. Friedrich
UN Executive Secretary (rtd.)
Kennedy-Ufer 1
D 5300 Köln

Helmut Giesecke
Director
Foreign Trade Department
Association of German Chambers of Industry and Trade
Adenauerallee 148
D 5300 Bonn 1

Wolfgang Hager
Special Projects Advisor
Robinson Linton Associates S. C.
36, rue Joseph II
Box 6
B 1040 Bruxelles
Belgium

Han Young-Soo
Director
Import Division
Bureau of International Trade
Ministry of Trade and Industry
Government Building Complex II
Kwacheon
Korea

Martin Hecker
First Counsellor
Permanent Mission of the Federal Republic of
Germany to the United Nations
C. P. 171
CH 1219 Genève 11
Switzerland

Manfred Hedrich
Head of Department
Senat Administration for Economics
Martin-Luther-Strasse 105
D 1000 Berlin 62

Jürgen Henke
ICT GmbH
International Cooperation and Transfer
Kurfürstendamm 46
Postfach 15 04 27
D 1000 Berlin 15

Fritz Hermanns
Member of the Board
Asia Pacific Society
Chairman
Board of Management
Stadtsparkasse Köln
Habsburgerring 2-12
D 5000 Köln 1

Franz Hesske
Principal Administrator
Directorate-General for External Relations
Commission of the European Communities (EC)
Rue de la Loi 200
B 1049 Bruxelles
Belgium

Achim E. von Heynitz
Senior Economic Researcher
Stiftung Wissenschaft und Politik (SWP)
D 8026 Ebenhausen

Ulrich Hiemenz
Director
Section for Developing Countries and World Economy
Kiel Institute of World Economics
P.O. Box 43 09
D 2300 Kiel

Wolfgang Hillebrand
Senior Industrial Economist
German Development Institute
Fraunhoferstrasse 33-36
D 1000 Berlin 10

Lutz Hoffmann
President
German Institute of Economic Research (DIW)
Königin-Luise-Strasse 5
D 1000 Berlin 33

Mei-Hwa Hsieh (Ms.)
Assistant Research Fellow
Chung-Hwa Institution for Economic Research
75 Chang-Hsing Street
Taipei 10671
Taiwan

Joachim Janke
Deputy Director-General
Federal Ministry of Economics (BMWi)
Villemombler Strasse 76
D 5300 Bonn 1

Friedrich von Kirchbach
Senior Advisor
Research Section
Division of Product and Market Development
International Trade Centre UNCTAD/GATT
Palais des Nations
CH 1211 Genève 10
Switzerland

Naoki Kuriyama
Research Assistant
International Institute for Labour Studies
International Labour Office (ILO)
C.P. 6
CH 1211 Genève 22
Switzerland

Rolf J. Langhammer
Chief
Research Division
Kiel Institute of World Economics
Düsternbrooker Weg 120
P.O. Box 4309
D 2300 Kiel 1

Tomas Lawo
Representative
Konrad Adenauer Foundation
65 A, Jalan Setia Raya
50490 Kuala Lumpur
Malaysia

Lee Young Sae
Director
Department of Special Studies
Korea Institute for Economics and
Technology (KIET)
Cheong Ryang
P.O. Box 205
Seoul
Korea

Theodor Leuenberger
Member of the Board
Asia Pacific Society
Director
Institute for Technology Management (ITEM)
University of St. Gall
Unterstrasse 22
CH 9000 St. Gallen
Switzerland

Günter Linden
Director
Marketing Department
Carl Duisberg Centren
Hansaring 49-51
D 5000 Köln 1

Wolf-Dieter Melzer
General Manager
DEG Deutsche Finanzierungsgesellschaft für
Beteiligungen in Entwicklungsländern
Belvederestrasse 40
D 5000 Köln 41

Jürgen Mohrhard
Third Secretary
Federal Foreign Office (AA)
Adenauerallee 99-103
D 5300 Bonn 1

Harald Mücke
Project Assistant
Asia Pacific Society
Postfach 19 03 27
D 5000 Köln 1

Syed M. Naseem
Chief
Development Planning Division
United Nations Economic and Social Commission
for Asia and the Pacific (UN ESCAP)
The United Nations Building
Rajdamnern Avenue
Bangkok 10200
Thailand

Suchat Prachimdhit
Counsellor
Department of Economic Affairs
Ministry of Foreign Affairs
Saranrom Palace
Bangkok
Thailand

Josef Puchta
Head
Development Cooperation Unit
Senat Administration for Economics
Martin-Luther-Strasse 105
D 1000 Berlin 62

Hans-Peter Repnik
Parliamentary State Secretary
Federal Ministry for Economic Cooperation (BMZ)
Karl-Marx-Strasse 4-6
D 5300 Bonn 1

Rhee Hak-Yong
Professor and Director
Institute of Economic Research
Korea University
5-1, Anamdong, Sungbuk-ku
Seoul 136-701
Korea

Hans C. Rieger
Senior Research Fellow
Southasia Institute
Department of Development Economics
University of Heidelberg
Im Neuenheimer Feld 330
D 6900 Heidelberg

Philippe Régnier
Research Coordinator
Modern Asia Research Centre
P.O. Box 36
CH 1211 Genève 21
Switzerland

Hans Martin Schmid
Counsellor
Federal Ministry for Economic Cooperation (BMZ)
Karl-Marx-Strasse 4-6
D 5300 Bonn 1

Lorenz Schomerus
Director General
Federal Ministry of Economics
Villemombler Strasse 76
D 5300 Bonn 1

Siegfried Schultz
Senior Economist
German Institute of Economic Research (DIW)
Königin-Luise-Strasse 5
D 1000 Berlin 33

Sharon Siddique (Mrs.)
Senior Fellow
Institute of Southeast Asian Studies (ISEAS)
Heng Mui Keng Terrace
Pasir Panjang
Singapore

Günther F. Sober
Member of the Board
Asia Pacific Society
Senior Advisor
MARUBENI Coop. Deutschland
Postfach 5505
D 4000 Düsseldorf

Soong Siew Hoong
Managing Director
Kwan Cheong Engineering Sdn. Bhd.
312, Jalan Sungei Besi
57100 Kuala Lumpur
Malaysia

Andreas von Stechow
Senior Counsellor
Head of Section
European Communities
Federal Foreign Office (AA)
Adenauerallee 99-103
D 5300 Bonn 1

Tan Keok Yin
Executive Director
Federation of Malaysian Manufacturers
P.O. Box 12194
50770 Kuala Lumpur
Malaysia

Augustine H. H. Tan M.P.
Associate Professor
Department of Economics and Statistics
National University of Singapore
10 Kent Ridge Crescent
Singapore 0511

Kanchana Thaichon (Ms.)
Chief
Foreign Affairs Division
Thai Chamber of Commerce
150 Rajbopit Road
Bangkok 10200
Thailand

Sho-Chieh Tsiang
Professor
President
Chung-Hwa Institution for Economic Research
75 Chang-Hsing Street
Taipei 10671
Taiwan

Wolfgang Veit
Development Economist
Southasia Institute
Department of Development Economics
University of Heidelberg
Im Neuenheimer Feld 330
D 6900 Heidelberg 1

Pairoj Vongvipanond
Dean
Assistant Professor
Faculty of Economics
Chulalongkorn University
Pyathai Road
Bangkok 10500
Thailand

Ulrich Weber
Head of Service
United Nations Industrial Development Organization (UNIDO)
Investment Promotion Service
P.O. Box 10 20 65
D 5000 Köln 1

Ponna Wignaraja
Coordinator
South Asian Perspectives Project
The United Nations University (UNU)
Participatory Institute for Development Alternatives (PIDA)
75, Kynsey Road
Colombo 8
Sri Lanka

Arthur K. Yeh
Vice President
Administration Division
Institute for National Policy Research
114, Chienkuo N. Road Sec.2
10433 Taipei
Taiwan

Young Soogil
Senior Fellow
Korea Development Institute (KDI)
P.O. Box 113
Chongnyang
Seoul
Korea

German Foundation for International Development (DSE)
Rauchstrasse 25
D 1000 Berlin 30

Hans-Rimbert Hemmer
Director-General

Secretariat

Development Policy Forum
Villa Borsig - Reiherwerder
D 1000 Berlin 27

Manfred Kulessa
Chairman

Götz Link

Irene Federwisch

Christa Baroth

Erika Funk

Gyda Thurow

MIX
Papier aus verantwortungsvollen Quellen
Paper from responsible sources
FSC® C105338

If you have any concerns about our products,
you can contact us on
ProductSafety@springernature.com

In case Publisher is established outside the EU,
the EU authorized representative is:
Springer Nature Customer Service Center GmbH
Europaplatz 3, 69115 Heidelberg, Germany

Printed by Libri Plureos GmbH
in Hamburg, Germany